THE TRIALS OF THOMAS MORTON

The Trials of Thomas Morton

An Anglican Lawyer, His Puritan Foes,
and the Battle for a New England

PETER C. MANCALL

Yale

UNIVERSITY PRESS

New Haven and London

Published with support from the Fund established in memory of
Oliver Baty Cunningham, a distinguished graduate of the Class of
1917, Yale College, Captain, 15th United States Field Artillery, born
in Chicago September 17, 1894, and killed while on active duty near
Thiaucourt, France, September 17, 1918, the twenty-fourth anniversary
of his birth.

Published with assistance from the foundation established in memory
of Calvin Chapin of the Class of 1788, Yale College.

Yale University Press books may be purchased in quantity for
educational, business, or promotional use. For information, please
e-mail sales.press@yale.edu (U.S. office) or sales@yaleup.co.uk (U.K.
office).

Set in Janson and Monotype Van Dijck types by Tseng Information
Systems, Inc.
Printed in the United States of America.

Library of Congress Control Number: 2019938841

ISBN 978-0-300-23010-9 (hardcover : alk. paper)

A catalogue record for this book is available from the British Library.

This paper meets the requirements of ANSI/NISO Z39.48-1992
(Permanence of Paper).

10 9 8 7 6 5 4 3 2 1

For Lisa, Sophie, and Nicholas,
Guides in the Wilderness

Our earliest American heroes were Morton's oppressors: Endicott, Bradford, Miles Standish. Merry Mount's been expunged from the official version because it's the story not of a virtuous utopia but of a utopia of candor. Yet it's Morton whose face should be carved in Mount Rushmore.

PHILIP ROTH, *The Dying Animal* (2001)

Contents

A Note on the Text

I have silently corrected punctuation and spelling in quotations in places to clarify meaning. Modernized quotations follow the guidelines presented in Frank Friedel, ed., *Harvard Guide to American History*, rev. ed. (Cambridge, Mass., 1974), 1:27–36.

Prologue

O N October 12, 1812, John Adams wrote to Thomas Jefferson inquiring about a Captain Wollaston, "who came from England with a company of a few dozen Persons in the year 1622." That Adams posed such a question to his onetime political rival is not surprising. They had been regular correspondents since 1777, when each played a central role in the American Revolution. Freed from the urgent matters of rebellion and subsequently their roles in governing the new nation, the two former presidents wrote to each other about a wide variety of issues, including history. Their letters were often thoughtful and long. Each embraced the idea, as Adams expressed it to Jefferson in 1813, that "You and I ought not to die, before We have explained ourselves to each other."[1]

On that October day in 1812, with the country again at war with Britain, Adams wanted to know what Jefferson could tell him about Wollaston, whom he believed had moved from a settlement on a hill overlooking Massachusetts Bay to Virginia in 1622. Adams could trace him no farther since Wollaston disappeared from any of the histories of New England that he could find. In his place, Adams knew, Wollaston left his followers under the command of a man named Thomas Morton, an English lawyer who would soon become one of the most notorious colonists in the region. Adams hoped that Jefferson might be able to fill in details about Wollaston, a mysterious figure to him, but he was more interested in Morton.[2]

Adams had heard stories about Morton for years. This was not unusual since Morton had figured as a foil to Pilgrims and Puritans in various histories of early New England. But Adams's interest had spiked just after he lost his epic battle with Jefferson in the presidential election of 1800. John Quincy Adams, his son, had gone to Europe as an ambassador for George Washington. When his administration was drawing to a close, the first president recommended to his successor that he keep John Quincy in Europe. Adams soon appointed his son ambassador to the mission in Prussia. While in Berlin, John Quincy dove deep into German literary culture. At an auction he purchased three books about early New England that had been bound together, a common strategy among book collectors, who often combined related texts into a single book. Two of the books in this set were well known: *New England's Prospect*, by William Wood, first published in 1634, and Edward Johnson's *Wonder Working Providence of Zions Saviour in New England* of 1654. Both had been published in London, the most important market for books about English North America. The third was Thomas Morton's *New English Canaan*, which had been published in Amsterdam in 1637.[3]

In his letter to Jefferson, Adams summarized Morton's book. He transcribed some of the prefatory verses that praised the author as well as Morton's prologue. Adams identified Morton as a follower of William Laud, the archbishop of Canterbury and infamous persecutor of the Puritans, and as an ally of Sir Ferdinando Gorges, a military commander and promoter of colonization who would eventually gain a patent to the area that became Maine. Morton's "design," as Adams saw it, "appears to have been to promote two Objects: 1. to spread the fame and exaggerate the Advantages of New England; 2. to destroy the Characters of the English Inhabitants, and excite the Government to suppress the Puritans, and send over Settlers in their Stead, from among the Royalists and the disciples of Archbishop Laud." Beyond the book's own allure, Adams added that his "curiosity has been stimulated by an event of singular Oddity." There were, he wrote, "a few Words in manuscript on a blank leaf, which, had I seen them in any other place, I should have sworn were in the hand Writing of my Father."[4]

Adams was no fan of Morton, whom he described as an "incendiary instrument of spiritual and temporal domination," a judgment supported by other early historians of New England. But he also recognized that Morton had much to offer about the region's past. He discovered that Morton had renamed Wollaston's settlement, Mount Wollaston, to Mare Mount (*mare* being Latin for *ocean*) because of "its Position near the Sea and commanding the prospect of Boston Harbour and Massachusetts Bay." Only later, as Adams wrote

John Quincy Adams.

NEW ENGLISH CANAAN
OR
NEW CANAAN.

Containing an Abſtract of New England,

Compoſed in three Bookes,

The firſt Booke ſetting forth the originall of the Natives, their
Manners and Cuſtomes, together with their tractable Nature and
Love towards the Engliſh.

The ſecond Booke ſetting forth the naturall Indowments of the
Country, and what ſtaple Commodities it
yealdeth.

The third Booke ſetting forth, what people are planted there,
their proſperity, what remarkable accidents have happened ſince the firſt
planting of it, together with their Tenents and practiſe
of their Church.

Written by Thomas Morton of Cliffords Inne gent, *upon tenne
yeares knowledge and experiment of the
Country.*

Printed at AMSTERDAM,
By JACOB FREDERICK STAM.
In the Yeare 1 6 3 7.

John Quincy Adams's copy of Morton's *New English
Canaan*, acquired in Berlin, would be read by at
least four generations of the Adams family.
(Boston Athenaeum.)

in his own history of the area, never published, did the Puritans change the name to Merrymount to reflect the fact that this was the place where Morton had erected an eighty-foot-tall maypole, a marker of his sin in the eyes of the Pilgrims. Morton, Adams informed Jefferson, had the pole dragged to the hilltop, attached a pair of deer antlers to the top, and danced around it with his small band of suspect English followers and a larger contingent of Algonquians. "A Barrel of excellent Beer was brewed, and a Case of Bottles, (of Brandy I suppose)," Adams quoted Morton, "with good Chear, and English Men and Indian Sannups and Squaws, danced and sang and reveled round the Maypole till Bacchus and Venus, I suppose, were satiated." This revel the Pilgrims of Plymouth could not abide. "The Separatists called it an Idol," Adams continued, "the Calf of Horeb, Mount Dagon, threatening to make it a woeful mount and not a merry mount."[5]

Only at the end of the letter did Adams reveal one of his motivations for pursuing his investigation of Morton. "It is Whimsical that this Book, so long lost, should be brought to me," he told Jefferson, "for the Hill is in my Farm." There was much more in Morton's book too, which Adams offered to share if Jefferson had any interest.[6]

As it turned out, Jefferson did want to know more. Though he had been at his rural retreat at Poplar Forest when Adams's letter first arrived, by late December he had returned to Monticello. Before he responded to Adams he read through the histories of early Virginia in his library in what became a futile search for news of Wollaston. Though Jefferson believed that there might have been a record of Wollaston's migration, he suggested it would be impossible to find since "our public records of that date" had been "destroyed by the British on their invasion of this state." On this point Jefferson was wrong, as was Adams. Wollaston had apparently never made it to Virginia. Still, eager to continue the dialog, Jefferson then transcribed six pages from Nathaniel Morton's *New-England's Memoriall*, a book by the nephew of Plymouth governor William Bradford (and no relation to Thomas Morton) that had been published in 1669. Those pages included the damning views of Thomas Morton that Bradford had put into his own history of the colony, a work that remained unpublished at the time Jefferson and Adams exchanged their views of early New England.[7]

In the months that followed, the two aging former presidents used Morton's *New English Canaan* as a tool to debate the origins of Native Americans. (In one letter he never finished, Adams raised questions relating to natural history and indigenous burial practices.) Adams called the conversation to a halt in late May 1813, writing that the time had come to leave Morton and his ilk aside "for the present." He then quoted from the fourth book of Virgil's *Eclogues:* "Paulo Multo majora canamus"—Let us sing a somewhat loftier strain. The two never wrote to each other about Morton again.[8]

When Adams and Jefferson exchanged these letters, the second president never informed the third that a decade earlier he had drafted his own history of his hometown of Quincy. Adams's manuscript was more like a commonplace book of snippets from other books than an original narrative history. But there was an arc to his story nonetheless. He began with an excerpt from the history of Massachusetts written by Thomas Hutchinson, the last royal governor of the colony and one of Adams's (and other revolutionaries') bitterest enemies a generation earlier. In his account, Adams wrote that Morton had "contrived to make himself chief" of those abandoned by Wollaston, "changed the name of Mount Wollaston to Merry mount, Sett all the Servants free, erected a May pole, and lived a Life of dissipation until all the Stock intended for trade was consumed." Adams, again following Hutchinson, reported that Morton had been accused of selling guns to the Natives and teaching them to shoot. He "made himself so obnoxious to the Planters in all parts," Adams continued, "that at their general desire the People of New Plimouth Seized him by an armed force and confined him until they had an opportunity of Sending him to England."[9]

While Adams extracted information from a variety of sources, the one that most drew his attention was Morton's *New English Canaan*. Adams wrote out long excerpts from the book, interspersing it in places with details drawn from other histories of the early years of Wollaston's settlement. He also included two long letters by Morton that had come into the possession of Governor John Winthrop of Massachusetts, who transcribed them into his journal, which Adams had in hand.[10]

Adams interspersed his own commentary throughout his manuscript. Among the topics that got his attention was the name of the place. "The Fathers of Plymouth[,] Dorchester[,] Charleston &c I suppose would not allow the name to be Mare Mount," Adams interjected in a section he had derived from Hutchinson, "but insisted upon calling it Merrymount, for the same Reason that the common People in England will not call Gentlemens ornamented Grounds Gardens but insist

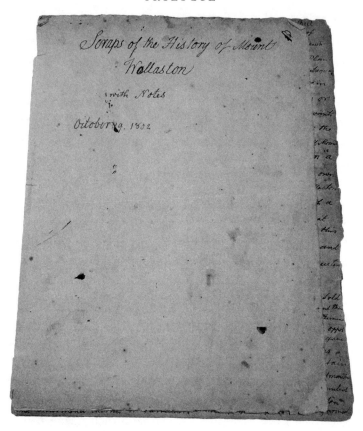

The title page of Adams's history of Mount
Wollaston, which he never published.
(Collection of the Massachusetts Historical Society.)

upon calling them Pleasure Grounds, i.e. to excite Envy and
make them unpopular."[11]

Adams was skeptical that the colonists reviled Morton
simply for being a member of the Church of England and
using the Book of Common Prayer, as Morton claimed. In his

history, Adams offered a different explanation. "Such a Rake as Morton, such an addle headed fellow as he represents himself to be," Adams wrote, "could not be cordial with the first people from Leyden, or those who came over with the Patent, from London or the West of England," a reference to the Pilgrims of Plymouth and the Puritan founders of the Massachusetts Bay Colony. He was certain that Morton's "Fun, his Songs and his Revells were provoking enough no doubt," but it was trading guns and ammunition to the Algonquians that "struck at the lives of the New Comers, and threatened the utter extirpation of all the Plantations." Adams, who reported that Puritan authorities put Morton's house to the torch after his arrest, presumed that the punishment reflected the fact that Wollaston lacked a title to the land, which meant that Morton had no legal claim to it either. The reason for burning his house, in this lawyer's opinion, "was to intimidate all persons in future from taking up Lands, without Titles."[12]

At the end of his manuscript, Adams transcribed a portion of King James's *Book of Sports*, published in London in 1618, which described popular customs in England. The excerpt noted the Stuart monarch's prohibition of Puritans' persecution of churchgoers who participated in "Dancing, Archery, Leaping, Vaulting, having May games, Whitson-Ales, Morrice Dances, *Setting up Maypoles* and other Sports therewith used, or any other Such harmless Recreations on Sundays after divine Service." As he wrote, "All ministers were obliged to read it in their churches," and "those who refused were Summoned into the high commission Court, imprisoned, and Suspended."

Adams left no doubt about why he concluded his history

with this excerpt. "I have extracted this Book of Sports," he wrote, "because it was so odious to our Ancestors, that probably it increased the hatred of Mortons Maypole at Mount Wollaston. They considered it as an Idol, a Dagon[,] a Calf of Mount Horeb"—language he took from Morton's book and would repeat later to Jefferson.[13] Adams might have been, as the historian Bernard Bailyn aptly put it, "a Puritan, at least to the extent of having unconsciously and unquestioningly accepted as his own the exacting behavioral standards of the Bible Commonwealth."[14] But that temperament did not blind him to the early New England Puritans' unwillingness to distinguish between frivolous celebrations and threats to their prescribed modes of behavior.

The second president was not the only member of the Adams family to read the copy of *New English Canaan* purchased by John Quincy in Berlin. On September 6, 1824, over twenty years after John had begun his history of Mount Wollaston, his grandson Charles Francis Adams woke up late after what he wrote in his diary was a "disturbed night." After breakfast, he retreated to his study to do some writing. He had turned seventeen in mid-August and would soon enter his final year at Harvard College as a member of the class of 1825. His father John Quincy, who was then serving as secretary of state under President James Monroe, would become the sixth president of the United States in February 1825 in an election determined by the House of Representatives.

Before noon on that day, Charles Francis picked up, as he put it, "a book called New Canaan or a description of New England by Thomas Morton[,] a man whose memory is well known in our family because he was the first inhabitant of the estate of Mount Wollaston." This Adams, unlike his grand-father, did not mention the rarity of the book. He called it "a singular book" that "displays much learning and satirical wit and feelings which may have become part of the soil, at least they agree with mine."[15]

Five years later, John Quincy Adams, who had just lost his bid for reelection, decided to read the same copy of Morton's book because it would be of use when he settled down to what he then believed would be his last major public act: preparing what he called a "biographical Memoir" of his father. That meant transferring his father's papers to his own library, a task that took several days. He planned to write one page each day of the "preparatory matter." But to get this right he thought he should reacquaint himself with the history of early New England. On August 6, 1829, three years and one month since the death of his father and only five months after his presidential term concluded, he picked up the "volume, which I accidentally purchased at Berlin." Here he drew on *New English Canaan*, which he described as a three-part book with the first section devoted to Natives, the second "a description of the country," and the third "a disguised and mystified narrative of his [Morton's] own adventures with the Colonists. But," he added, "it is told in a conceited and figurative style, with interspersions of poetry, or rather of rhymes, and satirical fictitious names applied to the principal persons" of the two early colonies. "This book is to be further examined," he wrote before turning his attention to the journal of John Winthrop and Cotton Mather's *Magnalia Christi Americana*, the ecclesiastical history of the region published in 1702.[16]

Probably none of these Adams readers—John, John

Quincy, or Charles Francis—knew that Morton's book had almost disappeared even before its publication, well before his ideas could have become part of the legacy of the town. Yet the teenage Charles Francis was right in his instincts. As his grandfather John had recognized earlier, Morton's life and book had had a deep impact on early New England, and a lasting influence on American culture.

On November 18, 1633, the Worshipful Company of Stationers of London recorded that an author named Thomas Morton registered the title *New English Canaan* for publication. The bookseller Charles Greene had intended to make the text available for sale in London, but he later wrote that "when some fewe sheets of the said booke were printed, it was stayed and those sheetes taken away by the meanes and procurement of some of the Agents for those of Newe-England." Greene claimed that he had lost four hundred copies.[17]

Despite the setback, Morton was undaunted. Four years later in Amsterdam, Jacob Frederick Stam published the book, which he advertised as written by an English gentleman who had spent ten years in North America. This time English officials tried to seize every copy that entered the realm, citing a new statute that forbade the sale of English-language works printed in another country. Their efforts almost succeeded. (Today the book is so rare that the asking price for a copy in 2017 was $125,000.) It is possible that only two copies were available in the United States in 1800 when Adams began his inquiry. One had been acquired by the botanist Peter Collinson, who was a book agent for the Library Company of Philadelphia. He shipped it to Benjamin Franklin in 1755 along with other early histories of the colonies, and it remains in the possession of the library today. Another was the copy acquired by John Quincy Adams, who bequeathed it to his son Charles Francis, who would eventually pass it to his own son, Charles Francis Adams Jr.[18]

For Morton, who was probably around sixty years old when Stam published the book, the battle to publish *New English Canaan* was the newest trial in a life that had seen many of them. Twenty years earlier he had married a wealthy widow only to find himself in court when the widow's son brought charges alleging that Morton had wed her in order to get his hands on her property. Within a few years of that incident he was accused of murder, though never arrested or tried for it. He likely made his first trip to Plymouth Colony in 1622, returning to England the same year. He went back to the colony in 1624, but colonial officials soured on the way that he administered a trading post on land claimed by Wollaston north of Plymouth and feared the close relations Morton had with local Natives.[19] He raised their ire even more in 1628 when he erected the maypole and his settlement descended into bacchanalian excess—at least in the eyes of the Pilgrim authorities.[20]

In 1628 Governor William Bradford declared that Morton had become a "Lord of Misrule" whose defiance necessitated his exile from the fledgling colony. The Pilgrims shipped Morton to England that year, but in 1629 he made his way back to Ma-re Mount, which then lay under the jurisdiction of the newly founded colony of Massachusetts Bay. Within a year he protested against the new colony's governing structure, which Morton believed did not acknowledge the authority of the king. Angered at his insolence, Puritan authorities including Governor John Winthrop (who knew about the murder allegation) ordered Morton back to England again. But Winthrop, like Bradford before him, soon learned that sending the man away did not solve the problems he represented. After his return to London, Morton reestablished links with a small group of English investors, led by the politically well-connected adventurer Sir Ferdinando Gorges, that was then working to undermine both Plymouth and Massachusetts Bay. It was during this period, in the early 1630s, that Morton began drafting *New English Canaan*.

In 1643 Morton returned to Massachusetts. But his book, which was simultaneously a work of natural history, an ethnography, and a critique of the Pilgrims of Plymouth and the Puritans of Massachusetts Bay—written with flashes of great wit, humor, and biting satire—had arrived first. Massachusetts leaders, enraged at the mocking accusations Morton had hurled against them in print, imprisoned him once again. After holding him for a year they sent him to a new English outpost at a place then called Acomenticus, the site of modern York, Maine, where he would no longer pose any danger. Morton did not escape this exile. He died there, probably in 1646.

In the years after his death, Morton became an outlier in the triumphant narrative of the establishment of colonies in New England. His seventeenth-century contemporaries, including two of the most prominent English colonists of the era— Bradford, the governor and first major historian of Plymouth, and Winthrop, who served eleven terms as the governor of

Massachusetts—castigated him in their eyewitness accounts of early New England.[21] Other members of New England's elite families picked up and retold the story. By the time of the American Revolution, Morton figured in Anglo-American culture as a miscreant who needed to be brushed aside for the colonies to succeed.

But the Puritans and their followers could not condemn Morton to permanent cultural exile. In the early decades of the nineteenth century a number of American writers rediscovered his story. Among them was the novelist Nathaniel Hawthorne, who in 1836, when he was thirty-two years old, published a story about Ma-re Mount in a collection called *The Token and Atlantic Souvenir.* (Fourteen years later he would achieve lasting fame with *The Scarlet Letter.*) Two years later the journalist, historian, and archivist Peter Force, who had been elected mayor of Washington, D.C., in 1836 and remained in office until 1840, included *New English Canaan* in a collection of primary sources from the colonial and revolutionary eras. This marked the first time the text had been printed since its publication in Amsterdam over two centuries earlier.

In 1883, Charles Francis Adams Jr., a member of the fourth generation in his family to come into possession of the book, used his grandfather's copy to produce a scholarly edition of Morton's work, revealing that its author was rather more truthful and the colonies' history more complicated than earlier critics had allowed. By the latter decades of the twentieth century, Morton had become an anti-hero—a back-to-nature idealist and a role model of political resistance in an age of anti-authoritarian rage. "Twice they shipped Morton to England to be tried for disobedience," the seventy-year-old protagonist of Philip Roth's 2001 novel *The Dying Animal* declares, "but the English ruling class and the Church of England had no use for the New England Separatists. Morton's case was thrown out of court each time, and Morton made his way back to New England. The English thought, He's right, Morton—we wouldn't want to live with him either, but he's not coercing anyone and these fucking Puritans are crazy."[22]

New English Canaan, the centerpiece of Morton's enduring fame but only one stage of his life's journey, suggested a different program for English colonization. Unlike expansionary plans predicated on the Christianizing pacification of Native Americans, Morton imagined a world based on indigenous values as well as English norms. He believed that the Pilgrims and Puritans, having exceeded their authority, should lose their charters. A contemporary reader of Morton's book would likely come away with the idea that those loyal to the king and national church would be better stewards of the territory than the religious dissenters who had already laid their claims.

During his life, Morton promoted an alternative path to colonization. As might be expected, he encountered stiff resistance from the religious enthusiasts who had both an uncompromising design for an ideal new society and what they believed were undisputed claims to pursue their plans. Morton—defiant, obnoxious, ego-driven—never accepted their view. His life suggests comparison with his near-contemporary Don Quixote, Miguel Cervantes's foolish yet idealistic hero unwilling to give up his vision, ever driven to joust with more powerful enemies. Morton defied authority time and again, not as a nihilist or a troublemaker but because he imagined a different future for the English colonies.

In Morton's New Canaan, positive relations between Natives and newcomers would create ample opportunities to acquire American natural resources and land for would-be migrants to establish new communities in territory that fell within Gorges's patents, which (as it happened) overlapped with those of the Massachusetts Bay Company. He wanted to bring this other kind of colony into existence. *New English Canaan* was not just another English account of North America but a weapon in an arsenal aimed at Morton's enemies. He worked with partners on both sides of the ocean to undermine the projects of Pilgrims and Puritans. Morton suffered three exiles because he threatened Plymouth and then Massachusetts. For those colonies to succeed, Morton had to go.

Morton failed to create a new promised land. Still, the record of his life opens a view to a very different history of New England than the familiar narrative rehearsed regularly over the last four hundred years. The trials he endured—including some in actual courtrooms—speak to the intimate nature of the early colonial period. Then, the actions of even small numbers of nonconformists prompted strenuous reactions from officials, who understood the fragility of their nascent settlements on land already inhabited by others. Morton's story suggests that seventeenth-century New England would have been far different had dissidents like him found a way to turn their schemes into reality.

CHAPTER ONE

Homelands

THOMAS Morton was probably born around 1575 or 1576 in the West Country of England, possibly in Somerset. There are no known details about his background, though one of his biographers has surmised that his family had sufficient means to send him to the Inns of Court in London to train as a lawyer.[1] With its long coastline facing Bristol Channel, Somerset sat between the busier cities of Bristol to its northeast and Plymouth to its southwest. At the time of Morton's birth, those ports, better situated to take advantage of transatlantic opportunities than London, bustled with ships coming and going across the ocean, especially to and from the rich cod fisheries of the Atlantic shelf off North America.[2]

Morton was likely at Clifford's Inn, which was part of the Inner Temple, in the 1590s. The Inner Temple was then one of the four pillars of the English legal education establishment. The Inner Temple and the Middle Temple, adjacent to each other in the City of London, were closer to the center of political life than the two other inns, Gray's and Lincoln's, situated in Camden. Had Morton ventured over to the Middle Temple, he might have seen the collection of Richard Hakluyt the elder, a lawyer deeply interested in the resources that could be found far from the realm. Hakluyt, who died in 1591, kept maps and books of cosmography (similar to the modern study of geography) in his rooms. As his younger cousin (also named Richard) testified, the lawyer could point to various parts of the world and recite the opportunities that lay there.[3]

Scholars like the Hakluyts and other readers who became absorbed in maps and accounts of travel to distant places understood that territory far from England might have resources that could improve the realm of King James I, who had ascended to the throne after the death of Queen Elizabeth in 1603. (Previously King James VI of Scotland, he assumed the crown of England because the queen left no direct heirs.) At some unknown point, Morton began to study that literature and prepare for a journey across the Atlantic Ocean. By the time he boarded the first vessel that took him to Plymouth in 1622, Morton was well aware that the region was already home to thousands of Native Americans. His own writings, based on firsthand observations and discussions with indigenous neighbors, provide additional details about the appearance of the region and the practices of its Native peoples on the eve of the arrival of European colonizers.

Long before Morton crossed the Atlantic, the Ninnimissinuok, the indigenous Algonquian-speaking residents of southern New England, understood the region and its resources with a level of sophistication that eluded the earliest English travelers to the region.[4] Their ancestors had settled there at least three hundred years before the English arrived. Unlike the newcomers, who tried to discern the Christian god's intent in the unfolding of daily events in the seventeenth century, the Ninnimissinuok believed that the land had been formed by multiple nonhuman spiritual forces. Various deities still remained active, including those controlling the movement of fish and animals and others that needed to be propitiated for a successful crop.

Indigenous views of the region survive in multiple forms. For example, archaeologists have provided details about aspects of these Algonquians' material culture. Their excavations point to precise moments when local lives changed, such as the years when European-manufactured items began to appear in grave goods. Still, what can be unearthed tells only part of a larger story of human occupation in this (or any other) region once settled by indigenous peoples and then claimed by newcomers who tried to erase most traces of the Native landscape. Fortunately, Ninnimissinuok oral history and folklore adds much about how the area's first occupants understood its resources and created sustainable economies there.[5]

By the time the English arrived on their shores, the Ninnimissinuok had created topographical maps of the region. Unlike the Europeans, they did not draw their maps on paper. Instead, they could be found in place-names. Such a strategy was common across much of North America. In the land of the Ninnimissinuok, many of these toponyms indicated local resources or specific geological features. Southern New England Algonquian dialects included the words *Connecticut*, meaning "on the long tidal river," *Skugamaug* (in modern Connecticut), "eel fishing here," and *Massachusetts*, "at the big hill." *Passagassawakeag* (a river in Waldo County, Maine) was a Maleseet word meaning "place for spearing sturgeon by torchlight." *Wessaguset*, the site of an early colonial settlement, meant "at the small saltwater cove." *Chicopee* referred to "violent water."[6]

Nature did not simply exist. What could be seen was one part of a complex relationship between humans and non-human forces. The gods who ruled in the homeland of the Ninnimissinuok had many names. Kautántowwit was, according to the linguist (and eventual founder of Rhode Island) Roger Williams, "the great *South-West* God, to whose House all soules goe, and from whom came their Corne, Beanes, as they say." Williams reported that the Algonquians named an eastern god (Wompanand), a western god (Checesuwànd), a northern god (Wunnanaméanit), and a southern god (Sowwanànd) in addition to the "house god" Wetuómanit. There was a god for women (Squáuanit) and another for children (Muckquachuckquànd). The Algonquians employed the term *manìt* to refer to a singular deity but the word also had a plural form, *manittówock*. They had a god of the sun (Keesuck-

---

(*opposite*) Indigenous peoples of southern New England, c. 1600, by Rebecca Wrenn, based on maps in William Sturtevant, ed., *Handbook of North American Indians*, vol. 15, *Northeast* (Washington, D.C., 1978), and Lisa Brooks, *Our Beloved Kin: A New History of King Philip's War* (New Haven, 2018).

St. Lawrence R.

St. Lawrence Iroquoians

Western Abenaki

Eastern Abenaki

Kennebec R.

Penobscot R.

Eastern Abenaki

Western Abenaki

Saco R.

Connecticut R.

Merrimack R.

Penobscot Bay

Casco Bay

Patucket

Nipmuck

Massachusett

Wampanoag

Atlantic Ocean

Pequot-Mohegan

Niantic

Narragansett

miles

0   40

quànd), the moon (Nanepaûshat), the sea (Paumpágussit), and fire (Yot·anit). The Natives named and worshiped thirty-seven gods in all. But, as Williams recognized, they claimed no monopoly on deities. They knew that others existed as well. "They will generally confesse that God made all," he wrote, "but then in speciall, although they deny not that *Englishmans* God made *English* Men and the heavens and the Earth there!" He added, "Their Gods made them and the Heaven, and Earth where they dwell."[7]

The Ninnimissinuok claimed to meet their deities as they slept. One such figure, called Hobbamock, was considered a devil by the colonist Edward Winslow, among the earliest English at New Plymouth and the author of a 1624 narrative entitled *Good Newes from New England: A True Relation of Things Very Remarkable at the Plantation of Plimoth in New England.* Hobbamock "appeares in sundry formes unto them," he wrote, "as in the shape of a Man, a Deare, a Fawne, an Eagle, &c. but most ordinarily a Snake." Yet while the English saw him as evil, the Ninnimissinuok understood that he was capable of curing illness and wounds. In their dreams Hobbamock told them that a failed cure was the fault of Keihtan, "the principall and maker of all the rest," the one who had "created the heavens, earth, sea and all creatures contained therein." No one claimed to have seen Keihtan himself in dreams, but legends of his prowess survived in oral history, passed from one generation to another.[8] One of those stories focused on the origins of humans. Kautántowwìt, Williams reported, "made one man and woman of a stone" but did not like the results, so "he broke them in pieces." Then he "made another man and woman of a Tree, which were the Fountaines of all mankind."[9]

Native deities played a variety of roles in the lives of the Ninnimissinuok. Among the more notable was Maushop (or Moshup), an ancient giant who once lived on what is today Martha's Vineyard. He pulled entire trees out of the ground for his fires and roasted whales on them. "To facilitate the catching these fish," a physician named William Baylies reported near the end of the eighteenth century, Moshup "threw many large stones, at proper distances into the sea, on which he might walk with greater ease to himself." This observation explained how the Natives understood the topography at Gay Head at the western edge of the Vineyard. Moshup had been much feared and the Ninnimissinuok once gave him all of the tobacco available on the Vineyard to appease him. Moshup smoked it and then "knocked the snuff out of his pipe, which formed Nantucket." Once all-powerful, Moshup became alarmed by the spread of Christianity on the islands and fled, never to return.[10]

These stories provide an opening into the worldview of the Ninnimissinuok in southern New England. So do archaeological remains, especially if read in the context of indigenous oral history. Surviving physical evidence reveals that Native burials in the area often followed a southwestern orientation, pointing toward a favorable spiritual locale and in opposition to the direction where nor'easters battered the shoreline. Archaeologists have also found dugout canoes submerged with rocks in local waters. In a region with substantial tidal shifts, such crafts were crucial for navigating what one archaeologist referred to as the "wet homelands" of Native peoples. Sinking canoes made sense where wide temperature fluctuations and sub-freezing winter weather might have cracked wooden vessels left exposed to the air. Kept underwater during the winter when they were unusable, these canoes survived from one season to the next, enabling the Ninnimissinuok to maintain access to coastal waters crucial to their economies.[11]

Archaeological remains also confirm broader aspects of the regional economy. Maize cultivation likely took hold there around 1300 C.E. Evidence of farming can be found in the skeletal remains of women, which reveal excessive wear around the wrist joints characteristic of participation in agriculture. Further, early English observers took note of Ninnimissinuok landscape practices. "Every *Sachim* knoweth how farre the bounds and limits of his own Countrey extendeth," Winslow reported, "and that is his owne proper inheritance, out of that if any of his men desire land to set their corne, hee giveth them as much as they can use, and sets them their bounds." Traces of fish used as fertilizer provide yet further evidence of farming practices that were sufficiently intensive that fields began to lose fertility, which prompted efforts to improve yields. Coastal Ninnimissinuok undoubtedly relied extensively on aquatic resources as well. During times of conflict they took refuge in low-lying areas, which provided religious as well as strategic advantages since the practice put them into closer proximity to nonhuman powers that could offer protection.[12]

Thomas Morton first encountered indigenous people in southern New England on a brief journey in the summer of 1622. When he later settled down to compose his own observations, he blended firsthand observation with information he had extracted from others. Here he drew on a series of reports generated by Europeans who had traveled to this territory in the first two decades of the seventeenth century. But he also relied on his own understanding of communities and cultures based on his conversations with local peoples.

Morton's book included what might seem like inaccurate details about these Algonquians' world. He claimed, for example, that they drew on words from both Greek and Latin, and noted how often they integrated *pan* in their own words and place-names, such as Pantneket (possibly Pawtucket) and Mattapan, no doubt an ancient way of showing reverence for "*Pan* the great God of the Heathens."[13] While he acknowledged that there existed no traces of the worship of Pan, he argued that the word's appearance in language revealed that "it is most likely that the Natives of this Countrey, are descended from people bred upon that part of the world, which is towards the Tropicke of Cancer, for they doe still retaine the memory of some of the Starres [on] that part of the Celestiall Globe, as the North-starre." Morton was not alone among English colonists in noticing that the Natives recognized specific stars and constellations and possessed a keen understanding of the phases of the moon.[14] Morton dismissed others' claims that the Native Americans might have once been Tartars, but he speculated that they could be the descendants of the ancient diaspora of the Trojans, though he perhaps made his observation in jest as a way to mock other Europeans' speculations about the origins of indigenous Americans.[15]

Morton, who could see how these Algonquians lived day to day, likened their houses to those of "the wild Irish." They erected poles in a circle and bent the top of them to form an arch, then bound the tops together with walnut bark, renowned for its durability. A hole at the top allowed smoke from their fires to escape. They covered the walls with mats consisting of reeds or sedge sewn together using needles fashioned from the leg bones of a crane and thread spun from hemp. Their beds were built of planks that rested twelve to eighteen inches above the ground, draped with blankets made from the skins and fur of beaver, otter, deer, bear, and raccoon, "all which they have dressed and converted into good lether, with the haire on, for their coverings." Bedclothes kept them warm at night, as did the perpetually burning fire, which the Natives used during the day to roast fish and meat. "The aire doeth beget good stomacks," Morton believed, "and they feede continually, and are no niggards of their vittels." Instead, they always shared what they had with visitors, who could also sleep inside their houses. "If you be hungry, there is meat for you, where if you will eate you may," he wrote. "Such is their Humanity."[16]

Morton recognized that the Natives migrated with the seasons. To stay in one place would have put too much pressure on local resources. So "after the manner of the gentry of Civilized natives," he wrote with a bit of sarcasm, they "remoove for their pleasures." During parts of the year they followed stocks of game animals. At other times they visited known fishing places, especially in the spring, when "fish comes in plentifully." They joined others during their travels for games, juggling, and "all manner of Revelles."[17] Their practice of burning undergrowth in the woods twice each year made it easier for them to hunt. Morton wrote that this practice improved the look of the landscape. "This custome of firing the Country is the meanes to make it passable," he wrote, "and by that meanes the trees growe here, and there as in our parks: and makes the Country very beautifull, and commodious."[18] Modern scholars, using a variety of sources, have confirmed the accuracy of most of Morton's assessment of the landscape, describing the varied and productive economies indigenous peoples created across southern New England in the era before Europeans arrived.[19]

Like other Europeans, Morton was fascinated by the appearance of Native Americans.[20] He wrote about their clothing and how they adapted it to each season—for example, leaving the hair on some skins so they could turn them inside out in winter for additional warmth. They worked other skins into supple leather and decorated the large skins of moose, which they also used to make shoes. If they had no moose skin, they used deer hides for their feet. After puberty, men used leather hides to cover "their secreats of nature, which by no meanes they will suffer to be seene." They wore aprons made of deerskin, tied by the tails, which they used to carry tools for making a fire, and donned more clothing so they would not scrape their skin during a hunt. Morton thought the men looked like "Irish in their trouses."[21]

If the men looked more handsome than the English, for their part, the women "have as much modesty as civilized people, and deserve to be applauded for it." Like the men, the women would not allow anyone to see them naked. Pregnant women carried large burdens on their backs up to the point of giving birth, and went back to work soon after, even if that meant needing to travel only one or two days later. Mothers carried their infants in cradles that were better than those employed by the English, evident in their excellent posture — "well propertioned not any of them crooked backed or wry legged." Morton claimed that girls and boys were white skinned at birth but that their mothers bathed them in a rinse of walnut leaves and husks that stained "their skinne for ever, wherein they dip and washe them to make them tawny."[22]

Morton's writing, like any observer's, reflected his own sentiments toward the Ninnimissinuok. He often praised their physical traits. They possessed eyesight so much sharper than the English that they could see ships arriving well before the newcomers. Their vision was so powerful that "one would allmost beleeve they had intelligence of the Devill, sometimes." Their sense of smell was remarkable too. Walking through the woods one day, Morton and an unnamed local came upon two recently buried deer. His ally dug both up and could smell the fresher one, which they then ate. Morton also claimed that a French writer reported that Native Americans could tell a Spaniard and a Frenchman apart by their smell.[23] They devised ways to preserve their food using holes in the ground, though Morton admitted that "if any thinge bring them to civility, it will be the use of Salte, to have foode in store, which is a chiefe benefit in a civilized Commonwealth."[24]

But while the Ninnimissinuok could learn from the English, the newcomers could benefit as well if they modeled their behavior on that of the indigenous Americans. Young men spoke in meetings, but everyone considered the opinions of the older men before taking action. "The consideration of these things," Morton wrote, "should reduce some of our irregular young people of civilized Nations: when this story shall come to their knowledge, to better manners, and make them ashamed" of their earlier treatment of senior members of their own communities. He praised as well the Natives' dedication to preserving their reputation and honor.[25]

On occasion Morton, like other travel writers, used analogous reasoning in his text, comparing what he saw with his eyes to practices that his readers would have already known, particularly when he attempted to probe the Natives' inner lives. He wrote that the Algonquians buried "their dead ceremoniously, and carefully," but then moved away "because they have no desire the place should put them in minde of mortality," a claim that perhaps suited the post-epidemic landscape of the early 1620s.[26] Nonetheless, Morton claimed that there were "weake witches" among them, called "Powahs," who had "some correspondency" with the devil and impressed large groups when they gathered together for their "Revels." Morton claimed they used sleight of hand to impress the credulous, such as one powah who made a "firme peece of Ice to flote in the middest of the bowle in the presence of the vulgar people," though such a trick could have been done only "by the agility of Satan his consort." Aside from such trickery, powahs performed cures for the ill—even, on occasion, for a colonist. One of them, Morton wrote, accepted a parcel of biscuits in exchange for healing one Englishman's swollen hand. The powah "tooke the party grieved into the woods aside from company, and with the helpe of the devill, (as may be conjectured,) quickly recovered him of that swelling, and sent him about his worke againe." Morton referred to a healers' use of "juggling tricks," employing the same idea that earlier English observers had applied when they saw healers use incantations to cure the afflicted.[27]

Given the fact that Morton had set up at Ma-re Mount to

trade with the locals, it is not surprising that he understood their commercial practices as well as any English observer. He recognized that the business they conducted did not rely on large sailing vessels. They lacked "the use of navigation, whereby they may trafficke as other nations, that are civilized, use to doe," so instead they "barter for such commodities as they have." Rather than money, they traded in beads made of white and purple shells known as wampum (or "Wampampeak" as he called it). Morton did not quite understand the unique ecology of this part of the Atlantic shelf, so he presumed that the shells could be found "in all the parts of New England, from one end of the Coast to the other." But if he overestimated the ease with which such shells could be found, he understood their value. "The white with them is as silver with us," he wrote, while the violet was equivalent to gold. Wampum was a medium of transaction with other indigenous peoples and also, as Morton noted, with the English as well, who understood that they could use wampum to obtain furs from interior groups that lacked direct access to the coastline. He also warned his readers that the locals had a keen eye and could detect imitation wampum.[28] Though no commodity was as valuable to the Ninnimissinuok as wampum, some Native artisans made small maple bowls for trade. Algonquians who lived along the coast dealt with those in the interior who harvested aquatic resources from fresh water, part of an elaborate economy based on extensive and long-lasting coastal expertise.[29]

There was some inconsistency within Morton's book when it came to the religious ideas of the Ninnimissinuok. Most surprising was his assertion that the indigenous peoples of New England lacked any sense of religion, despite the assertion of Cicero that there was "no people so barbarous but have some worshipp or other." Morton claimed that it was "absurd to say they have a kinde of worship, and not able to demonstrate whome or what it is they are accustomed to worship." He thought it more likely that elephants, the smartest of all animals, worshipped the moon. His reminiscences about Native religion ended with the notion that one "neede not the helpe of a wodden prospect for the matter," a snarky reference to the views of William Wood, whose book, first printed in 1634, had included a section on indigenous religious beliefs.[30]

Still, Morton's own evidence revealed deep and abiding spiritual beliefs among the Ninnimissinuok. He wrote that while the Algonquians were "without Religion, Law, and King," they were "not altogether without the knowledge of God (historically)." The latter point fit more easily into his evidence, especially when he claimed that indigenous religious practices often conformed to English beliefs. He reported that the Ninnimissinuok believed that "God made one man and one woman," and he instructed them to "live together, and get children, kill deare, beasts, birds, fish, and fowle, and what they would at their pleasure." But "their posterity was full of evill, and made God so angry that hee let in the Sea upon them, & drowned the greatest part of them, that were naughty men, (the Lord destroyed so)." Those banished were consigned to "Sanaconquam who feeds upon them, (pointing to the Center of the Earth: where they imagine is the habitation of the Devill)," while those who were spared in the flood "increased the world." When these men and women died, they traveled westward "to the howse of Kytan," a reference to the deity that Roger Williams called Kautántowwìt, "to whose House all soules goe." In that blessed afterlife they would have all provided for them as long as they worked. The Ninnimissinuok, Morton wrote, were convinced that it was Kytan who was responsible for trees, corn, "and all manner of fruits."[31]

He also added that these people believed in "the immortality of the soule" and had established rituals for marking the graves of their deceased, differentiating between those of "noble, and of ignoble, or obscure, or inferior discent." The more esteemed were buried in a kind of chest with wooden boards underneath on each side and on top of the corpse, and then something "in forme of a hearse cloath" placed on top. They marked the deaths and returned at certain times to hold ceremonies of remembrance. In contrast, Morton reported that the indigenous marveled "to see no monuments over our dead," which made them conclude that "no great Sachem is yet to come into those parts, or not as yet deade, because they see the graves all alike."[32]

This discussion provided a crucial opening for Morton to share his own belief that "wee that use the booke of Common prayer, doo it to declare to them, that cannot reade, what Kytan has commaunded us, and that wee doe pray to him with the helpe of that booke." This was no stray reference but instead a criticism of the Pilgrims and Puritans who disdained the use of this book and hence failed in their efforts to convert the locals to Christianity. Morton claimed that an unnamed Native who had lived with him before the man got married and had children asked Morton to let his son move in with him to learn how to read the Bible. Morton agreed. He "was a very joyfull man to thinke, that his sonne should thereby (as hee said) become an Englishman," Morton noted, "and then hee would be a good man." Morton asked this father what qualities made a "good man." Someone who would not lie or steal, he learned, which were capital crimes among the Ninni-missinuok. Those who led an honorable life would someday live forever with Kytan "in all manner of pleasure."[33]

By the time Morton observed these Algonquian peoples, the world they had known before the arrival of Europeans had already changed. English and other transatlantic travelers had been interested in the region since the late fifteenth century, when John Cabot—born Giovanni Cabota in Venice—first reached the North American mainland in 1497 on a ship out of Bristol. Over the course of the following century, Euro-peans realized the enormous bounty to be hauled from these seas, something known earlier to Norse sailors but not a major industry until after the decline of the Northmen. English fish-ing crews began to harvest cod off Newfoundland in ever-greater numbers after the mid-1570s.[34] From 1576 to 1578 the mariner Martin Frobisher led three expeditions to modern-day Nunavut, at first seeking the ever-elusive Northwest Pas-sage and then in the hopes of finding gold. The 1578 mission consisted of seventeen ships, the largest seaborne exploratory venture ever launched by the realm. Those involved sent home tons of rocks they believed contained gold, but assayers found them to be good only for paving roads or building walls. In 1583 a three-ship convoy led by Sir Humphrey Gilbert, a vet-eran of the violent conquest of Ireland, explored Newfound-land. But one of the ships sank off its shores and another went down in a mid-ocean squall, leaving but one boat of survivors.³⁵ Chronicles of these voyages and others circulated in England in the latter years of Elizabeth's reign, notably in the massive volumes edited by the younger Hakluyt, who became the most avid promoter of English overseas colonization during the 1580s and 1590s.³⁶ Though he did not publish another large collection of travel accounts after 1600, Hakluyt continued to gather materials that he hoped would spur others to engage in long-distance trade and settlement schemes.³⁷

Soon other reports started to appear that provided English readers with new details about the Atlantic coast of North America between 43 and 46 degrees north latitude, approximately from modern-day Portsmouth, New Hampshire, where the Piscataqua River meets the Atlantic, to the northeastern reaches of modern Nova Scotia. On May 14, 1602, Bartholomew Gosnold, who had trained in law at the Middle Temple and become acquainted with the younger Hakluyt, led an expedition that arrived in North America after a voyage that lasted about six and one-half weeks. John Brereton, a gentleman on the voyage whose account of the trip was printed in London later that year, praised the plentiful sources of fresh water and the richness of the soil, suggesting that "the most fertil part of England" was "barren" by comparison. He and his companions planted barley, oats, peas, and wheat on a small shoal they named Elizabeth's Island; within two weeks the seedlings were already nine inches tall. Brereton's narrative also included a list of trees, birds, animals, minerals, and plants (including many kinds of berries) available at the site. He singled out the abundance of copper in the region, which the locals used to make jewelry, cups, and arrowheads. The travelers, Brereton wrote, "were much fatter and in better health than when we went out of England." With that observation Brereton introduced what became a notable theme in English travel accounts of the region. This was, as William Wood later put it, a "medicinable climate." Most notable, perhaps, were the region's abundant aquatic resources, which exceeded those in Newfoundland.[38]

Brereton communicated with the Algonquians he met in sign language. This proved sufficient for most purposes, including the trade of English-manufactured goods for furs. The Natives were fond of tobacco, which they dried into a powder to consume or "drinke," as other contemporary Europeans had noted. He described how he had taught some English words to one and the man "suddenly spake so plaine and distinctly, as if he had beene a long scholar in the language." Brereton and his travel companions brought the English the first detailed information of a region they labeled Cape Cod in honor of the plentiful supply of the fish there.[39]

Three years later a mission led by George Waymouth, a native of Devon with extensive experience exploring along Britain's coasts, reconnoitered the shores of modern Maine. James Rosier's report of that mission detailed local resources, including shallow waters crowded with lobsters, oysters boasting pearls, abundant schools of fish, and small islands covered by thick forests.[40] He also described how the English and Algonquians communicated via sign language and how the Ninnimissinuok were eager to trade for manufactured goods such as combs and mirrors. He wrote about the joy the English felt encountering "the kind civility we found in a people, where we little expected any spark of humanity."

They were "a people of exceeding good invention," he noted, "quick understanding and ready capacatie." On one occasion Rosier claimed he conveyed to the Algonquians that he would provide them with knives if they brought him furs and skins. Such commerce promised a twofold advantage. The English would acquire beaver and deerskins, which they prized. Just as important, the newcomers would use the transaction to teach a lesson—namely, "to bring them to an understanding of exchange" so that the Algonquians "might conceive the intent of our coming to them to be for no other end." The English believed that the best way to advance their mission was to fashion alliances with coastal peoples.[41]

To do so, the English thought they should first establish their intellectual and technical superiority, as when they once used a lodestone to move an iron sword, which Rosier believed caused the locals to marvel at the English. "This we did to cause them to imagine some great power in us," he wrote, "and for that to love and fear us," using phrasing that other English travelers to North America had employed earlier.[42] To advance this plan the English decided it would be best to capture a handful of Natives as a defensive measure to prevent any possible assault. "Because we found the land a place answerable to the intent of our discovery, namely, fit for any nation to inhabit," he wrote, "we used the people with as great kindness as we could devise, or found them capable of."[43]

The Waymouth expedition never made it as far as the Kennebec River, which would later become a decisive locale for English colonists and their fur-trading operations. But Rosier's narrative of the journey added to the English stock of knowledge about a place that seemed to possess natural resources and friendly inhabitants. It was the kind of place, that is, that drew the interest of prospective investors.

On July 18, 1605, the explorer Samuel de Champlain, who had been sailing along the northeast coastline to establish a French claim to the region, spotted the coast of modern Plymouth Harbor. As they passed, he observed "a great many cabins and gardens." That day the winds were against his crew, so they decided to anchor in the bay as they waited for better conditions, a typical tactic used by European explorers along the Atlantic coast at the time. But while they waited for the winds to freshen, they were not alone. "There came to us two or three canoes," he wrote, "which had just been fishing for cod and other fish, which are found there in large numbers."[44] Champlain may have observed how easy it was to fish along the coastal shelf of the continent, but his writing was also likely informed by earlier European accounts about the bounty of those waters. Those vast numbers of fish remained for decades until Europeans and colonists developed ever more efficient ways to haul them in, eventually producing scarcity in what had been among the richest fishing waters in the world—or at least in the world known to Europeans.[45]

Champlain explained how Natives took advantage of these waters, praised their generosity (and described his willingness to accept their gifts), and wrote that these Algonquians embraced trade. He paid attention to geography as well, offering preliminary thoughts on which rivers a vessel could ascend. There would be no problems finding this locale again. "This place is very conspicuous from the sea," Champlain wrote, "for the coast is very low, excepting the cape at the entrance to the bay. We named it the Port du Cap St. Louis, distant two leagues from the above cape, and ten from the Island cape. It is in about the same latitude as Cap St. Louis." Champlain, as was his custom, drew a map of the region, which included a number of Native dwellings and the note that these were "cabins where the savages till the ground." The next day, July 19, he and his crew sailed off to continue their voyage.[46]

Nine years later, in April 1614, Captain John Smith departed London with a two-ship expedition to explore the same territory. Smith by then had long expertise in treating with coastal Algonquians, most famously during the earliest years of the settlement at Jamestown. This time his journey took him farther north, allowing him to describe the region from Penobscot Bay to Cape Cod.

Like many other European explorers, Smith went looking for natural resources, notably whales and possible copper and gold mines. "If those failed," he wrote at the start of his report, published in London in 1616, "Fish and Furres was then our refuge." The English, hapless at catching whales and incapable of locating minerals, turned toward more predictable sources of income. Smith and his crew hauled in about forty-seven thousand fish, drying forty thousand and salting the rest. They then traded with the Algonquians for pelts: eleven hundred beaver, one hundred marten, and approximately one hundred otter. He returned to England in October with one ship loaded with the salted fish, oil drained from cod livers, and furs. The other ship headed to Spain to sell the dry fish. By his own account, the American wares found ready purchasers.[47]

The cargo unloaded from those English ships was less sig-

Louys, diſtant dud. cap deux lieues, & dix du
cap aux iſles. Il eſt enuiron par la hauteur du
cap S. Louys.

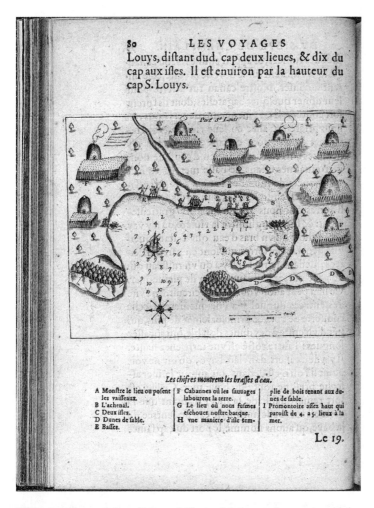

Les chifres montrent les braſſes d'eau.

A Monſtre le lieu ou poſent les vaiſſeaux.
B L'achenal.
C Deux iſles.
D Dunes de ſable.
E Baſſes.

F Cabannes où les ſauuages labourent la terre.
G Le lieu où nous fuſmes eſchouer noſtre barque.
H vne maniere d'iſle ſem-

plie de bois tenant aux du- nes de ſable.
I Promontoire aſſez haut qui paroiſt de 4. a 5. lieux à la mer.

Le 19.

This map from a 1613 edition of Champlain's travel narrative of the
place he named Port du Cap St. Louis featured houses surrounded
by fields and clearings, one of many places where indigenous
people along and near the coast maintained towns from spring,
when they planted maize, until autumn, when they harvested the
crop. Even a casual observer would have had to acknowledge that
the territory had been settled before the Europeans arrived.
(The Huntington Library, San Marino, California.)

nificant than the most important commodity Smith brought home—information about a coastline, its peoples, and the opportunities of a region not yet settled by any European nation. He counted forty Native settlements near the shoreline. Smith's expedition sounded twenty-five harbors, some large enough to berth five hundred to a thousand ships. Two hundred wooded islands lay nearby. Smith enumerated over twenty separate indigenous groups in the northern part of the region. All of them, he wrote, "differ little in language, fashion or government." Farther south the Massachusetts had established about twenty different towns scattered from the coast into the interior lakes of modern-day Maine. In the interior, Smith wrote, they hunted otter and beaver. The coastline itself was uneven, with clay or sandy cliffs in some places and stone quarries in others. Smith believed that the English would be able to find stones for building, slate for tiles, "smooth stone to make Fornaces and Forges," and limestone to extract from many cliffs. The region, which he thought resembled the Devonshire coast, would have ore to make fine iron and steel. He saw fields of maize, gardens, thick forests, abundant schools of fish, a moderate climate, and towns "well inhabited with a goodly, strong and well proportioned people." Smith boasted that he had seen four parts of the world—a reference to his earlier time in the Levant as well as Virginia—and if he had the chance to create a colony himself he would set it up in New England. Who, Smith wondered "can but approve this a most excellent place, both for health and fertility?" Only people incapable of taking care of themselves would fail here.[48]

Any reader of Smith's book would have come to an easy

conclusion: here was territory that the English could colonize more easily than the Chesapeake, where the Virginia Company had struggled to maintain a settlement since 1607. Smith compared the potential gains to be had here to the riches generated by the Venetians and the Dutch, other European powers that had built great wealth through long-distance trade.[49] Further, here was a place where colonists could grow rich from planting familiar crops that flourished at the same latitudes in Europe. It would take only three hundred men to launch a colony. They would buy corn from the Algonquians "for a few trifles," echoing (perhaps unintentionally) the economic logic employed by Columbus. If the Natives objected, thirty to forty men would be enough to subdue them, he argued. Two hundred others would be needed to take in fish for the next nine months until the rest of the economy took off.[50] Smith's details of the seasonality and richness of the local fishing industry strengthened his credibility. This natural advantage produced cultural opportunities. There was hardly a local boy over twelve years old who could not fish, and every girl could spin thread to make a fishing net. As Smith or the book's compositor noted in the margins: "Imployment for poore people and fatherlesse children." This was no random observation but instead a specific response to the concerns of policy makers since Elizabethan times.[51]

While the New England coastline varied—rocky here, sandy there, with shallow harbors that made some places off limits to oceangoing ships—one place was close to perfect. The "Countrie of the Massachusetts," Smith wrote, using the name of the local inhabitants, "is the Paradise of all those parts." This land presented the best opportunity yet for an En-

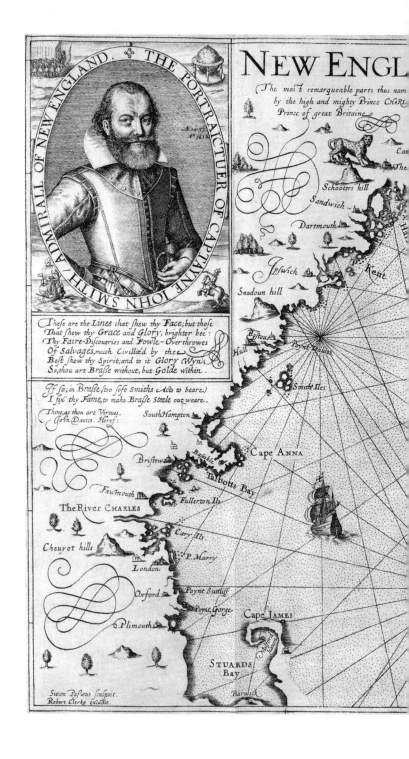

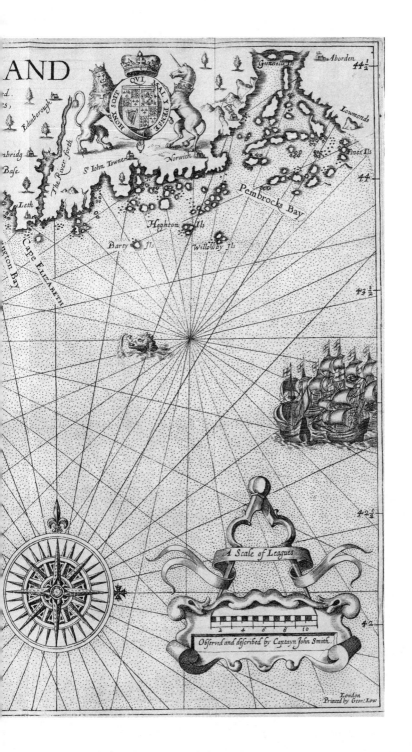

AND

Aborden

Gunnells Ils

44½

Edinborough

Lowmonds

bridg

Norwich

Innes Ils

Base

St. Iohn Towne

44

The River forth

Leth

Pembrocks Bay

Cape Elizabeth

Heghton Ils

ington Bay

Barty Ils

Willoway Ils

43½

43½

A Scale of Leagues

2   4   6   8   10

Observed and described by Captayn Iohn Smith

42

London
Printed by Geor: Low

glish colony. What's more, if the English were serious about their Reformed religion, then it was time "to shewe our faith by our workes" by converting the Natives "to the knowledge of God, seeing what paines the *Spanyards* take to bring them to their adulterated faith." Smith hoped that both honor and the possibility of profit would motivate the English gentry to invest in the region, which would also put the realm ahead of its European competitors. Wasn't it better, he opined, to serve "our God, our King, our Country, and our selves?" The future lay in exploring and planting "these North parts of America."[52]

Smith's map was the first to label the area "New England," a new region for an extended realm. Surely, it could become a bountiful homeland for the English as it had been for generations of Ninnimissinuok—a place ready-made, as Thomas Morton saw it, for migrants who would live in peace and prosperity with their Native neighbors.

(*previous pages*) This map, printed in Smith's *Description of New England* (London, 1616), gives place-names as labeled by Smith and Prince Charles. Some copies of the book include a page where Smith listed the "old names" and "the new." Although Gosnold had recently named Cape Cod, Smith and the prince renamed it in honor of the king—but the old name prevailed nonetheless. More commonly they replaced Algonquian names with English. In this scheme Accomack became Plymouth, the Massachusetts River became the Charles, Sagadahoc became Leeth, Pemmaquid became St. John's Towne, and Passataquack became Hull. Smith identified the location of Plymouth on the coast in the lower left corner of the map, four years before the Pilgrims arrived. (The Huntington Library, San Marino, California.)

CHAPTER TWO

Partners

O
N March 16, 1616, about the same
time that Captain John Smith's *Description of New England* was appearing in London, a member of the
Wiltshire gentry named George
Miller was putting the finishing
touches on his last will and testa-
ment. Miller owned multiple parcels of land and lived in what
some of his contemporaries referred to as a "mansion" called
Upmershmead. He owned land in the same town called Langlers as well as property in Collm, Stanford Coppice, Stanford
Hartley, Shinfield, and Whitley. But his main holdings were
in the small town of Swallowfield on the western edge of what
is today Berkshire.[1]

Like others of his community Miller, who owned one
of four manors in the parish, was supposed to provide some
funds for the local poor, in this case to those who lived in his
hometown of Croydon in Surrey as well as in Swallowfield.

That expectation was explicit in a series of articles that the leaders of the settlement had drawn up in 1596, possibly as a result of tensions that the elders of the parish hoped to contain before they became a source of social upheaval. (They were also concerned with public drunkenness, unmarried mothers, maintaining order at their meetings, preventing strife between neighbors, and hedge breaking—probably a result of the theft of wood for fuel.)[2] He also designated modest sums for his nurse, his servants, and his godchildren. But he bequeathed the bulk of his estate to his immediate family—a son, George Jr., and seven daughters: Anne, Mary, Margaret, Susan, Dorothy, Jean, and Prudence. They were all still minors. He named their mother Alice, then pregnant again, as the co-executrix of his estate. George Miller would never learn the sex of his unborn child, a boy. He died less than two weeks after he finalized his will.[3]

Soon after George Sr. died, his widow Alice hired Thomas Morton to help her with various legal issues relating to the estate. Four years later, the two married, prompting a series of legal claims and counterclaims pivoting on the troubled relationship between George Jr. and his mother. The litigants brought increasingly outrageous charges against each other, driving a wedge between Miller's other children. The cases that resulted from this war within the Miller clan sharpened Morton's understanding of how to win in a courtroom. This firsthand experience enhanced his legal education in ways beyond his formal training. He learned that courts did not always agree with each other and that litigants could bring cases into different venues. His legal study would have taught him that in theory there might be one overriding conception of the law, but in reality he saw what modern scholars have called "legal pluralism," which was prevalent in the early modern Atlantic world.[4]

The year Morton married the widow Miller corresponded with the first voyage of English Pilgrims across the Atlantic. They were religious dissenters, eager advocates of certain strands of Calvinist theology that put them in opposition to the Church of England. These Pilgrims were a subset of a larger group typically known as Puritans. By the 1610s, what differentiated these Pilgrims from their more numerous fellows was the fact that they had come to the conclusion that they could no longer practice their faith freely in England. After reaching that point, a number of them sailed east to the Low Countries and formed a community at Leiden. In 1620, approximately one hundred of them boarded the *Mayflower* along with other passengers bound for New Plymouth, the first English effort to establish a permanent settlement along the American coastline north of Virginia since the failure at Sagadahoc fifteen years earlier. From then until the dissolution of the so-called Old Colony in 1691, the Pilgrims and their descendants documented the progress of their settlement, their quest to establish a religious structure that would do honor to their god, and the vicissitudes that seemed to appear with regularity to test them. Among the problems they wrote about were those caused by Sir Ferdinando Gorges, a well-connected and highly decorated military veteran whose program for North America conflicted with the well-laid plans of the Pilgrims and Puritans. As luck would have it,

Gorges and Morton began to work together at some point in the early 1620s, likely in the aftermath of the 1622 round-trip voyage that Morton had made to New England.

Neither Gorges nor Morton subscribed to the religious precepts that drove the Pilgrims and Puritans. They were members of the Church of England, as were the vast majority of English colonists who had been traveling to North America since the founding of Jamestown in 1607. Even on board the *Mayflower,* famed in American lore as the ship that launched the Pilgrim settlement of New Plymouth, perhaps two-thirds were not religious dissenters.[5]

Gorges was an assiduous promoter of the English settlement of New England and a financial supporter of Captain John Smith on the ventures he undertook after his return in 1614. As early as 1606 he had been a partner in the Plymouth-based Council for New England, a group of investors who laid out an argument for why King James should allow them to claim most of the territory along the Atlantic coast north of the colony then planned to be planted on the shores of Chesapeake Bay. A shared interest in New England nurtured the relationship of Gorges and Morton.

Sometime after 1622, Gorges became Morton's primary supporter. Morton responded by using all of his literary abilities and his legal skills, tested in the battle for Miller's estate, to promote Gorges's plans. Morton had moved, that is, from one kind of partnership to another, and from the battlefield of the courthouse to a conflict that would shape New England's formative years. Gorges is largely forgotten today except in Maine, whose local historians have long understood the crucial role he played in establishing an English province there. But he posed more of a threat to early English colonial ventures than almost anyone else on either side of the Atlantic Ocean.[6] Still, however bitter his fight against the promoters of New Plymouth and Massachusetts Bay—the people he believed had taken control of territory that rightfully belonged to him and his allies—he understood that the experiences he had in warfare did not easily translate into legal and policy disputes. Gorges, like Alice Miller, came to believe that Morton was the partner he needed to advance his agenda.

Like other members of his social class, George Miller Sr. knew the rules for taking care of his family. He understood that prevailing laws dictated how he needed to allocate the vast majority of his property among his family members. As his widow, Alice would be entitled to one-third of his holdings, including income to take care of her for the rest of her life. According to the will, she would inherit the principal residence at Swallowfield as well as the rest of that property, including its barns, orchards, and gardens. She also inherited six enclosed arable fields of undetermined size and another meadow. Wanting to ensure that Alice had the funds to educate his children and provide for them until they turned twenty-one or, as he may have expected for his seven daughters, until they married, George Sr. set aside a part of his property called Langlers, in Swallowfield, to generate rents for the family until his youngest daughter reached twenty-one or all of the girls were married. Further, if his son George Jr. died before the age of twenty-one—he was seventeen at the time—then Alice would maintain Langlers for the duration of her life. Alice was also to receive one-half of the possessions in the house in addition to cattle, swine, and two mares.

The provisions for his daughters were unexceptional. Each was to receive £300 when she married or turned twenty-one. Should one of them die before reaching her majority, the remainder would be divided among the girls equally. George Sr. understood that the outlay here—£2,100 for the bequests to the girls alone—was substantial. To make sure there would be enough, he charged Alice with taking in annual rents of £100 each year from five of his properties. His brother Robert would get a separate house and pay Alice rent. (His other brother was not so lucky. All he got was a ring, which George had himself inherited from their deceased brother Leonard.) George Sr. also made provisions for the child Alice would soon bear. If it was a son or twin boys, he or they would inherit land; if a daughter or twin girls, she or they would receive £300 each, to put them on a par with the other girls.

Other than Alice, the person who would most benefit from George Sr.'s will was his son George Jr. He was to inherit the other half of the goods in the estate that had not already been encumbered. George Sr. specified that the boy would also serve as co-executor with his mother. This clause, however unproblematic it might seem, would prove central to George Jr.'s ferocious relationship with Morton.

George Jr., court records revealed, was an angry young man. In 1620, three years after his father died and before Morton married his mother, he was charged with assault for an attack inside the church at Swallowfield. The object of his fury was a wooden pew that his grandfather and father had used. He apparently did not realize that the pew traditionally belonged to the family that owned Sheepridge Manor, then controlled by a man named John Phipps, who had not used it for some years. When the younger Miller arrived during a service and found the pew occupied, he broke open the lock on its door. Mrs. Phipps, no doubt alarmed, told him to stop, and seemingly insulted him in the process. As the court record put it, George Jr. shot back, "Does thou call me boy? Gods wounds! If I were in bed with thee thou should knowe that I were no boye." Still in a rage, George Jr., according to one version of the incident, then "leaped over the door and tumbled on the heads and necks of the 'gentlewomen' seated with the Phipps family." He landed, of all places, on the lap of Mrs. Phipps. She protested but he refused to leave. "Then he picked her up bodily and through her over the railing into the aisle," the record continued, "in sight of a Justice of the Peace who offered no remonstrance or help and only laughed at the proceedings."[7]

Though the incident might have amused some witnesses, it hinted at the rage that lived within George Jr.—a fury that was not satisfied by embarrassing an older woman sitting in a disputed pew. Soon enough, George Jr. would train his anger on a more dangerous nemesis.

The problems began, Morton claimed in court documents, soon after the wedding. Morton knew from George Sr.'s will that Alice and George Jr. were to be the co-executors of the lands in Swallowfield and the rest of the estate. Alice took on her role as executor, but George Jr., according to Morton, refused to do so, even after he turned twenty-one. More troubling, the younger Miller formed an alliance with a yeoman from Kent named Thomas Humphrey (also spelled Humfrey or Humfreyes in court records) who had married George's sister Mary, and with Thomas Hilman, "who had," so the records of one court recount, "a desire to have married with one other of the daughters" in the family. Their plan was to find a way to extract an additional £300 on top of the amounts already promised to each of the girls.

To gain the funds, George Jr. and Hilman filed a suit against Morton and Alice, claiming that she had already promised Humphrey the money. Though Alice admitted that she could not "Certainely Remember what words did passe" between herself and her son at the time she married Morton, she added that she did not believe she had ever made such a promise. Moreover, she had had extraordinary expenses during the years before George Jr. turned twenty-one and her estate had suffered while she struggled to take care of her large family. Morton and Alice were themselves owed £100 from rented properties, but their adversaries had been urging the estate's tenants not to pay up.[8]

As Morton told the story, this effort to interfere with the proper payments to Alice was only one of George Jr.'s unlawful and uncharitable actions toward his mother. Morton claimed that the young man had publicly stated that if Alice died, none of his sisters would "have one penny of their [portions] payed [unto] them." He was a terrible son, Morton continued, who sought "to vex and molest" his mother and "thereby to shorten her life." With his mother out of the way, he might find a way to get their portions, "Contrary to lawe, equity and good Conscience." Morton even claimed that George Jr. had "abused" his mother "by beating and kicking her, havinge not the feare of God before his eyes or any manner of reverence, regard or respect of dutye" toward her. Having hatched his "malicious plotte," he "Covetously" wanted to enjoy "the benefitt of her estate" because he had no concern for his mother's "welfare life or prosperity."

On May 24, 1622, Thomas Morton appeared before the Chancery Court, which had sat in Westminster since the reign of Edward III and which, among its other duties, handled issues relating to estates. Chancery was unlike a common law court, where decisions were bound by precedent, so litigants often turned to it with the hope that the unique circumstances of their case would produce a favorable verdict. Morton recounted the travails he and Alice had experienced at the hands of George Jr. and his allies, hoping that the court would rule that the estate owed the couple the disputed funds and agree that Alice had lost an additional £300 in trying to protect the estate. The two petitioners also wanted the court to judge that the defendants were at fault for generating "this unnaturall suite."[9]

The defendants, as might be expected, denied everything Morton alleged. Humphrey stated that he had been married to Mary Miller for six years, an unlikely claim since that would have meant they were married when George Miller Sr., was still alive, which his will failed to mention. He claimed that Alice had promised him £300, which was to be paid in three installments, but the last third had still not been paid. He added that he thought Morton and Alice had received more than they claimed.[10]

A month later, with the case still pending, Morton filed

a brief affidavit in the Chancery Court asserting that he had subpoenaed George Jr. to pay 30 shillings for his court costs. According to Morton, the young man had rebuffed the claim and "scornefully denyed the same cyringe twittle twattle," a phrase suggesting that George Jr. had responded in an offhand manner. As might have been expected, George Jr. had a different view of events. He filed his own claim against his mother and her new husband, noting that he had already paid the 30 shillings. Both parties agreed to submit their claims to binding arbitration, which was to be handled by two attorneys at Gray's Inn, one of the inns of court that was likely less well known to Morton.[11]

The contest between George Jr. and Morton and Alice remained unresolved and eventually came before the Star Chamber in Westminster. The original purpose of this court, established during the early decades of the fifteenth century, had been to provide less powerful litigants with a chance to press a case against more prominent members of their communities who, some feared, might escape justice if tried only in local communities. Although the Star Chamber would collapse in the 1640s in the face of political changes associated with the rise of a more activist Parliament, it was a powerful body when, on June 3, 1622, George Jr. arrived in Westminster, pressing his claim against his mother and Morton.[12]

As George Jr. told the Star Chamber, about a year earlier, his mother had been "earnestly solicited to intermarry with one Thomas Morton a person of noe certaine abode." He claimed that Morton, a solicitor, had been a "troblesome person to the Comon weale" who had been "expelled out of an issue of Chauncery for his lewd and wicked behavior." He added that his mother, after this incident, had come to regret her marriage to "soe base a person and of noe worth" who had tried to defraud her children of their inheritance. He also claimed that Alice had made a protective arrangement with her son, granting him a fifty-year lease to Swallowfield, so that even if she married Morton, her new husband would be incapable of causing havoc and cheating the son's estate. He claimed too that when he was absent from Swallowfield, Morton had convinced Alice to search the house for that lease.

Under pressure, Alice broke into the young man's "cupbords, tronkes and chests" so that Morton could "deface and cancell" the lease. He added that it was only after his mother had the lease in hand that Morton married her. He stated further that Morton and armed confederates tried to take possession of the main house in Swallowfield. They managed to get everyone out except George Jr.'s pregnant wife and her maid, who had locked themselves into a room. Morton, the young man claimed, burst into their chamber, tossing out the two women even though his pregnant daughter-in-law was naked at the time. In an effort to save his wife, George Jr. claimed, he wrestled with a gun-bearing Morton, but no one was injured. Morton and his confederates, the young man claimed, shot at the group, but divine intervention prevented any injuries even when George Jr. leapt at an armed Morton.[13]

Morton remembered things differently, according to his account. As was common in any court, he rehearsed his argument in depth. He began with an assessment of the capacity of the estate, a necessary calculation if he wanted to argue that there were funds adequate to pay his claim. He deviated from the story of the dispute to mention he had been doing some legal work for Alice when some of her relatives implored him to marry her, which she agreed to since she had known him for some time. He also said that he would have been willing to sign a lease with George Jr. for Swallowfield if it had allowed for Alice to handle the sale of any livestock or crops if George Jr. was otherwise employed. But the lease never materialized, he claimed, and Morton returned to London to attend to his own business. But his primary concern was the improper behavior of George Jr., who had set out to "abuse his mother," even though this made him "a Comon Spectacle to the world." He added that he never had any intention of defrauding any of the Miller children. If anyone had committed a fraud, it was George Jr.[14]

Subsequent actions, Morton claimed, proved that he was telling the truth. An earlier court order had specified that Alice and George Jr. were to share the resources of the estate. But George Jr., Morton testified, would not allow his mother to bake or brew, to take water from the well, or even to live in peace on the property. Morton argued that he had received only 26 shillings in rent since marrying Alice, and that was supposed to go toward the support of her children. George Jr. even sold off his mother's cattle and took the corn she had growing in her fields. Morton reported that Alice had concluded that the only way to obtain justice was to confront her son in court. Morton, for his part, believed that George Jr. sought nothing less than her ruin and quick death since he had been telling others "that he is sicke of the mother, sicke of the mother in lawe, sicke of the uncle, sicke of the Aunt." Matters got worse when George Jr. turned twenty-one, at least in Morton's telling. He alleged that George Jr. had threatened to withhold any money to his sisters if Alice died. He also offered a point-by-point refutation of George Jr.'s claims. He did admit that he carried a gun to Swallowfield, but since it was not loaded it could not have discharged in the way that George Jr. had asserted. (Two witnesses supported Morton's claims.) The reporter for the court noted that all of the defendants denied George Jr.'s claims relating to "the Ryotts, Routs, unlawfull assemblyes, breaking upp of cupboards, trunks, Chestes, doores walles and unlawfull Entreys, defacing or cancelling of deeds, obligacons or writinges" and every other misdemeanor mentioned in the original complaint. The court agreed and dismissed all charges against them. George Jr. had failed to make a convincing case against Morton.[15]

A month later, the Star Chamber, as was its practice, sent a message to the king rehearsing the details of the case. The report characterized George Miller Jr. as a "younge man of an untemperate condicon and most [incorrigible]" whose "evill carriage and behaviour towards his parents" had earlier led George Sr. to move to disinherit him, an action prevented only because Alice had intervened. The summary also noted that George Jr. and his wife had moved out in the middle of November.[16]

If he had the patience to read the entire summary, the king would have learned that any semblance of order soon dissipated. Allegations of assault, forced entry, theft, men exposing themselves and uttering profanities filled the record, including a charge that George Jr. had beaten his mother when she was pregnant, presumably with Morton's child, but soon miscarried. Morton claimed personal injuries too, with assailants lunging at him at Swallowfield, tearing off his clothes and ripping out his hair. Morton pleaded with the court to set a stern punishment to serve as an example to prevent "all other unnaturall children and ill disposed persons" from committing similar crimes. The court officer agreed and sought the arrest of the alleged offenders. Appearing in person, George Jr. and the others denied everything, claiming again that Morton had tricked his mother.[17]

In June the Chancery Court, after hearing from all of the parties, ordered that George Jr. should gain possession of a farm known as Wivalls and also that he must pay Alice a rent of £50 every year until her death.[18] In mid-November 1623, almost a year after Morton alleged George Jr. had orchestrated the most egregious assault on Alice, the son apparently prevailed, in large part because Morton could not be found. Morton later refused to comply with the court's dictates and instead sought "to find out holes whereby to elude performance of these things." That is, the lawyer used his training in an effort to evade the judgment.[19]

The court proceedings, however voluminous they might seem for this series of cases, contain no mention of what went on outside of legal chambers. Unbeknownst to Chancery or the Star Chamber and perhaps even to the mediators from Gray's Inn, Morton had made a fast trip to New England in 1622. Since he alluded to this trip only later and with more brevity than was characteristic of his normal style, the reasons for this voyage remain mysterious. But given the clamor of the case with his son-in-law, Morton was likely eyeing his next opportunity. Sometime in 1624 he left England again, this time intending to stay in North America.[20]

Morton's departure left unresolved his dispute with his

son-in-law. Legal records suggest that George Jr., in the aftermath of Morton's exodus, continued to battle other members of his family. In late May 1636 his sister Margaret and her husband Richard Blagrave, a haberdasher from London, brought suit in the Chancery Court against George Jr. for £300 that was due to Margaret, as had been specified in George Sr.'s will almost twenty years earlier. The dispute would continue until 1640, when George Jr. apparently paid a smaller amount. This time neither Morton nor Alice was involved. Alice had died even before this round of proceedings had begun in 1636. Morton, for his part, was back in England then, but now working with Gorges. He had apparently long given up whatever plans he had had for Swallowfield.[21]

Morton realized that the time had come for the next chapter in what was already proving to be an exceptional life's journey. What he might not have understood quite yet was the value of the courtroom experience he had gained. The judgments of the courts, taken together, led Morton to conclude that he might have better prospects outside of England than within it. But he left having learned precious lessons. A setback in one court did not mean defeat, nor did a favorable judgment mean that one would prevail as one hoped. Morton learned too about the individuals who worked in and around the courts, especially in London. That experience, invisible in the surviving records, made him ever more valuable as a solicitor and honed his ability to make an argument, either within a courtroom or to a wider public.

In 1605, well before George Jr. and Morton were engaged in their intricate legal proceedings, the English sea captain George

Waymouth landed in Plymouth, England, after a voyage that had taken him to the coast of modern Maine and back. Along with news about the coastline and its resources, Waymouth brought back five Eastern Abenakis the English had taken captive. He soon left three of them—Maneddo, Skicowaros, and Sassocomoit—in the charge of Ferdinando Gorges.[22]

Until that time Gorges was best known for his efforts battling the Spanish in the Netherlands, commanding the defense of Plymouth, and playing a minor role in the Earl of Essex's plot against the aging Queen Elizabeth I. Gorges, whose family traced its origins in England to the Norman invasion of 1066, had been briefly imprisoned for his part in the plot until King James granted him a pardon and reappointed him to his position at Plymouth. Gorges had sought glory through service in the military, which likely explains his enlistment when he was eighteen years old. He had earned a knighthood for his valor.[23] But at the dawn of the new century, with his active years on the battlefield behind him, he was in search of a new challenge.[24]

Gorges was thirty-seven when Waymouth returned. By then, he was well aware of the colonization schemes circulating among Bristol's merchants, spurring the king in 1606 to support the establishment of two colonies in North America, one on the Chesapeake and one located farther north. The southern colony was organized by the privately financed Virginia Company, which in 1607 established a settlement on the banks of the James River, a tributary of Chesapeake Bay, where after a generation of exploratory and failed ventures in Carolina, Newfoundland, and Maine, the English grabbed a toehold in North America. Gorges would concentrate his efforts on the other potential colony, which the English then referred to as Northern Virginia, the name it would bear until the circulation of Smith's book in 1616.[25] He remained committed to that northern colony despite having been defrauded by one would-be English explorer and also no doubt knowing of the series of travails Smith had borne: a fierce storm, an encounter with pirates, incarceration in a French prison.[26]

When he wrote about this period of his life some years later, Gorges drew on the kind of logic that would make him a natural ally of Morton's. According to his recollection, he saw the arrival of the Abenaki captives as pointing to the future course of English colonization in North America. "I seized upon" them, he wrote in his account of early New England's history. "They were all of one Nation, but of severall parts, and severall Families; This accident must be acknowledged the meanes under God of putting on foote, and giving life to all our Plantations."[27] Because of the long peace England had experienced since James's accession in 1603, it was now possible to promote the highest religious calling Gorges could imagine: spreading Reformed Christianity among America's indigenous peoples or, as he put it, "advanc[ing] the Crosse of Christ in Heathen parts." Further, the arms of the English king would be planted in North America and, as a result, repulse the "infernall spirits, which have so long kept those poore distressed creatures (the inhabitants of those parts) in bondage."[28]

When Waymouth left those three Natives with Gorges, he likely did so with the widely held English belief that indigenous peoples of the Western Hemisphere were inferior to Europeans. Whatever his own beliefs, Waymouth apparently felt no hesitation in kidnapping the five Abenaki men. In his mind, bringing them to England was for their benefit and the future happiness of their people. He had no plan, as others at the time did, to put Native Americans into bound labor. Instead, he wanted to observe their behavior and customs. He presumably believed that they could teach the English their language and perhaps provide some details about how the Natives lived that might be useful to English sailors exploring the region. Gorges's own views of indigenous Americans, which first took shape when those captives came into his home in 1605, influenced much of what he hoped to accomplish in North America on behalf of the Council for New England, and later in his partnership with Morton.

In 1606, members of the Council for New England, eager to maintain their claim, sent a sea captain named Henry Challons to the Maine coast, along with the returning captives Maneddo and Sassocomoit, who bore "credible informations" about the region.[29] But the voyage failed when the English expedition encountered Spanish sailors who seized the ship and stole the cargo.[30] Sir John Popham, then lord chief justice of England and the prospective leader of a new colony in the Northeast, had outfitted another vessel and sent it westward, but it returned after surveying the coast.[31]

The English supporters of the cause were undaunted. In 1607 they sent two more ships with one hundred men under the leadership of Popham's son George and Rawley Gilbert, who was the brother of the president of the council. They also took along Skicowaros. This time they carried both provisions and ordnance they would need for defense. But once again the effort failed. The winter of 1607–8 was brutal, one colonist observed, with a deep frost across Europe. It was just as bad, perhaps worse, along the Maine coast. The English hunkered down, unable do much more. At some point Popham died, possibly along with others. The resupply ship arrived, presumably in early summer, with Captain R. Davies, who had commanded its return in 1607, still in charge. He found that the English had managed to gather many furs and a large supply of sarsaparilla. But he also brought word that Captain Gilbert's brother John had died and so he needed to return home.[32]

At that point the English were forced to make a decision. They had completed a fort and had even managed to build a thirty-ton pinnace, which they christened the *Virginia*. But they had not located any ore needed to forge metal tools and it was unclear if the travelers could produce enough food to keep going. Crucially, they feared the next winter. If it was anything like the one they had just endured, then prosperity, or even survival, seemed doubtful. Rather than take their chances, they boarded the *Virginia* and sailed for home. "This," the chronicler William Strachey concluded, "was the end of that Northerne Colony" on the Kennebec.[33]

The news of the English troubles at Sagadahoc struck a blow at Gorges and those who supported the venture. Though Popham was, in Gorges's telling, the only English traveler who had perished that winter, others suffered as well from an assault that Gorges did not describe other than to mention that "their lodgings and stores were burnt, and they thereby wondrously distressed."[34] No English accounts described what might have been an assault by locals, but a French Jesuit later claimed that the Natives had used witchcraft to kill the English captain, and the English then turned on the indigenous at Sagahadoc. "They drove the savages away without ceremony," Pierre Biard wrote in 1612, and then "beat, maltreated and misused them outrageously and without restraint." In response, the Native Americans launched an attack on three English fishing vessels, taking eleven lives. The action prompted the English to flee. Their departure ended all talk of settling this part of the coast, leaving it open for the French to build forts and establish links with the Natives.[35]

Having received news of the debacle at Sagahadoc, Sir Samuel Argall, who would later become deputy governor of Virginia, sailed northward and took the three forts the French had already erected. He seized their weapons, stole their cattle, and raided one of their ships, hauling everything back to Virginia, where English newcomers were still struggling to survive. Just as important, Argall's victory opened the sea lanes in northern New England, which Gorges believed would facilitate settlement on Nova Scotia.[36]

When the *Gift of God* arrived in Plymouth Harbor on February 7, 1608, those on board brought news of the harsh winter and little else. Gorges, who understood that launching a colony would take time, realized the myriad benefits that the English could have if they were patient. Colonization, he wrote at the time, would lead to the "increase of the king's navy; the breeding of mariners; the employment of the people; the filling the world with expectation and satisfying his subjects with hopes, who now are sick in despair, and in time will prove desperate through necessity." Colonizing that region would expand the realm and hence keep that land out of the hands of a rival European nation. Presumably he had in mind the designs of the French who, Gorges knew from reports he had received, had already been in the area trading with Natives along the coast.[37]

But whatever optimism Gorges initially sustained faded once the remainder of the colonists returned later that year, bearing news of the bitter winter they had experienced. "All our former hopes," he wrote years later, "were frozen to death." The Council of the Virginia Company wrote to Gorges to inquire about his interest in the southern colony, but he passed on the opportunity. Soon afterward, the *Virginia*, the ship the Sagadahoc colonists had built, sailed back to North America from Plymouth in 1609.

Its destination was Virginia, not Maine.[38]

The ensuing years proved difficult for Gorges's cause. The events from 1605 to the early 1610s, from Waymouth's first landing through the death of Popham and the initial success of the French, had proven that the region was going to be hard to settle. These occurrences, as Gorges put it, made "manifest that wee are so farre from making a Monopoly of all those lands belonging to that coast (as hath beene scandalously by some objected) *That we wish that many would undertake the like.*" The English had also come to learn that winter was especially difficult in this part of the coast, another disincentive for those who might have been inclined to invest in a new venture.[39] Still, Gorges resolved "to put new life into that scattered and lacerated Body" that remained from the initial colonization efforts in the north.[40] As it turned out, the English had kept some of Waymouth's captives, and over time

Gorges came to believe that there was real hope that a settlement on those far shores would enable the English "to prosecute a worke so pious and honourable." With that motivation in mind, the council organized another expedition.[41]

This expedition, like the previous, included one Native American Gorges knew well, a man named Epenow who had been captured from the island Capawack (or Capawick, modern-day Martha's Vineyard). No Spaniard would purchase Epenow since he, and apparently several of the others, were "unapt for their uses." Gorges got Epenow from the ship captain Edward Harlow (a.k.a. Henry Harley), though he admitted that he did not know how Harlow had gotten possession of him. But Gorges had heard about Epenow, who "had been shewed in *London* for a wonder," a reflection of the then current practice of Europeans displaying Native American and other captives. (Captain John Smith would later write that Epenow "was shewed up and downe London for money as a wonder, and it seemes of noe lesse courage and authoritie, then of wit, strentch, and proportion.")[42] Epenow had apparently dazzled crowds with his command of English, enough "to bid those that wondred at him, welcome, welcome." But eventually the crowds grew tired and so Epenow no longer had to entertain them. He came to Gorges's house, where he lived alongside Sassocomoit (referred to by Gorges as Assacumet), one of the original three Abenakis Gorges had met.[43]

Gorges understood that Sassocomoit and Epenow had both come from the northern parts of the coast but that they did not speak the same dialect. At first, Gorges later wrote, they hardly understood each other. But then they found a way to communicate, leading Gorges to conclude that the disparity in their speech "was no more then that, as ours is betweene the Northern and Southerne people," a reference to what some English in the seventeenth century referred to as the "dark corners" of the north where locals resisted the inroads of urban culture and new religious trends.[44] Gorges came to believe that the information Epenow shared with Sassocomoit was sufficiently accurate that he should relay it to acquaintances planning an expedition to New England who took the two with them on the voyage. By the time the ship embarked it had a man named Wenape on board too, "another Native of those parts sent me out of the Isle of *Wight*," Gorges wrote, "for my better information in the parts of the Country of his knowledge."[45]

In his second narrative about early New England, Gorges wrote that he observed in these three men "an inclination to follow the example of the better sort." The way they comported themselves "shewes of great civility," he added, "farre from the rudnesse of our common people." They learned how to communicate quickly and thoroughly, sharing information about their homeland that would be of use to the English, "especially when I found what goodly Rivers, stately Islands, and safe harbours those parts abounded with." He reported that he spent three years with them in order to find out details that mattered. "I made them able to set me downe what great Rivers ran up into the Land, what Men of note were seated on them, what power they were of, how allyed, what enemies they had, and the like of which in his proper place." He took careful note of the time Epenow spent with him, seeing in his linguistic abilities a sign of how the Natives of the northern coast might be at least as sophisticated as the residents of northern Britain.[46]

Gorges had hoped that these Algonquians would become intermediaries for the new expedition. "But as in all humane affaires," Gorges wrote, "there is nothing more certaine, then the uncertaintie thereof." He described how an English vessel captained by a man named Thomas Hunt, "a worthlesse fellow of our Nation" who had been sent to sea by merchants who were not satisfied with the profits to be made from either the fisheries or the fur trade, had arrived on the coast before the council's expedition. Hunt, "more savage" than the indigenous, in Gorges's opinion, captured twenty-four Natives and stowed them under the hatch of his ship. He then set sail for "the Straights, where hee sought to sell them for slaves, and sold as many as he could get money for." Eventually local friars intervened and seized those he had not yet sold, ruining the completion of Hunt's "divellish project."[47]

Although Hunt's scheme failed, the news of what he had done spread quickly—including to Epenow and Maneddo (whom Gorges called Manawet). The two of them, as Gorges reported, "presently contracted such an hatred against our whole Nation" that they immediately sought revenge. As it turned out, Maneddo died shortly after the English landed. That left the plan in Epenow's hands. Once on land, he convinced locals to come rescue him. During a subsequent skirmish, Epenow was wounded. A master of one of the English ships was also injured but survived. Enraged by what had transpired, the English fought back, killing an unspecified number. Soon enough they decided to return to England, Gorges wrote. The ship captain "brought home nothing but the newes of their evill successe"—a reference to Hunt's actions—"of the unfortunate cause thereof, and of a warre now begunne between the inhabitants of those parts, and us."[48] The legacy of Hunt's action stained relations between English and Algonquians for generations.[49]

The years that followed brought intermittent hope of creating an English colony in the region. The council funded another expedition by Captain John Smith, but he encountered violent seas, more violent pirates, and then spent time in a French prison before he could be redeemed—a story that Smith told himself in his *Description of New England.* By then, Gorges reported, the council members decided it would be prudent to clarify their claim to the region. That meant sending a petition to the king. But in the process of filing it, they learned that their claims were being contested by those associated with the Virginia Company. It took two years to resolve the issue. In the meantime, Captain Thomas Dermer, who also worked with Gorges, decided to press ahead on the coast. While there he ran into a new group of Native Americans— Gorges did not specify who they were or where they came from, though one report claimed that Epenow was among them. Dermer survived for a time and sailed back to Virginia, but died soon after from what Gorges called "the infirmities of that place," likely a reference to the ravages produced by typhoid fever and dysentery. Gorges mourned Dermer who had, over the course of those two years, mended relations between the English "and the Salvages, that so much abhorred our Nation, for the wrongs done them by others."[50]

Gorges remained optimistic about the prospects for

settlement, despite "the many disasters, calamities, misfortunes, oppositions, and hinderances we have had." Relying on a then current European idea that places at the same latitude should be similar, he reminded his readers that this part of the American coast had "the same climate and course of the Sunne" as Rome and Constantinople, "the Ladies of the World," as well as France and Italy, "the Gardens of Europe." The climate was better for the English than that of their home, as could be measured by assessing the healthy state of colonists in North America. The soil was fertile, the harbors navigable, the woods full of desirable trees, the waters teemed with fish and the land with fowl, game, and fur-bearing mammals. Pearls and ambergris could be found, as could "great numbers of *Whales.*" The abundance of tall trees and naval stores suggested that the English should think about moving their shipbuilding industry across the ocean. Gorges was especially taken by moose, which the indigenous hunted by setting fires and driving them into the sea, but which he believed the English could tame like oxen. And, as Gorges knew from firsthand experience, the Natives were "tractable (if they bee not abused) to commerce and Trade withal, and as yet have good respect of us." This part of the American coast and the adjacent interior would be perfect for English settlements and a feudal system in which local barons would rule, as they once had in England.[51] No English colonist ever put that idea into effect in North America, though it had been discussed among promoters of colonization in Elizabethan times.[52] But the rest of Gorges's report came to serve as an early version of the narrative about regional resources that would constitute a major part of Morton's book a decade later.

In 1619 the king's council decided to establish a patent for a territory to be known as New England.[53] In 1620 Gorges's petition to the king led to a patent for a group of forty men, based in Plymouth in Devon, to create a colony to be called New England in America. The patent specified that the land stretched from 40 to 48 degrees north latitude from the Atlantic across the continent. The group had the power to create its own government and could divide the land as it saw fit. The patent specified that the primary goal of the venture was "the Conversion of and reduction of ye people in those p[ar]tes unto the true worship: of god & Christian Religion." Gorges and the members of the company believed that the English could claim this territory by right of discovery and the fact that the lands remained unoccupied by any Christian nation.[54] Soon after, Gorges and a small group of others laid out their own reasons to reconfirm the patent.[55] Gorges feared that the success of the Jamestown settlers posed a threat and that other English who had begun to trade along the coast were undermining the gains the council had made in American waters.[56] Other members of the council shared his concern. In September 1621 they sent a warning to the mayors of Bristol, Exeter, Plymouth, Dartmouth, Barnstable, and Weymouth instructing them to advise all merchants and ship owners to warn off anyone who lacked the permission of the council.[57]

The primary function of the new patent was to shore up the northern colony against possible inroads from English migrants to Virginia, which was still under the control of the private Virginia Company. Yet since their initial explorations in 1607, the authors of the petition acknowledged, the Native population of the region had dwindled substantially.

"Within these last Yeares," they wrote, "there hath by God's Visitation raigned a wonderfull Plague, together with many horrible Slaughters, and Murthers, committed amoungst the Savages and bruitish People there." As a result of this "utter Destruction, Devastacion, and Depopulacion" of the region, there was no longer a substantial population that could challenge the English. Nor could any other European sovereign claim the territory. Hence the petitioners were convinced that the moment had come to press their claim since God had "thought fitt and determined, that those large and goodly Territoryes, deserted as it were by their naturall Inhabitants, should be possessed and enjoyed by such of our Subjects and People" who would go there.[58]

The patentees had only a partial understanding of the region, but they were right that this epidemic had taken a horrific toll. The victims suffered from nosebleeds, headaches, fever, and lesions on their skin. While some of these symptoms could have been caused by smallpox, there was already sufficient knowledge of that illness that chroniclers would likely have identified it. Instead, it appears that the outbreak of this disease was perhaps caused by the bacteria leptospirosis. Modern medical historians come to that conclusion based on the symptoms, which suggest that this potentially lethal Old World bacteria spread via rats, frequent companions on ships that crossed the Atlantic. Once the bacteria was in New England, Natives could have become exposed either through rodent feces on the ground, which could enter a body through cracks on the feet, or via rat urine in bodies of water frequented by Algonquians. In either scenario, Natives were more likely to be exposed than any English. In addition, as the epidemic raged, Natives spent a large amount of time with deceased relatives or friends, which meant that practices intended to smooth the transition from the worldly existence into the realm of the spirits might have had the tragic effect of providing more frequent chances for opportunistic bacteria to find new hosts. While this disease could also have killed Europeans, there were few in the region at the time so the mortality was borne almost entirely by Natives.[59]

The pace of death must have been terrifying. Most epidemics, even of highly contagious diseases like the plague, typically leave survivors.[60] But this series of infections apparently killed almost everyone. The high death toll likely led to an inability to produce crops, hunt game, or fish along an often-dangerous coastline. Here, as elsewhere, the result could have been food shortages, which would have weakened the Ninnimissinuok physically and made individuals even more likely to succumb to bacterial infection.[61]

Under the circumstances, it was perhaps not surprising that the New England epidemic of 1616–19 figured prominently in English descriptions of the region. English writers did not celebrate the fact of the epidemic, but many quickly realized, like Gorges, that it provided an opening for would-be settlers that English colonists lacked elsewhere. As Smith noted in *New Englands Trials*, a small book he wrote eight years after the publication of his first volume on the region, "God had laid this Country open for us, and slaine the most part of the inhabitants by cruell warres and a mortal disease; for where I had seene 100 or 200 people, there is scarce ten to be found." He claimed that there were fewer than twenty Natives in the area between Penobscot Bay and Casco Bay, another thirty between there and Cape Ann, and only about forty from Salem Harbor to the Charles River. He added that none of the English became ill, but that one Frenchman had succumbed to the disease.[62]

The devastation altered both the demography and psychology of the region. According to Robert Cushman, a leader of the Pilgrims who made a brief journey to Plymouth in 1622 and then returned to England to act as an agent for the nascent colony, a "great mortality" had arrived among the Natives in 1619. He estimated that the epidemic, combined with "their own civil dissensions and bloody wars," resulted in perhaps only 5 percent of the original population remaining alive. The decline reversed the odds for the English, who, Cushman understood, could have been eliminated by the Algonquians when they first arrived but no longer faced such an existential threat.[63] One visitor to Plymouth in 1623 claimed that there had been two thousand Natives there a few years earlier, but "not one living now."[64] Morton, too, dramatized the human suffering. He accepted the English idea that the "hand of God fell heavily" on the Ninnimissinuok "with such a mortall stroake that they died on heapes as they lay in their houses and the living: that were able to shift for themselves, would runne away and let them dy, and let there Carkases ly above the ground without burial." There were few survivors of this once well-peopled region, he added. "Crowes, Kites and vermin" feasted on the corpses.[65]

While there were obvious strategic advantages for the English, Gorges and his fellow petitioners emphasized that the establishment of the second colony would be to the benefit of the Natives as well. This was to them "a hopefull" kind of work, "which tendeth to the reducing and Conversion of such Savages as remaine wandering in Desolacion and Distress, to Civil Societie and Christian Religion." The result would be an expansion not only of the English kingdom but also the territory under the control of those who practiced Reformed Christianity. Such an argument was not new. The logic here fit the rhetoric and practice of other English promoters of colonization who argued that the English would instill the virtues of the Protestant faith, which would serve to tame the wilder natures of the indigenous population. To make sure the strategy worked, the English would make all migrants sign the oath of supremacy recognizing the king as the head of the church, a plan that would prevent Catholics from joining the venture. The conversion of the local populace to the Protestant faith would remain one of Gorges's obsessions, eventually leading him to send a young cousin, Thomas Gorges, to a small outpost at Acomenticus, modern-day York, Maine, to advance his agenda.[66]

In 1622 Gorges wrote *A Briefe Relation of the Discovery and Plantation of New England*, a book that combined historical reports with advocacy. As he put it, the time had come "to vindicate our reputation from the injurious aspersions that have been laid upon it, by the malicious practises of some that would adventure nothing in the beginning, but would now reape the benefit of our paines and charges." In other words, with English migrants then making regular voyages to New England and with New Plymouth recently established, the time had come for Gorges to assert the primacy not merely of English claims to North America, but those of the Council for New England.[67]

In the early 1620s—those same years that Morton was battling with George Miller Jr. and looking for a way out of that morass—Gorges realized that he and his associates needed to move forward on their plans. He had initially feared expansion of the Virginia settlements, but that threat disappeared when the Powhatans attacked the English on March 22, 1622, killing 347 of them. Reports of the calamity circulated through London, feeding the ambitions of some in the capital who had already grown skeptical about the company's abilities. In May 1624, the company lost its charter. Crown authorities reorganized Virginia as a royal colony in 1625.[68]

During these same years, Gorges came to understand that English settlement in North America was perhaps more fluid than fixed. No one, he knew, could predict with any certainty what would happen thousands of miles away. Would the harsh winters prove an obstacle as they had elsewhere?[69] Gorges thought not, since he understood that there were flourishing civilizations farther north than New England.[70] Would locals decide to rise up against the newcomers in an effort to force them out—as had occurred in Virginia? With the situation perpetually in flux, Gorges comprehended something that has often eluded historians of the early colonial period: the decline in the number of indigenous people and relentless propaganda about the resources along the American east coast provided an opportunity for success, not a prefiguration of it occurring. Colonization remained available to those who would seek chances, just as it had seemed in the 1570s and again at Sagadahoc and Jamestown. The trick was to master what is perhaps best understood as the moment of colonization, the time when possibilities remained open. In that effort, few were as well positioned as Gorges, an adventurer with knowledge of at least some indigenous Americans. Gorges was willing to take risks, an attitude that lay behind his aggressive efforts to claim New England. He was also in an ideal position to shift the direction of colonization in the region using the resources and political clout of the Council for New England.

Gorges concluded that he was in the best position to organize a settlement in New England. New Plymouth existed, but to that point it had attracted fewer than two hundred migrants. Gorges understood that he would need partners, not only in boardrooms in Plymouth or London but individuals who would serve as his agents on the ground, on the seas, and possibly in courtrooms to advance his claims against other contenders. That need solidified his relationship with Morton, a man with a troubled past who was endlessly on the make and ready to take the one action that Gorges had to that point avoided: cross the Atlantic and live among the emigrant English and the Ninnimissinuok. In the years to come, Morton proved a far more able partner to Gorges than he had ever been to the widow Alice Miller.

CHAPTER THREE

Exiles

THE circumstances surrounding Morton's departure from England after his legal entanglements with the Miller family remain a mystery. There is no known evidence of any divorce proceedings. Rather, Morton seems to have abandoned the widow and her children. Perhaps it was during his transatlantic sojourn of 1622 that he decided life in New England would be more satisfying—and certainly free, he might have hoped then, of the legal morass that had dominated much of his time since he first met Alice.

When Morton returned, likely in 1624, he became an irritant to his neighbors in Plymouth, and especially to Bradford, who would eventually send Morton to England.[1] But the exile came back to New England, returning to his old household, which soon fell under the jurisdiction of the new colony of Massachusetts Bay. Again he ran afoul of local leaders, battling with them over the legitimacy of their charter. Morton, who had earlier been undaunted by the relentless taunts and violence of George Miller Jr. and his unwholesome band of confederates, would now face far more powerful foes.

While it is tempting to see the English communities scattered along the shores of Massachusetts Bay as isolated outposts of a putative transoceanic power, from the start every colonial village had connections to others.[2] Ships moved back and forth between New England and Virginia, carrying not only individuals but also information. News and rumors traveled even more quickly on the smaller skiffs and shallops that the immigrants paddled or sailed near the New England coast, echoing indigenous communication networks. Some individuals left Plymouth on their own, setting up makeshift camps. Few tried to live apart from the world. Every English man and woman understood that survival depended on maintaining good relations with Algonquians. The newcomers realized too that their lives would be better, and day-to-day survival easier, if they maintained access to goods coming from England. These practical and psychological desires—for safety, for material goods, for connections to their prior homeland—bound Pilgrims and fellow travelers together. Such emotions also tempted them to eliminate anyone who posed a threat.

Morton's travails in New England in the mid- to late 1620s reveal the persistence of a stubborn man. But his story makes sense only when seen in the context of the English religious dissidents' efforts to establish a homeland far from what they believed was the corrupt society of the known world. Such a journey was always going to be difficult, especially since the migrants needed to find a way to reimburse their creditors for the cost of their passage across the Atlantic. Anyone who might interrupt their divine quest needed to be removed.

On September 6, 1620, the Pilgrims, after traveling from their religious refuge in Leiden to Southampton and then experiencing troubles with one of their two vessels, set sail from Plymouth on the *Mayflower.* They endured a long and difficult journey but managed to reach Cape Cod on November 9. The sighting of the shoreline pleased William Bradford, who wrote that the view "much comforted us, especially, seeing so goodly a Land, and wooded to the brinke of the sea, it caused us to rejoice together, and praise God that had given us once again to see land." The travelers stayed near modern Provincetown for five weeks, then sailed to what became New Plymouth. The first winter was brutal for the newcomers, half of whom died by the following summer.[3]

While anchored in November, many of those on board agreed to certain principles for self-government, which became known as the Mayflower Compact. Signatories to the pact asserted that they had sailed across the ocean for "the glory of God, and advancement of the Christian Faith and honour of our King and Countrey." They had arrived to "plant the first Colony in the Northerne parts of VIRGINIA." With their signatures they agreed, in the eyes of the almighty and one other, to form into "a civill body politicke" for their common good and that they would follow all laws passed there. They chose John Carver, who had previously been a merchant in London but had migrated to Leiden in 1610, to be their first governor. But in April 1621, as Bradford later wrote, Carver became ill when working in a field on a hot day. After complaining of a splitting headache, he lay down "and within a few hours his senses failed." He died a few days later and was replaced as governor by Bradford, who would become both the colony's political leader and its ablest historian.[4]

The Pilgrims were a subset of the larger group of dissenters known as Puritans. The differences between Pilgrims and the other Puritans hinged on close reading of scripture and religious commentaries, particularly relating to whether it was acceptable to become Separatists or whether such an act constituted schism, which was unacceptable (the view of the other Puritans as well as of the Church of England). The Leiden congregation avoided that problem by arguing that the Church of England was not a legitimate church, and therefore it was permissible to become Separatists. In contrast, religious dissidents who chose to remain in England criticized the Anglican establishment but still believed that, as one historian put it, "within the bloated, corrupt, putrefying body of episcopacy there were the ghostly breathings of real churches."[5]

The congregation at Leiden was composed of English Pilgrims who felt they needed to leave their homeland and find a place where they could worship in peace. The Dutch allowed them to pursue their own vision free of any state interference, which enticed several hundred to migrate to the Netherlands in the early years of the seventeenth century. By 1620 there were about four hundred members of the Pilgrims' church at Leiden, many of whom never subsequently crossed the ocean to New England. (By 1628 there were only about two hundred Pilgrims in the new colony.) There were also several hundred other English and Scots émigrés in Leiden who were members of nonseparating Reform churches. These

latter Puritans were doctrinally similar to most English dissenters, who believed it was better to remain in England, at
least for the time being. By 1630 thousands of this latter group
who had been facing persecution for their beliefs from Archbishop Laud and who confronted novel economic challenges
relating to the development of the cloth industry and com-
petition from other Europeans, concluded that the time had
come to leave. Rather than travel the relatively short distance
across the English Channel, these Puritans headed to the new
Massachusetts Bay Colony. The migration of Puritans to New
England totaled around twenty-one thousand by the time it
came to an end in 1642 as a result of the English Civil War
and the rising prominence of onetime dissenters in England,
which encouraged Puritans to remain at home rather than risk
an ocean crossing to an unfamiliar land.[6]

The Pilgrims' Atlantic passage in 1620 had been difficult.
One of the non-Pilgrims on board had apparently sworn at
the seasick dissenters and told them that he looked forward to
tossing their corpses into the sea. Fortunately, as Bradford saw
it, God took care of his true flock: the "lusty" man fell ill and
died halfway across the ocean. The survivors threw his body
overboard. "Thus his curses light on his own head," Bradford
wrote years later, "and it was an astonishment to all his fellows
for they noted it to be the just hand of God upon him."[7]

Bradford understood that arriving safely in New England
did not mean that the Pilgrims' hoped-for new life would un-
fold easily. Instead, landing upon the shores made him realize
the magnitude of the challenge they faced. In one of the crucial passages in his history of New Plymouth, Bradford looked
back at that moment of arrival with uncanny clarity. "Being

thus passed the vast ocean, and a sea of troubles before in their preparation"—a reference to the Pilgrims' prior difficulties in Europe as well as perhaps to chapter 10 of the book of Zechariah—he proclaimed that the migrants "had now no friends to welcome them nor inns to entertain or refresh their weather-beaten bodies; no houses or much less towns to repair to, to seek for succor."

Using a common strategy among writers with a religious bent, he drew on scripture for telling analogies. Here he turned to Acts 28, which taught that it was "a mercy to the Apostle and his shipwrecked company, that the barbarians showed them no small kindness in refreshing them." He then adapted that notion to his new circumstances. "These savage barbarians," he wrote in reference to the Natives of the region, "when they met with them (as after will appear) were readier to fill their sides full of arrows than otherwise." His description of open hostilities departed from earlier English views of indigenous people in the region, a sign that Bradford used his memoir to make both historical and religious points.[8]

The Natives posed one kind of threat to the newcomers, the region itself another. Just as Gorges had wondered if the English could endure the fierce winter of the Maine coast, so Bradford understood the dangers of the climate. They had arrived late in the year, with winter upon them, "and they that know the winters of that country know them to be sharp and violent, and subject to cruel and fierce storms, dangerous to travel to known places, much more to search an unknown coast." Though other English writers had chronicled the cataclysmic epidemic that had devastated the region from 1616 to 1619, Bradford described "a hideous and desolate wilderness, full of wild beasts and wild men — and what multitudes there might be of them they knew not."[9]

Yet even Bradford had to acknowledge that there were far fewer Algonquians than had lived there earlier. In the summer of 1621, as the newcomers went in search of locales to expand their initial settlement, they arrived at a place forty miles away where they found "the soil good and the people not many, being dead and abundantly wasted in the late great mortality, which fell in all these parts about three years before the coming of the English, wherein thousands of them died." Witnessing the most ghoulish traces of the epidemic, he wrote that the victims had been unable "to bury one another, their skulls and bones were found in many places lying still above the ground where their houses and dwellings had been, a very sad spectacle to behold."[10]

But emphasizing the tragic recent past did not fit Bradford's agenda. Vast and unavoidable danger still lurked here, as he saw it. The new migrants could not, Bradford wrote, "go up to the top of Pisgah to view from this wilderness a more goodly country to feed their hopes" — a reference drawn from Deuteronomy 34:1-5.[11] Unlike Moses, who could look down onto the promised land but not descend to enjoy it, the migrants saw only menace, "for which way soever they turned their eyes (save upward to the heavens) they could have little solace or content in respect of any outward objects."[12]

The moment held little promise, Bradford lamented, "for summer being done, all things stand upon them with a weather-beaten face, and the whole country, full of woods and thickets, represented a wild and savage hue." Once again, the unique sense of foreboding that comes from being lost in a dense wood engulfs the reader, as Bradford intended. If the migrants "looked behind them," he continued, "there was the mighty ocean which they had passed and was now as a main bar and gulf to separate them from all the civil parts of the world." They were no longer adrift, but they were more alone than any of them had been before. But, Bradford wrote, there was one sure way forward. "What could now sustain them," he asked rhetorically, "but the Spirit of God and His grace?" Drawing on the language of Psalms 107:1–8, he wrote, "Yea let them which have been redeemed of the Lord, shew how he hath delivered them from the hand of the oppressor. When they wandered in the desert wilderness out of the way, and found no city to dwell in, both hungry and thirsty, their soul was overwhelmed in them. Let them confess before the Lord His lovingkindness and His wonderful works before the sons of men."[13]

Bradford's take on the initial moments of colonization revealed how he understood the world the Pilgrims inhabited. But while they might not have known it, they had arrived in an ideal place at a perfect time to create a colony. The indigenous population had declined in the epidemic and their fields had not yet become overgrown with forest. There was clean water, which gave these English an advantage over those who had gone to Jamestown or remained in crowded towns and cities at home. And there were abundant fur-bearing mammals to be captured and sent home to pay off the debts that the Pilgrims had accrued to finance their migration.[14]

Bradford would have dismissed such a naturalistic explanation. As he saw it, the Pilgrims survived despite the dangers only because a forgiving God had planned for this to happen,

just as that beneficent deity had designed all events to un-
fold. From that premise, Bradford knew, moving forward demanded obeisance to God.

He understood better than anyone how difficult the
first few years at Plymouth were for the newcomers. Wary
of trouble with their Algonquian neighbors, the residents of
New Plymouth erected a fort by 1623 as well as a blockhouse,
though their actions did not erase the resistance they faced
from some Ninnimissinuok.[15] Further, the English community lacked a minister for half of the time during its first fifty
years, a situation that posed a series of problems for those who
wanted to receive sacraments and limited efforts to launch
effective missionizing activities among the Algonquians. The
lack of a proper minister likely accounted for the low number
of members in the church. It had about fifty after that first terrible winter and numbered only forty-seven in the late 1660s.[16]

The migrants had more worldly concerns too. English
officials had authorized them to settle only within the bound-
aries of the Virginia Company's patent, which stretched to
41 degrees north latitude, a line that made sense on a map
drawn in London or Plymouth but did not account for the
fact that these newcomers had landed in a more favorable setting slightly to the north. New Plymouth, as the Pilgrims recognized, lay within territory that had been granted earlier to
the Council for New England. In November 1621 a new patent
arrived, which provided some measure of assurance that they
would be able to remain despite the fact that they were, as
some English would later argue, in the wrong spot.[17]

Bradford often linked the fate of New Plymouth to the
prospects of the Leiden émigrés. Early on, he understood

that the search for spiritual perfection could proceed only if the economic base of the new settlement was secure, which meant trying to establish good relations with their Native neighbors, who controlled access to the fur-bearing mammals eagerly sought by European customers. But he knew that there were English migrants who did not embrace the Pilgrims' beliefs. Some were Puritans, others adherents of the Church of England, and perhaps still others who had no interest in any religion. In 1623 ninety new colonists arrived from Europe, thirty of them from the congregation at Leiden. But among the others were ten known as "particulars" who, having paid their own way, were not part of the company or members of the church at Plymouth.[18] Some of these non-Pilgrims had dreams of becoming "great men and rich all of a sudden," as Bradford sneered. But they agreed to leave the fur trade alone, at least until such time as the community decided it could move away from its initial corporate mode of settlement, known as the "communality."[19]

According to Bradford, one group of migrants organized by Thomas Weston, a London ironmonger turned investor, set up a nearby settlement they called Wessaguset at what the Pilgrims would later call Mount Wollaston. The colonizers had arrived well equipped for survival but soon faced economic collapse because of what Bradford called their "great disorder." Some of these "Adventurers" cavorted with local Native women, while "others (so base were they) became servants to the Indians, and would cut them wood and fetch them water for a capful of corn." Some sold their bedding and their clothes to the Algonquians, while still others turned to stealing their indigenous neighbors' goods, a development that created new tensions. But even that failed to help them. "In the end," Bradford reported, "they came to that misery that some starved and died with cold and hunger. One in gathering shellfish was so weak as he stuck fast in the mud and was found dead in the place." So they dispersed, combing the ground for nuts and digging for clams to eke out an existence.[20]

Bradford's history detailed the early years of the colonization of New Plymouth. By 1624 or 1625, Wollaston, like Weston, had come and gone and the small outpost fell under the control of Morton. But though the governor wrote about that event, he only rarely seems to have had knowledge of the day-to-day work of the Council for New England, which in March 1620 had reaffirmed its claim to the region and much beyond.[21] By 1622 the principals of the council, a group that included Gorges, were detailing plans for establishing English communities on their holdings. In May of that year the council members discussed a plan to transport "youths from Parishes, that have not been taynted with any villanyes or misdemen[o]rs," to New England, where they could be bound out as apprentices "to such as shall have occasion and meanes to imploy them," a suggestion that the communities they envisioned might bear a close resemblance to the English households along the Chesapeake. Much of their discussion focused on the allocation of lands to specific individuals. But they had other concerns as well. In July 1622 they decided that they would set aside two large islands in the River of Sagadahoc (the modern Kennebec River) for a "publike planta[ti]on" and land between the two primary branches of the river would become "a publike Citty."[22]

In October 1622 the council established rules for the fishing fleets that worked the New England coastline. They decreed that each crew should give the council 5 percent of its haul. Further, they wanted to make sure that only English fishing crews would have the ability to dry fish there, something that had been (they thought) an English monopoly since the Dutch and French in the area cured rather than dried their catch. If those Europeans imitated the English, the commerce might collapse. In addition, each ship of at least thirty tons had to transport at least one migrant to New England, who would be left behind when the crews returned. Larger ships would take more colonizers on them. Such a plan would require more than depositing someone on the shoreline, so the council decided that it should negotiate with the fishing crews for transporting cows, swine, poultry, and goats across the Atlantic. They also wanted to ensure that their agents left in the region would have a supply of fish, bread, salt, and fishing equipment.[23]

In the early 1620s the members of the council began to sketch out plans for how to people and then manage these new communities. On November 16, 1622, they discussed sending a letter to the lord mayor of London seeking one hundred children, presumably to send across the ocean as servants. That same day they discussed, again, their desire to control the actions of fishing crews, though this time they wanted to find a way to prevent these other English from trading with New England's indigenous peoples. They wanted to make sure that no one sold them "any Armor, wepons, powder, Shott, or such like furniture for warr." Three days later they arranged for the transportation of a Native boy they referred to as "papa Whinett belonging to Abbadakest Sachem of Massachusetts" back to his homeland. Soon after, the council approved Gorges selling subscriptions for a ship being built at Whitby in Yorkshire.[24] Gorges also took charge of communications with ship owners. The council members wanted to encourage fishing in these rich waters, but wanted each captain to negotiate with them first. Such agreements would prevent the kind of trouble caused by an English captain employed by the Virginia Company who had sailed to New England, kidnapped an unknown number of Natives, and stole their furs. Fortunately, he did not get far. Not knowing how to navigate the shallow waters of Cape Cod, his ship became grounded in the sand. The captives jumped off and "made great exclama[ti]on against the present planters of New England" to Gorges and others.[25]

By late 1622 the members of the council had recognized that they needed to lay out more details about their planned communities. On December 30 they awarded a patent for the land "known by the name of Massachusett" to Robert Gorges, the son of Sir Ferdinando.[26] Within weeks they were discussing the best strategies for colonizing the entire region they believed they owned. They would recruit three groups of English: gentlemen who would bear arms and assist the governor, artisans, and farmers. On February 18 the council members concluded that their business would benefit from taking in poor children to become apprentices and that the king supported a plan to draw the destitute from across the realm to be sent to New England. A week later they approved a scheme to fund a 180-ton ship owned by Lord Gorges—the father of Sir Ferdinando who was also a member of the council—to be used to transport migrants to New England. On June 29,

1623, members of the council traveled to Greenwich and presented King James with "a Plott of all the Coasts and lands of New England" to be assigned to twenty patentees. The list included a number of members of the English gentry: the Lord Duke of Richmond, the Earl of Arundel and Surrey, the Earls of Middlesex, Warwick, Holderness, and Carlisle. Sir Ferdinando Gorges and his father were among the patentees.[27]

This was the New England that Gorges had wanted to create: a vast territory that arced from 40 to 45 degrees north latitude, with an institutional base in London capable of crafting contracts with fishing crews, transporting poor children to better their lives, and handling the paperwork that came with large capital investments like ships. But before they could launch their enterprise, they needed to attend to the English who had already crossed the ocean, especially Weston.

In 1623 Robert Gorges crossed the ocean to press the council's case against Weston, who had defrauded his father and the council. He arrived bearing the title of governor-general of New England, a designation that suggested more authority than he had. He was keen to prosecute Weston for violating his agreement to transport armaments for a fort to be built. Weston had instead sold the arms for his own gain, "for which," Bradford wrote, "the State was much offended, and [the younger Gorges's] father suffered a shrewd check, and he had order to apprehend him for it." Weston beseeched Bradford to intervene on his behalf, which he did, and in the end Gorges did not arrest him. But although the incident passed, it stuck in the mind of the older Gorges, who printed the patent his son took with him to demonstrate the family's claim to the area.[28] The younger Gorges, who had second thoughts about arresting Weston, eventually gave up on that task and even on New England, "not finding the state of things here to answer to his quality and condition," as Bradford archly noted. Weston, for his part, left for Virginia and eventually went back to Bristol, where he died in an epidemic.[29]

Sir Ferdinando Gorges and his colleagues on the council did not find a way to establish durable communities in New England in the early 1620s. But even the more successful Pilgrim colony had problems too. During the first years at New Plymouth, some English men and women returned home, just as Weston had done. Some of them made public complaints about what they saw as shortcomings of the English colony. By the spring of 1624, there was enough concern in England about developments in New Plymouth that James Sherley (or Shirley), a London goldsmith who was an early investor in the Plymouth Colony, sent a letter to Bradford outlining a series of specific allegations. Some of the emigrants' concerns focused on religious issues, such as individuals in the colony not attending church on Sunday and the lack of sacraments, including baptism, available to those who sought them— problems caused by the fact that the community had yet to attract a permanent minister. Those who sailed home had reported that there was no formal educational system, which meant that children could learn neither the catechism nor to read. They complained that many members of the settlement would not work for the common good, that the water was "not wholesome," that the soil was infertile, and that there were problems in the fishing industry. They grumbled about the mosquitoes and feared wolves and foxes. Reflecting their lack of knowledge about North American geography, they also moaned that the Dutch "are planted near Hudson's Bay and are likely to overthrow the [fur] trade." The place-name was wrong. Sherley was presumably referring to the recent Dutch purchase of Manhattan Island.

Bradford refuted each allegation. There had been no problems with religious practice, he asserted, and the Pilgrims had plans to set up a school. In response to a claim that the colonists were stealing from one another, Bradford replied that this was hardly unique. "Would London have been free from that crime," he riposted, "then we should not have been troubled with these here." The water was as good as any water in the world, though Bradford joked it might not be "so wholesome as the good beer and wine in London." Was it likely, he asked, that there were problems with the fishing industry given the fact that so many fishing ships arrived there each year to haul in a catch to take home? The cattle imported from England to New Plymouth were all fat, a sign that the ground produced sufficient grass for the current herds and likely could support many more. Certainly there were mosquitoes, but Bradford believed that the population of these stinging insects would decrease since "the more the land is tilled, and the woods cut down, the fewer there will be, and in the end scarce any at all." While he was wrong on that last prediction, his understanding of local ecology was precise: a decrease in wetlands, a by-product of the extension of European-style farming, would have lessened the number of mosquitoes in the area, though this deforestation also altered the regional climate with far-reaching consequences.[30]

The confident tone of Bradford's history here does not

betray a sense of anxiety. Still, the depth with which he described certain aspects of the earliest years of the American settlement suggests that he knew, even when he was writing for posterity, that he had to be ever vigilant—or at least wanted his readers to believe that he was. The list of failed English colonies was long—Baffin Island, Newfoundland, Roanoke, and Sagadahoc had all gone under, and the events along the Chesapeake in 1622 hardly built confidence. Hence he reacted strongly to those who he felt caused trouble, including two—John Oldham and a minister named John Lyford—who Bradford believed had been undermining the new community by writing to England about the missteps of those running the Plymouth Colony. Bradford likened Lyford to a villain from the book of Jeremiah who "went out weeping and met them that were coming to offer incense in the house of the Lord, saying 'Come to Gedaliah' when he meant to slay them." [31]

Soon after their arrival, Oldham and Lyford set out to destroy New Plymouth. That, at least, is how Bradford saw it. He accused them of plotting secretly against the Pilgrims. Through such tactics, as Bradford wrote, they "brought others as well as themselves into a fool's paradise." To advance their cause they wrote a series of long letters, which they sent via the *Charity* when it sailed for London. [32]

But unbeknownst to these plotters, Bradford and his friends were paying close attention. Fearing that such letters might do real damage if they reached England, the governor and others clambered into a shallop and paddled out to the *Charity* to retrieve them. The shipmaster, William Pierce, an ally of Bradford, agreed to help and so handed over twenty of the letters. When Bradford opened them, he found Lyford's messages, "large and full of slanders and false accusations," aimed at the "ruin and utter subversion" of the colony. They copied the letters and sent the copies to England, holding on to the originals so that they could more effectively prosecute the authors. It proved more difficult to sort out Oldham's intent since "he was so bad a scribe as his hand was scarce legible," but Bradford had no doubt that he was as deep into the scheming as Lyford. These men, the governor concluded, "intended a reformation in church and commonwealth, and as soon as the ship was gone, they intended to join together and have the sacraments, etc." Soon they even called their own meeting on a Sunday, a sign that they had decided "now publicly to act what privately they had been long plotting"—namely, the establishment of the Church of England in New Plymouth.[33]

With the letters in hand, Bradford struck. The colonists hauled Lyford and Oldham into court in the summer of 1624 and confronted them with the evidence against them.[34] The defendants counterclaimed that they were the victims and that the authorities had plotted to deprive them of their rights to live peacefully. They announced that they had come to Plymouth at considerable personal expense "to enjoy the liberty of their conscience and the free use of God's Ordinances." Lyford denied having any part in the letters, but when the accusers produced the originals and read from them, Bradford claimed, "he was struck mute." Oldham, in contrast, "began to rage furiously because they had intercepted and opened his letters." He threatened Bradford and the others, believing that his associates would rise to his defense. "But all were silent," Bradford wrote, "being strucken with the injustice of the thing." Bradford then told the court that he had a responsibility to open the letters "to prevent the mischief and ruin that this conspiracy and plots of theirs, would bring on this poor Colony."[35]

The letters, Bradford wrote, were read aloud in the court and Lyford was asked to respond. After trying to pass blame onto others, he collapsed. He "burst out into tears," Bradford recalled, "and confessed he 'feared he was a reprobate, his sins were so great that he doubted God would not pardon them, he was unsavory salt, etc.'" Through his tears he acknowledged that he could never make sufficient amends. That confession sealed the affair. The court decided to exile him immediately. Local authorities allowed Oldham to remain another six months before he too would be "expelled [from] the place," a delayed sentence that gave the convicted an opportunity to go to church to confess his sins.[36] While the exiles continued to cause some grief for Plymouth's leaders—Lyford through circulating yet more information about clerical affairs in the colony and Oldham, who returned and had to be sent away again—they no longer posed a threat.[37]

Lyford and Oldham were gone, but Bradford recognized that the problems they created remained. Some of the associates of the newly exiled broke away from the settlement and set up their own fishing establishment. Those who left also sent word via the *Charity*, soon bound for England, explaining their reasons for splitting from a group of London-based investors Bradford called "Adventurers." In that report, which Bradford apparently saw and summarized for his history, they voiced concerns about the administration of the church. They also declared, per their understanding of the original patent, that they were "partners in trade, so we may be in government" as well.[38]

Still, considering the travails they had experienced, Bradford believed that the year had not been a complete disaster. Plague roiled London, he heard from those on a recently arrived ship, but the Pilgrims enjoyed "peace and health and contented minds." They produced surplus corn that year, which they sent up the Kennebec for trade on one of the shallops that their carpenter had recently built, which included a small deck over the central portion to keep the crop dry. The traders returned bearing seven hundred pounds of beaver and other furs. That report pleased Bradford, who from the moment the Pilgrims landed had been eager to secure trade with the Algonquians.[39]

With the English colony's self-inflicted wounds diminishing, the next couple of years were less fraught for its members, who continued to find ways to improve their finances. During 1628 they had multiple contacts with the Dutch from the recent settlement at New Amsterdam to the south.[40] More important, the English had discussions about how to retire the debt they still had at home and also how to raise yet more funds to bring their associates across the ocean. Bradford, Myles Standish, the colony's military commander, and Isaac Allerton, who had become Bradford's assistant after Carver's death, formed themselves into a company and signed an agreement with the colony of New Plymouth. The three agreed to assume all remaining debts that the colony still had. In exchange, they gained exclusive use of a pinnace recently constructed at Manomet and a shallop, as well as trade goods already in store and similar commodities that were on their way. Crucially, the three gained exclusive control of the fur trade for six years. Allerton took a copy of the signed agreement with him to England, where he had the authority to bring others into the partnership and also to try to organize the passage of like-minded potential colonists still in Leiden.[41] In the months that followed, the company (which also included William Brewster and Edward Winslow) contracted with Sherley, who enumerated the accounts of Plymouth for 1628, and John Beauchamp, a salter who also lived in London, to be their English agents. The partners also received a patent for land on the Kennebec, where they soon set up a trading house.[42]

Their discussions with the Dutch also opened up an unexpected opportunity to join in what they soon realized was the lucrative wampum trade. Before 1628, as Bradford recalled, the English of Plymouth knew little about those shells. Wampum consisted of strings of polished quahog shells, which could be found only in Narragansett Bay and Long Island Sound. Before the arrival of colonists, indigenous peoples used wampum strings in various rituals. One group would present some strings to another in ceremonial acts, for example, during condolence rites that typically preceded negotiations. Strings could also communicate specific messages, though colonists did not know how to read them. One historian has estimated that by the eighteenth century some colonial merchants, recognizing their value in making deals with Natives, gathered millions of the small shells. Other enterprising colonists, who similarly saw the importance of strings of small beads, imported glass beads from Europe, often in colors other than the natural white, black, and purple shells that came from the Atlantic.[43] Soon enough Bradford and the others came to realize that the Pequots and Narragansetts had grown "rich and potent" by the commerce, adding that "it may prove a drug in time." The Narragansetts in particular embraced the business, producing wampum and selling it to the English, who then used it in the fur trade. The Natives used wampum to purchase guns, initially from Dutch and French traders as well as some English. Before long King Charles forbade the English from trading arms to the Natives, though by then they already had guns in their possession.[44]

In late 1628 the Pilgrims recognized that Morton's settlement at Mount Wollaston had become a problem. Soon after gaining control of the community there, Morton—in Bradford's telling—began to act in ways that the Pilgrims could not tolerate. "They fell to great licentiousness and led a dissolute life," Bradford wrote, "pouring out themselves into all profaneness." Bradford claimed that Morton and his followers engaged in one noxious behavior after another. They gained wealth by trading with the Ninnimissinuok, which threatened the new agreement that Bradford and his partners had signed with the residents of the nascent colony. With their newfound wealth Morton and his companions purchased alcohol and drank "in great excess," even in the mornings.[45]

More alarming to the Pilgrims, they erected an eighty-foot maypole and cavorted with the locals, "drinking and dancing about it many days together, inviting the Indian women for their consorts, dancing and frisking together like so many fairies, or furies, rather; and worse practices." To Bradford, it looked like the second coming of "the Roman goddess Flora, or the beastly practices of the mad Bacchanalians." Morton compounded his crimes by writing salacious poems and attaching them to the maypole. They also sang a bawdy song.

> Drink and be merry, merry, merry boyes;
> Let all your delight be in the Hymens joys;
> [L]o to Hymen, now the day is come,
> About the merry Maypole take a Roome. . . .
> Lasses in beaver coats come away,
> Yee shall be welcome to us night and day.

Morton also dropped the name Mount Wollaston and began, Bradford wrote, to call this settlement "Merry-mount, as if this jollity would have lasted for ever." In this den of impiety, Morton himself figured as the "Lord of Misrule, and maintained (as it were) a School of Atheism."[46]

While he reported few specifics about Morton's antics, Bradford's readers would have been quite familiar with the meanings attached to the character of the Lord of Misrule. Dancing around the maypole had a long tradition in England, where such rites brought communities together.[47] The practice was considered harmless fun to many, but maypoles angered English Puritans. According to the Puritan pamphleteer Phillip Stubbs, writing in *The Anatomy of Abuses*, first published in 1583, the erection of a maypole was an excuse for debauchery, and the Lord of Misrule was "odious both to God and good men." Stubbs claimed to have seen such characters himself, men who had been selected by "all the wilde-heds of the Parish" and crowned king of their festivities. The celebrants wore colored scarves, ribbons, and lace, tied jewels and bells around their legs, and carried bright handkerchiefs. With pipers and drummers accompanying them, they disrupted church services, screaming and prancing "like devils incarnate, with such a confused noise, that no man can hear his own voice." Their festivities spilled out into the adjoining

(*above and opposite*) This Flemish tapestry and English stained
glass suggest the common acceptance of maypoles across much
of western Europe. The eighteenth-century tapestry is by Peter
van den Hecke after a seventeenth-century painting by David
Teniers II. The stained glass, from the sixteenth or seventeenth
century, is from the Betley Window, Staffordshire, England.
(Getty Research Institute, Los Angeles [97.P.7];
© Victoria and Albert Museum, London.)

churchyard. The Lord of Misrule would solicit money and
alcohol to "maintaine them in their hethenrie, diverlie, whor-
dome, drunkennes, pride, and what not."[48]

But the revelries became even more reprehensible sometime around Pentecost (known to the English as Whitsunday).
Stubbs reported, "All the yung men and maides, olde men and

wives, run gadding over the night to the woods, groves, hils,
& mountains, where they spend all the night in plesant pastimes." In the morning, they came back to town again, bearing
birch and other branches to decorate their gatherings. "But
the chiefest jewl they bring from thence," he continued, "is
their May-pole, which they bring home with great venera-

tion." The pole was so large that it needed to be hauled by a yoke of twenty to forty oxen, each bedecked with "a sweet nose-gay of flowers" on its horns. Two to three hundred men, women, and children followed along and watched as the maypole soared into the sky. Then they danced around their new idol. Stubbs added that two-thirds of the young women who had spent the night in the forests had sex there. "These be the frutes which these cursed pastimes bring foorth." Such behavior was beneath that of Turks, Jews, Saracens, and pagans. Years later, when they controlled Parliament, the Puritans ordered all maypoles chopped down.[49]

This is the vision Bradford had in his mind when he described Morton's settlement at Ma-re Mount. But it was not only the maypole that offended him. Morton, so the governor reported, had learned that fishing crews and French traders had made a good profit from selling arms to Natives, and so he followed suit. He also taught the Algonquians how to use these guns. The Natives quickly incorporated the weaponry into their hunts and "became far more active in that employment than any of the English, by reason of the swiftness of foot and nimbleness of body, being also quick-sighted and by communal exercise well knowing the haunts of all sorts of game." Once they realized the power of guns, Bradford continued, they no longer wanted to use bows and arrows even though it was likely that their traditional weapons were more accurate.[50] When Morton was confronted with the danger that his actions posed to other colonists, Bradford wrote at the time, he "took it in great scorn, and said he would do it in the dispite of all."[51] Though Bradford worried about the sale of firearms, such transactions were legal. Prohibitions on colonists selling guns to Natives only later became a crime in the colony.[52]

Nonetheless, such behavior signaled disaster to Bradford. He feared that in time of war the Algonquians would be able to outgun the colonists of New Plymouth, especially since the Natives possessed molds to make new bullets and had almost enough knowledge to produce their own powder. "O, the horribleness of this villainy!" Bradford despaired. "How many both Dutch and English have been lately slain by those Indians thus furnished, and no remedy provided; nay, the evil more increased, and the blood of their brethren sold for gain (as is to be feared) and in what danger all these colonies are in is too well known." Bradford wanted to punish such "gain-thirsty murderers, for they deserve no better title, before their colonies in these parts be overthrown by these barbarous savages thus armed with their own weapons, by these evil instruments and traitors to their neighbours and country!"[53] Morton's neighbors grew alarmed as well, pleading (Bradford claimed) with the English at New Plymouth to help suppress the sale of guns to the Natives. "We told them we had no authority to do any thing," Bradford wrote, "but seeing it tended to the utter ruin of all the whole country, we would join with them against so public a mischief."[54]

In Bradford's mind, Morton posed a threat to the very survival of the colony. In addition to arming the Natives with the weapons he had on hand, he had also, so the governor claimed, sent word to England to procure more. Other English migrants in Plymouth likely shared Bradford's anxiety about armed Ninnimissinuok. Bradford also believed that Ma-re Mount would be a magnet for wayward indentured servants since Morton "would entertain any, how vile soever, and all the scum of the country or any discontents would flock to him from all places, if this nest was not broken." As Bradford saw it, the English faced as great a threat from "this wicked and debased crew as from the savages themselves."[55]

As fear spread among the scattered English hamlets, a growing number of colonists sought a remedy for what they came to see as the danger Morton posed. English immigrants from Piscataqua (New Hampshire), Nantasket, and Naumkeag (Salem), among other locales, sent funds to New Plymouth to organize an action. The group first sent Morton a letter "in a friendly and neighbourly way," as Bradford put it, "to admonish him to forebear those courses." "But he was so high as he scorned all advice," Bradford recalled, "and asked who had to do with him, he had and would trade pieces with the Indians, in despite of all, with many other scurrilous terms full of disdain." The colonists wrote again, pleading that his actions undermined all of their communities "against their common safety," Bradford reported, "and against the King's proclamation" of 1622 aimed to crack down on "disorderly trading" with the Natives. Morton responded as a lawyer might, arguing that James's proclamation was not a law since it carried no punishment for those who violated it. They responded that actions like his would earn the "displeasure" of the monarch. "But insolently he persisted and said the King was dead and his displeasure with him, and many other like things." He warned them that he was prepared to defend the settlement if the others came after him.[56]

Despite the threat, the leaders of New Plymouth organized a small force under Myles Standish and marched on

Ma-re Mount, which then had only seven men in residence. Bradford reported that Morton and his associates had barricaded their doors and all of them were armed, with bullets and powder laid out on a table. But they had also fortified themselves with substantial quantities of alcohol. "If they had not been over-armed with drink," Bradford wrote, "more hurt might have been done." When the Pilgrims finally persuaded Morton to come out, he and some of his fellows approached the invaders. Morton had intended to shoot Standish with a carbine, Bradford claimed, but he was too drunk to lift it. No shots were fired that day, and no one injured—except, as Bradford wrote, "one that was so drunk that he ran his own nose upon the point of a sword that one held before him, as he entered the house; but he lost but a little of his hot blood."[57]

The authorities arrested Morton and deposited him on the Isles of Shoals off modern Portsmouth, New Hampshire. They left him without any supplies, but he survived with the support of local Natives and presumably by harvesting maritime resources since this location was, as one colonist wrote in 1660, "one of the best places for fishing" in New England. After Morton had spent a month offshore, an English ship picked him up.[58]

Meanwhile, Bradford sent a letter to the Council for New England, informing it about Morton's actions at Ma-re Mount. The letter, carried by none other than the exile John Oldham, noted that Morton had already been warned "not to trade or truck with the Indians" but to no avail. The Pilgrims complained too about their inability to police the actions of the crews of fishing vessels and testified to their fears of the local Natives, who were preparing "some affront upon us," possibly because of Morton and his allies' practice of "abusing the Indian women most filthily, as it is notorious." In 1629 John Endecott, who had just arrived with the seal of the Massachusetts Bay Colony and would later be a founder of Salem as well as governor, went to Ma-re Mount and ordered the maypole cut down.[59]

Bradford and his associates, presumably unaware that Morton was by then working with Gorges, also sent a letter addressed to Gorges. At that moment, they believed that Gorges was a crucial supporter of New Plymouth. Bradford wrote to his putative patron that Morton and his "seditious crew" had sold guns "to the natives, who can use them with great dexterity, excelling our English therein." Those arms had "spread both north and south, all the land over, to the great peril of all our lives." Morton had ignored the Pilgrims' requests to halt the trade. Now Bradford beseeched Gorges to bring Morton to justice.[60]

The colony's authorities also asked that Morton be prosecuted in England, presumably for violating the king's order about giving arms to the Natives. But Morton proved too wily. As Bradford wrote in his history, the captive "went for England yet nothing was done to him, not so much as rebuked, for aught was heard." Even worse, he came back the following year. At least by then, as the governor remembered, "some of the worst of the company [at Ma-re Mount] were dispersed," leaving behind "some of the more modest." The whole episode depressed Bradford, even years later when he wrote his history. "I have been too long about so unworthy a person," he concluded, "and bad a cause."[61]

Morton returned in 1629 with Isaac Allerton, who had gone to England to represent the Pilgrims' interest when their first patent expired in 1627. By the time Allerton returned, Bradford had grown disenchanted with him, in part because Allerton had failed to get a new patent despite the expense of his journey. Further, Allerton had also begun to profit from private trading, which displeased the governor. Worse still, he offered hospitality to Morton, who stayed at Allerton's house and worked as a scribe. For unexplained reasons, Allerton soon decided that Morton had to leave. But instead of remaining in the town, Morton returned to what Bradford called "his old nest in the Massachusetts"—his former residence at Ma-re Mount.[62]

By the time Morton made the short journey he was already a figure bathed in suspicion. Before crossing the Atlantic, John Winthrop had served from January 1627 to June 1629 as one of the attorneys in the Court of Wards and Liveries in London. He first heard about Morton there. On November 27, 1627, a man named William Stuart from Stratfield Turgis testified in that court that a Thomas Moreton previously residing in Swallowfield in Wiltshire had gone into business with a man named Thomas Wigge. But after a year or so, Stuart stated, Wigge died. Winthrop wrote in his notes that he was "supposed to be made awaye by the said Moreton, and one Edwardes who was layd in prison for it, but Moreton fledd."[63] Despite the allegations, there is no evidence that Morton ever faced murder charges in England or New England.[64]

Winthrop had no doubt learned much else about Morton by the time he arrived in the new colony, especially given the

John Winthrop's note from the Court of Wards and Liveries
reveals that he was aware of allegations that Morton had committed
murder even before the Pilgrims exiled him from New Plymouth.
(© The British Library Board. Add. Ms. 35124, f. 023.)

frequent passages between New Plymouth and its neighboring settlements in Massachusetts Bay. Without providing details, he wrote in his journal that Morton had again angered local officials, this time in the jurisdiction of the new Massachusetts Bay Colony. He was "adjudged to be imprisoned till he were sent into England," Winthrop wrote, "& his house burnt downe, for his many injuries offered to the Indians, & other misdemenors."[65] The Massachusetts Court of Assistants provided more details. First, he should be shackled in a bilbo, an iron bar attached to the ground to confine someone for public humiliation. Then he was to be sent back to England on the *Gift*, his goods auctioned off to pay for his passage and any debts he had incurred and to reimburse an unidentified group of Natives for a canoe Morton allegedly stole from them. Crucially, his house was to be burned to the ground "in the sight of the Indians, for their satisfac[tion],"

because of his actions toward them.[66] Thomas Dudley, then
deputy governor of Massachusetts Bay, added that the Puritan authorities had sent Morton back in the hope that the lord
chief justice might give him the death penalty "for fouler mis-
demeaners there perpetrated," presumably a reference to the
alleged murder of Wigge.[67] The captain of the *Gift* refused
to take Morton on board—for reasons that Winthrop did not
specify—but the *Handmaid*, which left in December, took him
back, presumably to face charges.[68]

Bradford, looking back, wrote that Morton "lay a good
while in Exeter gaol" after this exile, possibly because "he was
vehemently suspected for the murder of a man that had ad-
ventured moneys with him when he first came into New England." He linked the murder accusation to unspecified mis-
demeanors and claimed that the Massachusetts authorities had
burned his house not as a punishment but so "that it might be
no longer a roost for such unclean birds to nestle in."[69] Morton was, as it happened, the first colonist expelled by the Massachusetts Bay Company, though he would not be the last.[70]
In 1635 Massachusetts authorities banished the minister Roger
Williams, who refused to swear an oath to the colony and
criticized it in public. He left Massachusetts and helped lay
the foundations for the new English colony of Rhode Island.
Two years later they tried and banished Anne Hutchinson, a
lay preacher accused of the heresy of antinomianism, or the
belief that one could receive God's will directly. She went to
Rhode Island and then to New Netherland, where she died in
Kieft's War in 1643.[71]

And so Morton headed eastward yet again. But Winthrop
could not forget him. In June 1631 a shallop arrived from Pas-

catawye (presumably Piscataqua) carrying letters that had been brought across the Atlantic, including a packet intended for Winthrop. Among them was a letter from Gorges who, Winthrop noted in his journal, "claimes a great parte of the baye of mass[achuset]tes." There was also a letter addressed to Morton, presumably sent before Morton had arrived back in England. Winthrop justified opening the letter because it was "directed to one who was our prisoner, & had declared himself an ill willer to our Government."[72]

In the years to come, Winthrop would learn much more about the relationship between Morton and Gorges, none of it pleasing him. But for the moment, at least, Morton was gone, reputed to be imprisoned thousands of miles away. The fact that he was deported based on somewhat specious charges that he had acted against the interest of the region's Native peoples was unimportant. Bradford and Winthrop alike recognized that Morton posed a threat, whether to their religious practices with the dancing around the maypole or to their security by selling guns to the Ninnimissinuok.

The revels at Ma-re Mount made Morton an easier target than he might otherwise have been. But his actions there convinced the Pilgrims and Puritans that exiling him was a necessary step in creating a pious and prosperous homeland in New England. Unlike Lyford and Oldham, Morton survived his first—and his second—exile. Bradford and Winthrop would soon come to realize that he was more dangerous to them in London than in New England.

CHAPTER FOUR

Cutthroats in Canaan

O N August 4, 1634, John Winthrop wrote in his journal that a colonist at Wessaguset named William Jeffrey had showed him a letter he had received from Morton, who was then in England. Jeffrey and Morton had met in the late 1620s, when both were in contact with Sir Christopher Gardiner, an associate of Gorges's who had arrived in Massachusetts in the spring of 1629.[1] Winthrop wrote that the letter, dated three months earlier, detailed a series of proceedings that Morton had initiated relating to his experience in the Massachusetts Bay Colony. Morton claimed that he had at last "obtained his longe suit, & that a Comission was granted for a general Governor to be sente over, with many rallyinge speeches & threates against this plantation, & mr winthrop in particular." Winthrop reported the contents to Governor Thomas

Dudley and the council of the colony. He also kept a copy, or perhaps the original, and wrote its contents into his journal.[2]

With Morton in England, Winthrop had no way to confront him about the accusations in the recent correspondence. But as Winthrop knew from the letter, Morton's second exile had led him into a close alliance with Gorges, who was unhappy with how settlement had progressed in the years since he had helped organize the Council for New England. The council itself had mostly faded from significance, but Gorges still held fast to the dream that he would someday lay claim to vast American territory. The recent establishment of the Massachusetts Bay Company posed a problem for him since its charter claimed exclusive access to much of the most desirable part of New England. In 1634 he wrote to Charles I with a plan for a reorganized New England under the direction of a "lord governor, or lord lieutenant." In order to proceed, Gorges first got the members of the Council for New England to surrender their claims under their grant of 1620, a feat that proved simple since some of the original patentees had died and others had lost interest. With the legal way cleared, or so it might have appeared at the time, the king agreed with Gorges and named him "lord governor," though without initially attending to the fact that the Massachusetts Bay Company had already organized colonial settlements on lands that Gorges believed he owned.[3]

Even with that appeal, Gorges needed to find a way to undermine the now-launched colonization of Massachusetts. How perfect for him, then, that Morton, seething at his treatment at the hands of Winthrop, was back in England. Here was the ideal partner—a lawyer who had been on the ground in North America, who understood it well, and who resented those who had exiled him from a life of apparent joy and economic gain.[4]

But Morton was not the only possible addition to the Gorges circle. Bradford had written at some length about the arrival of Christopher Gardiner in Plymouth in 1631, along with two servants and "a comly yonge woman, whom he caled his cousin, but it was suspected, she (after the Italian maner) was his concubine." He had settled first in Massachusetts, but ran into trouble and reportedly went to live among the Natives. Bradford claimed that some of the Algonquians came to inform him that Gardiner was living among them and they had thought about killing him, though the governor did not mention why.

Since Gardiner was well armed, the Natives decided to confront him when he had paddled out into a river in a canoe. During the struggle his canoe hit a rock, dumping him and his weapons into the water. He still had a small dagger, so they beat him with long poles until he dropped it. By the time he made it back to Plymouth, his arms and hands were swollen from the assault.[5]

Gardiner denounced the Natives for their treatment, though they responded later that "they did but a litle whip him with sticks." Bradford directed Gardiner to a house where his wounds could be "bathed and anointed," and soon enough he felt well again. But during his recovery, a small book fell out of Gardiner's pocket "or some private place," as Bradford put it, "in which was a memoriall what day he was reconciled to the pope and church of Rome, and in what universitie he tooke his scapula, and shuch and shuch degrees." Bradford wrote of his discovery to Winthrop, who sent John Underhill and Samuel Dudley, two officers, to bring Gardiner back. (In writing to authorities in England after Gardiner's arrest, Winthrop noted that it "was a spetiall providence of God to bring those notes of his to our hands.") Eventually Gardiner left Massachusetts a free man, and arrived in Bristol in mid-August 1632. There he reportedly complained about how terribly he had been treated in New England, a perfect complement to the case that Gorges and others were building against Winthrop.[6]

At the same time, Thomas Wiggin, one of Winthrop's allies in Bristol, had learned that Gardiner had returned from New England. Wiggin claimed that Gardiner had two wives in London but had gone to New England with a third woman. Hearing that he was to be arrested, Gardiner had allegedly fled to New Netherland but, Wiggin claimed, local Natives caught him and brought him back. Gardiner fetched up again at Bristol on August 19, spreading calumnies against Winthrop and the Puritans, claiming they were "noe less then traytors and rebels agaynst his Magestye wth Divers other most scandels and aprobrious speeches." Wiggin knew such charges to be false. What, he might have asked, would one expect from a bigamist who reputedly had once swum for his life to avoid being hanged by the authorities?[7]

Concerned that Gardiner, Gorges, and others were determined to undermine the colony, Wiggin, less than three months later, wrote to a member of the Privy Council, repeating the charges against Gardiner. For good measure, he also added a complaint about Morton, claiming that he had heard from his wife, her son, and others that he had fled to New

England "upon a foule suspition of Murther" but continued his nefarious ways there, where he fell "out wyth some of the Indians" and "shott them with a fowling piece." This was the crime, Wiggin claimed, that prompted Massachusetts Bay authorities to burn his house and banish him.[8]

Despite Wiggin's appeal, the Privy Council took the complaints it had received about Massachusetts Bay seriously. Specifically, it heard the allegations brought by Gardiner, Gorges, Morton, and their allies. In January 1633 the councilors acknowledged the severity of the charges, which if true and allowed to continue "woulde tend to the great dishonor of this kingdome, and utter ruine of that plantation." But in the end the council rejected the legitimacy of the claims. While it held open the possibility that the matter might be subsequently reexamined, the council found that the king remained committed to the original leadership of the colony and continued to hope "that the countrie would prove both benificiall to this kingdom, and profitable to the perticular adventurers." The council added that the king was willing to "supply any thing further that might tend to the good governmente, prosperities, and comforte of his people ther of that place."[9]

But although the Privy Council members had thus showed their renewed support for Winthrop, Morton's letter revealed that the nightmare for the Massachusetts Bay Colony had only begun. As agents for the Massachusetts colony soon understood, the Privy Council proved willing to hear additional evidence. Winthrop learned through Morton's letter to Jeffrey that this exile claimed he had been summoned to England— not exiled, as the Puritans knew—"to make complaint against Ananias and the brethren." Here Morton drew on scripture to compare Winthrop with the biblical Ananias (of Acts 5:1-5), whom God struck dead for lying, and the Puritans as his fellow travelers. During his first exile he had only "superficially (through the brevity of time)" made an adequate complaint against those leading the Massachusetts Bay settlement. But now, as he had written to Jeffrey, he was free to make a stronger case.[10]

Morton sketched out his argument in his long letter. He referred to himself as Jonas now back on land, able to cry, "Repent you cruel separatists, repent, there are as yet but forty days," a paraphrase of chapter 3 of the book of Jonah.[11] He believed that the Massachusetts charter had become void, though he knew that the leaders of the colony denied it with "their boasting and false alarms . . . with feigned cause of thanksgiving." Their crimes would soon be punished "like Sampson's foxes with fire-brands at their tails," a reference to Judges 15:4-5, which details Sampson sending foxes to burn down the fields of the Philistines.[12] Morton cast himself in the role of Perseus reborn: having "uncased Medusa's head," he "struck the brethren into astonishment."[13]

And it had worked, or so he claimed. Despite the fact that Winthrop and the others had friends in England, the king and the Privy Council now understood "their preposterous loyalty and irregular proceedings, and are incensed against them." Morton was convinced that everyone left the meeting "with a pair of cold shoulders." After a thorough reading, Morton claimed, the patent to the Massachusetts Bay Company "was declared, for manifest abuses there discovered, to be void," and the king had ordered that a new governor of New England be appointed. While Morton exaggerated the impact of his plea, which resulted in a royal authorization for the archbishop of Canterbury to monitor developments in New England, the threat posed to the continuation of the Bay Colony remained, at least in theory.[14]

Morton was writing to Jeffrey now, he explained, because he thought his friend might fear that he had "died in obscurity," as the Puritans, "abusing justice by their sinister practices," had hoped. Jeffrey needed to know that the English had no respect for "King Winthrop with all his inventions and his Amsterdam fantastical ordinances, his preachings, marriages, and other abusive ceremonies, which do exemplify his detestation to the church of England, and the contempt of his majesty's authority and wholesome laws, which are and will be established in those parts," even against Winthrop's will.[15]

When Winthrop saw Morton's letter, he no doubt recognized that Morton, rather than festering in jail, had become an avowed enemy not only of Plymouth but also of Massachusetts. More alarming, he seemed to have access to those who could, should they so choose, undermine the Bay Colony. What could be worse than someone who spread such calumnies at court?

As it turned out, Morton was just getting started.

During the early 1630s, Morton, Gorges, and their associates developed a legal strategy that they believed would convince the king to demand the return of the original charter, the physical parchment that carried the royal seal that Endecott had taken across the ocean in 1629.[16] But although that process would take several years, the council did not wait to make a decision. As early as late 1631, Gorges and the others had begun to allocate lands within their patent. (A late seventeenth-century copy of their meeting notes survives, allowing unusual access into the plan to derail the Massachusetts Bay Colony.)[17] They recorded the patent issued to Gorges and Captain John Mason that provided the legal basis for their action against Massachusetts and noted other land allocations as well. In subsequent meetings they specified who would own what parcel and how much these patentees would need to send back to the council, such as one-fifth of any silver and gold they found. The council's goal, as the minutes specified on December 2, 1631 (and on other occasions), was "to builde a Towne, and settle divers Inhabitants for the generall good of that Country." Specifying that requirement indicated that they did not intend to allocate land for speculative purposes but instead hoped to lure investors who would create new communities.[18]

On November 6, 1632, the president and council laid out a detailed plan for how the region should be colonized. They wanted the king to issue a new patent for the area and agreed to hire a solicitor to prosecute their case. All previous patents needed to be returned and then confirmed by the council. No more migrants could go to Massachusetts without a license from the council. They wanted to ban all fishing crews from engaging in trade with the Natives, nor should they be allowed to cut any timber for their ships without a license. The time had also come for the Earl of Warwick to send the council the great seal so that the proper certifying wax marks could be placed on the new patents. On June 26, 1634, they reported the movements of Dutch ships and possible interference coming from the English at New Plymouth. And they complained, not surprisingly, about the refusal of the Massachusetts Bay Company to return its patent despite the fact "that they had oftentimes written for it to be sent hither."[19]

The members of the Council for New England likely knew that in January 1633 the Privy Council, in response to rumors of disorder in New England, had ruled that the early progress of the Massachusetts colony was strong and that the king would "supplie anie thing further that might tend to the good Government of the place, and prosperity, and comfort of his people there."[20] With that resolution barring the way, the council decided in 1635 to bring a quo warranto, a legal effort to have the charter for the Massachusetts Bay Company sent back to London, which would invalidate the company's claim to the region. They took the case to the King's Bench in November 1635.[21] The council members were confident, as one reported in the minutes on May 5, 1635, that "when the surrender of ye said Patent is made his Maj[est]y shall be moved by joint request to those whom it concerns for the confirmation of their Deeds under the Greate Seale of England." At that point they put their faith in Morton, who was then their solicitor.[22]

The doctrine of quo warranto had emerged in England in the thirteenth century as a way to regulate relations between the monarch and corporations, which included any incorporated town. By then, parchment bearing the signature and seal of the king was the proof of a chartered entity's right to claim a particular place or operate in a certain way. This obsession with the physical charter had likely not always existed but instead emerged as a response to the growing number of charters appearing in England by the fourteenth century and the fear that forgers might copy them. Multiple documents relating to the same grant could sow confusion. A seal added power since it could be understood by someone who could not read the text, a crucial point in an era of limited literacy.[23]

At its core, the legal concept of quo warranto posed a question: by what warrant does a chartered body have the right to do something? When invoked, it presumed that those bringing the charge believed that a corporate body had exceeded its authority as defined in a founding text. Given the time and expense of preparing a case, which could be in court for weeks, a quo warranto hearing was not a casual matter, especially since all involved knew the high stakes. A successful case might result in the monarch revoking a charter, not to seize power for himself—a particular concern of those who feared Charles I was trying to expand the role of the monarch—but instead to place the rights of the corporation into the hands of others who would not exceed the authority the corporate body possessed. At the time that Morton and Gorges challenged the Massachusetts Bay Company, most cases went to the King's Bench. In legal parlance, they were known as "information in the nature of a quo warranto." While the procedure had been rarely used during the sixteenth century, more such actions were appearing before this court by 1630. The arguments put forward by the council members would not have been unusual in this moment of legal challenges to chartered authorities and heightened use of this court to find satisfaction.[24]

Gorges and his allies, including Morton, drafted a petition that they sent to the king in April 1635. (It is likely that Morton crafted the document, given his expertise.) The legal brief identified the twenty-four associates of the colony and

detailed the privileges they possessed as a result of the charter, including the right to control territory, sell it when they
chose, ship arms to settlements there, levy taxes on residents,
and monopolize trade in the region by prohibiting others from
becoming involved. Charles I accepted their argument, concluding that he had "been credibly informed of the many in-
conveniences and mischiefs that have grown & are like more
& more to arise" in New England. The judgment declared
that the rights assigned in the charter "should be seized into
the King's hands." The colonists in Massachusetts needed to
return their charter and Gorges would then become the governor of the region. Having invested in the region and already
demonstrated his loyalty to the Crown, Gorges was the obvious person to guide the colony forward. He alone, according
to one of the king's proclamations, would have the authority
to decide who could take up residence there.[25] At a subsequent
meeting at Gorges's house, the council decided that Morton,
because of his extensive courtroom experience, would lead the
legal charge to recover the charter and pursue the suit against
the Massachusetts Bay Company.[26] Morton served as his own
agent as well. On June 21, 1636, Morton had appealed to King
Charles seeking royal intervention in order to reclaim funds
he had lost in Massachusetts, having been sent away "from
those forraign parts by the mallitious practice of the separatists there," who had "seized and taken away" his property.[27]

But while the Privy Council, the King's Bench, and even
Charles I could demand that the colonists in Massachusetts
send the charter back, putting the revocation into action
proved more difficult. Immediately the colonists voiced vig-
orous opposition. Edward Winslow went to London to battle

The charter of the Governor and Company of the
Massachusetts Bay in New England of 1629 was signed by
King Charles I and brought to North America by John
Endecott, who took it to Naumkeag, which later became
Salem. The king's agents demanded that the colony return
this document in 1635, but it never left American shores.
(SC 1/series 23X. Charter of the Governor and Company of the Massachusetts
Bay in New England, 1629. Massachusetts Archives. Boston, Massachusetts.)

the plan, which had been driven forward by Gorges and
Mason with Morton's assistance. He learned that the Gorges
group had the support of the archbishop of Canterbury who,
Winslow feared, wanted to vacate the New England patents

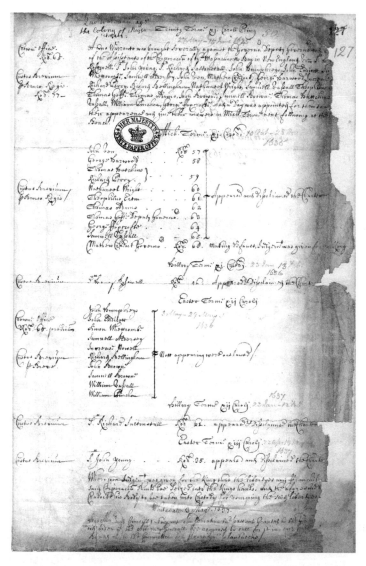

Minutes taken during the hearing about the Massachusetts
quo warranto case of 1635. The verdict appears on the
reverse side: "Judgmt to seize their Franchise."
(The National Archives.)

and bring the Puritans' churches under his control. Winslow needed to answer questions raised by Morton's accusation of errant ministerial practice in the colonies. Winslow admitted that the lack of sufficient clergy led some laypeople, including himself, to "exercise his Gift to healp the edification of his bretheren when they wanted better meanes which was often." This meant presiding over marriages, which Winslow noted should be a civil and not religious function.[28]

In September 1638 the Massachusetts General Court, the governing body of the colony, assembled and discussed the order they had received from the Lords Commissioners for Plantations to return the charter. Rather than comply, the court resolved that surrendering the parchment would send a message to their allies in England that they would accept a new form of government and they would, as Winthrop wrote, "be bound to receive such a governour and such orders as should be sent to us, and many bad minds, yea, and some weak ones, among ourselves, would think it lawful if not necessary, to accept a general governour."[29]

Rather than sending the charter, the court instead sent a petition, arguing that surrendering their charter would have four disastrous consequences. First, residents of the colony would lose whatever protections they had against potential enemies. Second, if Massachusetts Bay failed, then other English colonies would as well, leaving the region open for the French and Dutch. Third, such an action would become a disincentive to anyone who had thought about migrating to North America. And finally, if they agreed to surrender their charter, the colonists there would conclude that they no longer needed to be loyal to the king and would presumably "be ready to confederate themselves under a new government," sending a dangerous signal to all other Britons in North America. Given what they took to be the superiority of these claims, the petitioners asked that the quo warranto not be put into force.[30]

Their strategy worked, though not in the way they had intended. In 1635, a ship that Gorges and Mason had financed and that Gorges planned to use to establish his position as governor never made it out of the dock. According to the Puritan-leaning antiquarian diarist Sir Simonds D'Ewes, the ship was central to Gorges's plan to transport one thousand soldiers to New England to support his new government. But though the English god "had carried so many weak and crazy ships" across the ocean, he reported, it seemed like divine intervention when "this strong new-built ship in the very launching fell all in pieces." After the ship's demise Gorges never commissioned another, perhaps concluding that a military invasion was too expensive to mount.[31]

The great ship's failure disappointed Gorges and the Council for New England, but the problems of enforcing the order had more to do with changing circumstances. By the time the king issued his rule that Gorges should sail to Massachusetts as governor-general, Mason had died and the Crown offered no financial assistance to prosecute its own request for the return of the charter. Charles had also become distracted by more pressing issues at home, including the violent Scots reaction to the introduction of a prayer book that the king and Laud introduced in an effort to minimize Presbyterian practices in the north. A riot broke out in St. Giles Cathedral in Edinburgh on July 23, 1637, the first instance of open rebellion against what many Scots saw as an effort by Charles and Laud to impose a Roman-style liturgy. By the next year the English and Scots were deep into the so-called Bishops' Wars, a conflict that occupied the king's time and drained the state's finances. Though no one could have known it then, the ensuing crisis helped trigger the rise of Puritan power in England, the Civil War, and the execution of the king in 1649.[32]

The council had won its quo warranto case in court, but there was no way for it to win on the ground as long as authorities in Massachusetts refused the order to return the patent. Eventually, Gorges came to the realization that he was too old, and his financial resources stretched too thin, to make the journey across the ocean to take matters in hand. Instead of putting the king's order into action, he remained in England, where he continued to mount a legal battle over the territory he believed he and the council owned. In 1636 he sent his nephew William to be the governor of a settlement to be called New Somersetshire, which John Winthrop claimed would extend from "Cape Elizabeth to the Sagadahoc." The younger Gorges soon began the process of establishing a community near modern Saco, Maine.[33] On November 1, 1638, the last meeting reported in the minutes, the council decided to grant Sir Ferdinando and Lord Gorges an additional sixty miles "further up into the maine land." All of their hopes and expectations hung on their case that the Massachusetts Bay Company had violated its charter and hence invited the quo warranto.[34]

Thomas Morton, having suffered firsthand in ways that Gorges never did, still sought to undermine the Puritans. He realized that additional legal actions in London, where he, Gorges, and Mason had prevailed, would do no good. He decided to pursue his cause through a literary assault—a case brought not in a court of law but in a book.

Before the petition from Massachusetts arrived in London, Stam's press printed Morton's book in Amsterdam. Morton could not have known then that the quo warranto case would fail, but he understood that if the authority of the Massachusetts Bay Company disappeared, a replacement would need to be created. In some sense, this notion lay at the heart of *New English Canaan*. English readers needed to understand that this region could have a different future once the Pilgrims and Puritans lost their authority.

In many ways, Morton's book followed the rules of the genre of the travel account. Ever since the appearance in 1493 in Barcelona of Christopher Columbus's first report of his transatlantic voyage, European printers had produced an ever-greater number of accounts of journeys to the Western Hemisphere.[35] In the mid-1550s the Venetian geographer Giovanni Battista Ramusio gathered together a large collection of European travel writings, including one volume devoted to reports about the Western Hemisphere, which contained the first printed pictures of a pineapple, maize, and a hammock, an invention of the Tupinambás of Brazil.[36] The first collection of such writings in English appeared in London in 1555.[37] Other efforts followed.[38] In 1589 Richard Hakluyt the younger, who modeled his efforts after Ramusio's and became among the most devoted promoters of English exploration, trade, and colonization schemes in the latter decades of the sixteenth century, printed his first large collection of such accounts. He published an expanded edition in three volumes from 1598 to 1600, with the last volume devoted to narratives from expeditions to the Western Hemisphere.[39] In the years that followed, English readers learned about the myriad journeys of Captain John Smith and of the famed, and doomed, explorer Henry Hudson.[40] The best-known study of New England before the publication of Morton's book was William Wood's *New England's Prospect*, which was published in London in 1634, with a second edition—a sign that the first one had likely achieved some popularity—appearing in 1635, and a third edition following in 1639.[41] And of course Morton had one other text available: Gorges's history of the region, though that contained secondhand information rather than eyewitness testimony.

In the first part of *New English Canaan*, Morton focused on the mores of the indigenous peoples of southern New England, especially those he knew best, along with a description of what Morton declared on the title page was these people's "tractable Nature and Love towards the English." The second part extensively discussed the regional environment, including the commodities the region could produce. The final section, as the title page also announced, focused on "what people are planted there, their prosperity," and the "remarkable accidents" that had transpired since the Pilgrims and Puritans arrived, as well as information about the "Tenents, and practice of their Church." Morton identified himself as a gentleman of Clifford's Inn who possessed a decade of "knowledge and experiment in the Countrie." That was a clever bit of self-promotion—a single statement indicating his prominence as a trusted observer and the fact that he had spent considerable time on the ground there, as opposed to others who made only brief excursions across the Atlantic and then claimed to be experts. The claim was also false: Morton had probably spent no more than five years in New England. The assertion on the title page likely referred to the passage of time from his first expedition of 1622 to the year the manuscript went to the English printer Charles Greene, or about a year after Morton's second exile.

From the opening there was no doubt that Morton had fallen in love with New England, a "Rich, hopefull and very beautifull Country, worthy the Title of Natures Masterpeece." In his dedication to the Privy Council he likened his offering to the widow's mite, a reference to the books of Mark (12:41–44) and Luke (21:1–4) describing Jesus's proclamation that the modest gift of a poor woman was superior to a large donation from a wealthy person. But he was compelled to press on because "all that wrong and rapine" in New England required he do his best to serve the king. While such protestations were common, Morton's explicit association with those who gave money in the ancient temple signaled less his actual sense of modesty, which was likely false, and more the religious tropes through which he would be telling his story. This was no accident. Having been exiled twice by English migrants who prided themselves on the purity of their religious mission, Morton needed to establish that he was just as devout. The book itself, then, was "an offering, wherewith I prostrate my selfe at your honorable footstoole."[42] He added that his book drew on his long experience in America, which would distinguish his account from those who had offered only superficial reports, a possible reference either to Wood's *New England's Prospect* or to Bradford, whose first brief history of the original settlement had appeared in print in London in 1622.[43]

Morton had two audiences in mind when he wrote his book. First, he believed that his text would prove invaluable to those contemplating the arduous task of migrating to the new colony. But he also knew that there would be curious readers, perhaps the vast majority of those who picked up the small book, who read it because they were "inquisitive after novelties." For selfish reasons, other authors had kept the truth about New England's peoples and resources to themselves. Morton sought to create in his book a verbal picture "more punctually to the life." Among those who praised the text was Christopher Gardiner, the man who had met Morton and Jeffrey on the shores of Massachusetts Bay in 1629.[44]

Morton launched his work with details about the climate and opinions about the origins of Native Americans, two topics that would fascinate European writers well into the eighteenth century.[45] The English, he argued, needed to avoid places that were too hot (the "Torrida Zona") or too cold (the "Frigida Zona") and settle in a temperate climate (the "Zona Temperata"), which was suitable for "the Ant and Bee," a reference to then current natural histories favoring these two insects because of their industriousness.[46] Fortunately, the English had a man who could guide them, "the noble minded Gentleman, Sir Ferdinando Gorges, Knight, zealous for the glory of God, the honor of his Majesty, and the benefit of the weale publicke." Morton argued that the perfect place to settle lay between 40 and 45 degrees north latitude, an area that corresponded directly to the patent that Gorges had sought and still dreamed about claiming. Just as important, God had made it easier for Gorges to organize the settlement of New England by sweeping "away by heapes the Salvages," a reference to the epidemic of 1616 to 1619.[47]

Though the English had already established settlements in North America, this territory, more beautiful than any other, was "not to be paraleld in all Christendome." The "sweetnesse of the aire, fertility of the Soile, and small number of the Salvages" prompted discerning authorities to conclude that this was "the principall part of all America, for habitation and the commodiousnesse of the Sea." (As an additional benefit, English ships would not suffer from worms that attacked their vessels in Virginia, though Morton did not explain how he had reached that conclusion.) Massachusetts, at the center of this region, provided excellent anchorages. Morton likened his report to "a Landskipp, for the better information of the Travellers," who could study it and "plainely perceave by the demonstration of it, that it is nothing inferior to the Canaan of Israel, but a kind of paralell to it, in all points."[48]

After writing in some depth about indigenous beliefs and cultural practices, Morton laid out an argument for how Natives and newcomers could coexist, a claim that stood in stark contrast to the opinions of other English visitors to the region. His views no doubt stemmed from his close association with the Algonquians—the very relationship that so angered Bradford. That proximity allowed Morton to come to know a Massachusett named Cheecatawback, a regional sachem who claimed sovereignty over a large area. One day,

Morton reported, a group of one hundred Narragansetts arrived in Cheecatawback's territory with plans to spend the winter. They hunted deer and turkeys, which was customary, but they also hunted beaver, which were far more prized. On occasion, Morton noted, the Narragansetts would offer full beaver skins, a present usually fit only for a sachem, to the English at Wessaguset.[49]

Cheecatawback was not pleased by the Narragansetts' poaching so he devised a plot. According to Morton, he reported to the English that the Narragansetts had come to find out how many of the newcomers had arrived and to look for an opportunity "to cut us off, and take that which they found in our custody usefull for them." He also told the English that the Narragansetts would burn their houses, a plan he allegedly uncovered after capturing one of the invaders, Meshebro. Cheecatawback told this story to the English, asking in return that they protect his own wives and children from the onslaught. The English readily agreed and armed for battle, putting on "corslets, headpeeces, and weapons defensive and offensive."[50]

Cheecatawback then arranged for some of the Narragansetts to come to the English on the pretense that they would engage in trade. "The Salvage that was a stranger to the plott," Morton wrote, "simply comming to trade, and finding his merchants, lookes like lobsters, all cladd in harnesse, was in a maze to thinke what would be the end of it." He quickly sold all the furs he had, taking whatever the English offered before trying to flee from their trading shack. The English persuaded him to share a meal before he left, which gave him an opportunity to see more of his hosts' arms. He bolted for freedom as soon as he could, but Cheecatawback was not done. Soon enough, the entire Narragansett party fled and the Pilgrims, so Morton claimed, were so "gulled by the subtilety of this Sachem" that they "lost the best trade of beaver that ever they had for the time."[51]

By reporting this story in some depth, Morton managed to accomplish two distinct goals. First, he demonstrated without any doubt the intellectual capacities of the Ninnimissinuok. "These people were not (as some have thought[)], a dull or slender witted people," he wrote, but instead "very subtile."[52] Second, he revealed that he was better suited to deal with the locals than any of the other English, including the dullards at Wessaguset whom Cheecatawback had played so skillfully. Telling the story of the encounter with the uninvited Narragansetts was no mere accident but instead a rhetorical strategy Morton used to reveal his particular knowledge of southern New England. The Pilgrims and Puritans lacked this local knowledge and so behaved badly. He illustrated that point by describing English desecration of the grave of the mother of none other than Cheecatawback, an incident that led to violence.[53]

Morton understood that these Algonquians had their faults, claiming they could not resist alcohol if traders made it available to them and that one inebriated man put a long gun into his mouth and pulled the trigger with his foot. (Obviously knowing the accusations that had been made against him, he reported that he had given alcohol only to local leaders since, he claimed he told them, "it was amongst us the Sachems drinke.")[54] But despite such failings, the Natives seemed more content than colonists or Britons in general. They suffered no want. They had ample access to game animals and to fish and did not strive after the fineries that consumed Europeans. They worked when they wanted and secured all they needed. "If our beggars of England should with so much ease (as they,) furnish themselves with foode, at all seasons, there would not be so many starved in the streets, neither would so many gaoles be stuffed, or gallouses [gallows] furnished with poor wretches, as I have seene them."[55] Morton here, consciously or not, invoked one of the central ideas that had motivated the English colonization of North America over the past half century. England was overcrowded, some promoters of overseas settlements argued, and able-bodied young men who might cause domestic unrest would better serve the realm if they were sent across the Atlantic. This idea would later become embedded in the policy known as "transportation," which provided convicted criminals with the option of passage to a North American colony and time as a bound laborer in lieu of a long prison term or the death sentence.[56]

Ninnimissinuok disdain for material wants proved the superiority of their culture. They possessed a grander sense of the possible than the Pilgrims and Puritans, Morton averred, and shared what they had with others. "Platoes Comonwealth is so much practised by these people," he wrote. "According to humane reason guided onely by the light of nature, these people leade the more happy and freer life, being voyde of care, which torments the minds of so many Christians." The Algonquians should not be scorned but rather emulated and joined. If only the poor English could "goe from the good ale tap, which is the very loadstone of the lande by which our English beggers steere theire Course," they would prosper in this newfound Canaan.[57]

Morton's discussion of the suitability of this region for English migrants emphasized the bounty to be found there, often reading more like a promotional offering than a realistic critique of an actual landscape. "The more I looked, the more I liked it," he wrote of his survey of the area. "And when I had more seriously considered, of the bewty of the place, with all her faire indowments, I did not thinke that in all the knowne world it could be paralel'd." He stood in awe of the region's rich forests, gentle hills, large meadows, and abundant clean streams. Dense flocks of birds flew overhead and thick schools of fish crowded the waters. "If this Land be not rich," he exclaimed, "then is the whole world poore."[58] Morton understood that his task was to share the knowledge he had gathered abroad with his countrymen, who might likewise come to understand that New England was "in a paralell with the Isrealites Canaan, which none will deny, to be a land farre more excellent then Old England in her proper nature."[59]

Morton wrote at length about local resources that could be harvested. He extolled the benefits of white and red oak, which could be used to build both houses and ships. Local ash would be ideal for barrel staves and oars. The English could construct chairs and trenchers with beech and employ walnut to make hoops. The nuts would feed the swine they would import. Elm, chestnut, and pine were abundant, as was cedar, which could be used to erect temples like those of ancient Jerusalem. Northern New England boasted an "infinite store" of spruce ideal for masts, another benefit for a nation committed to navigation. Fruit trees, berry bushes, and vines bearing grapes added to the bounty hidden in the woods.[60]

The birds to be found in New England were even more varied than the trees and bushes, and like the plants they too had special properties that could be harvested. Seemingly every bird that lived on both sides of the Atlantic was superior in New England. Ducks, quail, partridges, and other game birds were every bit as tasty as those at home—and bigger. American geese were fatter than those to be found in England, with feathers that made better down beds than his readers might have ever experienced.[61] Turkeys, native to America, could be found in abundance; they often walked right up to the doors of new settlers' abodes. Morton claimed he had seen one that weighed forty-eight pounds and that a local boy had told him he once saw a thousand turkeys in a single day, and none fled even when someone shot among them.[62] He praised New England's hawks and falcons, species familiar to his English readers as hunting birds, which could have gained the attention of the elite gentlemen Gorges and the council wanted to attract. (Morton might have known that in 1635 the Council for New England ordered hawks sent to Charles I from New England.) Morton also called attention to hummingbirds "no bigger then a great Beetle," whose "fethers have a glasse like silke" and changed color. Other Europeans had also been captivated by these iridescent creatures found across much of the Western Hemisphere, from Brazil northward, which were, as Morton noted, "admired for shape, co-loure, and size."[63]

As might be expected from someone who had made a living, however briefly, as a fur trader, Morton knew much about the animals that roamed New England's forests—otter, lynx, marten, raccoon, fox, and even wolves, a dangerous predator with a luxurious fur that made a fitting present.[64] But two animals especially drew his sustained interest. One was the moose, which Morton (like Gorges earlier) believed could be used as a draft animal. Moose skins made excellent leather, so the Ninnimissinuok used them for shoes. Morton claimed that these large and powerful animals were not especially quick and they were so abundant that the locals had given a half dozen to "one English man whome they have borne affec-tion to"—a likely reference to a gift that Morton himself had received.[65] The other notable creature was the beaver, at home on land and in water alike, a natural engineer that shaped the environment to its needs. The flesh was excellent and Mor-ton praised its castor sacs, which produced the fluid used by the beaver to scent its territory. "This beast is of a masculine vertue for the advancement of Priapus," he noted, and its fur was "the best marchantable commodity, that can be found."[66]

Morton fleshed out the rest of his catalog of New En-gland's natural endowments with descriptions of minerals, fish, and the healthy quality of the region's waters. There was a coastline along the northern shores of Massachusetts Bay that had already been named Marble Harbor (modern Mar-blehead) because of the beauty of the striped rock to be found there.[67] Abundant slate for roofs for houses could be found, ore to produce lead and iron, and a stone that the locals called "cos" employed to fashion tools that held an edge. He claimed that tin, silver, and gold mines could be found there, perhaps unwittingly reinforcing an idea already in circulation among English promoters of colonization that Britons in North America would locate the same riches that the Iberians had found farther south.[68]

Morton's writings on the abundant fish off the coast of New England added little to the voluminous writings by promoters who had already extolled the aquatic riches of these waters. Still, he noted that there were already up to three hundred European ships plying the area each year, primarily for cod, which he claimed was "a commodity better than the golden mines of the Spanish Indies; for without dried Codd the Spaniard, Portingal and Italian, would not be able to vittel of a shipp for the Sea." He was certain that the sale of dried fish as well as the fish's oil "will enrich the inhabitants of New England quicly."[69]

The notion of a land and sea of abundance carried through the final pages of his natural history. Bass were so numerous in one place, Morton claimed, that when the tides changed one could walk on their backs without getting wet. Locals, including colonists, had already figured out that the use of shad as a fertilizer could triple their corn yields. Lobsters were so plentiful that groups of Ninnimissinuok camped by the seaside for four to six weeks, taking in five hundred to a thousand of the crustaceans, which they ate fresh and also dried to consume later. Ponds and rivers proved just as rich, with carp, trout, and eels, among others. Even the colonists' pigs enjoyed the seemingly endless number of clams. The Ninnimissinuok, Morton claimed, recognized the superiority of English fishhooks and traded for them, with a single hook worth a beaver skin, a remarkable deal for the newcomers.[70]

New England, in a word, beckoned. The air was superior to what the English breathed in fetid Virginia, and those who left the Chesapeake ill would recover quickly in this region once they could breathe its clean air.[71] Anyone could sink a well for fresh water more abundant than that to be found in the ancient Promised Land. At Ma-re Mount, the place he knew best, Morton boasted that there was a spring that produced water to cure "Melancolly probatum"; at nearby Wena-semute (modern Chelsea) the local waters cured barrenness; and at modern Quincy (which he called "Squantos Chappell") the locals drank a water that put them in a deep sleep for two days, during which local healers would have visions and then share them with their communities.[72] The rains and winds were more moderate than in England, the harbors safe for ships, the soil superior.[73] Images of the biblical paradise flowed from Morton. Getting necessary goods was cheaper here than in England so it was time, he wrote, "to come out of Sodome, to the land of Canaan, a land that flowes with Milke and Hony."[74]

Morton set his writings on nature into a trans-European perspective. He argued that the English should try to claim Lake Champlain, an area where, so he had heard, the French had already set up a booming fur trade—one shipment went home with twenty-five thousand beaver skins. Now that some of the colonists could speak with the locals, the English could compete with their rivals.[75] As a result, they would not lose ground to the French and the Dutch, who Morton feared might monopolize the fur trade since they had explored the waterways that drained eastern New England. The Dutch had already found a passage from the north to their new settlements, he claimed, thereby giving them a dangerous head start. They were possibly taking twenty thousand pounds of beaver each year. The English could not allow these "intruders upon his Majesties most hopefull Country of New England" to continue.[76] He imagined a world that generated the kinds of wealth extracted from New Spain and even Virginia, but set in a New England whose colonial economy was not yet determined—if only it could be controlled by people like him (and presumably Gorges), who would know how to set it up for maximum gain.[77]

Near the end of the book Morton launched an assault on the Separatists' religious practices and the ways that they explained their actions to the world. In effect, this was an extension of the logic of the quo warranto case: by what warrant had the religious dissenters who went to New England behaved as they did? He made no distinction here between the Pilgrims of New Plymouth and the Puritans of Massachusetts. In his eyes, their practices might as well have been identical. The pages here seethe with his anger and mark the book as unique, not only as a screed against those who appear as heroes in other contemporary accounts but also as a work of history. Morton's concluding section marked his most important contribution to the politics of the early 1630s, the moment when Gorges's efforts to undermine the patent of Massachusetts Bay might still succeed.[78]

True to his earlier praise of the locals, Morton time and again described the Ninnimissinuok in a positive light and disparaged the misdeeds of the religious dissenters. One of Thomas Hunt's captives who had learned English was crucial in early discussions between Algonquians and colonists, he wrote. Another Native who spoke English purportedly told a sachem that the English had stored plague in a hole and would release it, a claim sure to alarm those who had suffered the horrors of 1616 to 1619.[79] Morton repeated the story of the desecration of Cheecatawback's mother's grave, which enraged the local sachem. He added that his informant had had a vision in which his mother begged him to do something about "this theevish people" now resident in the region, revealing to his English readers his exasperation at how the Pilgrims had violated Ninnimissinuok spiritual beliefs.[80]

Morton's version of history took a dark turn when he recounted a bloody assault that took place in 1623. Some of the Pilgrims invited three Ninnimissinuok men to join them in a feast at Wessaguset and then stabbed them to death. The malefactors, so Morton wrote, had done this because they thought the Algonquians posed a threat to Weston. The Massachusetts did not accept this version of events. Instead, Morton claimed, from then on they called "the English planters Wotawquenange, which in their language signifieth stabbers or Cutthroates."[81] Morton later added that the English had grown increasingly suspicious of the Natives, though he himself had "found the Massachusetts Indian[s] more full of humanity, then the Christians."[82]

Morton also offered a brief history of the exiling of Lyford and Oldham. Lyford, he wrote, had gone to New Plymouth as a minister, but the Pilgrims denounced him, calling him "hereticall and Papisticall." Unlike the Pilgrims, these two men "did maintaine the Church of England, to be a true Church, although in some particulars (they said) defective." But even a nod toward the imperfections of the Anglican Church was not sufficient for the religious of the colony, who had separated from it because they believed it had become a false church.[83]

In Morton's mind, the Pilgrims and Puritans, consumed by their zealotry, could not understand how fortunate they were in their new home. In only seven years as many English children had been born in New England as in twenty-seven years in Virginia, despite the fact that there were relatively few adult women among the earliest colonists in New Plymouth.[84] During one winter a group of Ninnimissinuok, looking to purchase some food, came upon a seemingly abandoned storage shed, so they broke into it and stole the contents. Later they offered restitution to the owner. Such action prompted Morton to write in a marginal note, "The Heathen more just, then the Christians."[85] In another instance, a colonist had fled for his life from a group of indigenous, leaving his shoes behind in his haste. When the Ninnimissinuok returned the shoes to Wessaguset, where they thought the man had gone, the English feared the worst. What colonist would dash off barefooted unless threatened by grave danger? Soon enough the man reappeared and the English celebrated his return. "By this you may observe," Morton told his readers, "whether the Salvage people are not full of humanity, or whether they are a dangerous people," as the Pilgrims claimed.[86]

To Morton, the group lacking humanity was the Pilgrims. He wrote at some length about how they mocked his settlement at Ma-re Mount, likening the celebration around the maypole to the Calf of Horeb instead of seeing the event for what it was—"harmless mirth made by younge men" eager to have wives. They drank and sang merrily around the pole, but these carefree acts infuriated the authorities of New Plymouth. Morton could not grasp how they missed that he was a pious man who "indeavoured to advance the dignity of the Church of England." They vilified him and his use of the Book of Common Prayer, which Puritans believed errant because that text recommended exclusion from a church of only "an open and notorious evil liver," a standard for entry too low for those who believed that only the elect should be allowed to join a church.[87]

The English opposition to Morton had been harmless enough earlier, when there were fewer of them, but now they had become "like overgrowne beares" and appeared "monsterous" when they captured him. When Morton briefly escaped, Myles Standish—whom Morton insisted on calling Captain Shrimp—erupted in anger. Morton, so he reported, had only walked home to Ma-re Mount to prepare to defend himself. When Standish and eight others arrived, Morton surrendered, though that did not stop the Pilgrims from beating him, imprisoning him in New Plymouth, and then dumping him without any supplies on a remote island awaiting passage to England, where he had been kept alive only through the kindness of Natives.[88]

"[T]o their terrible amazement," Morton wrote with satisfaction, he returned, first to New Plymouth and then to Massachusetts.[89] Even by his own account he stirred trouble in Massachusetts. He wrote that the Puritans demanded that each colonist sign a set of agreements that "*in all causes, as well Ecclesiasticall, as Politicall, wee should follow the rule of Gods word.*" Morton insisted that there be an additional clause to read "*So as nothing be done contrary, or repugnant to the Lawes of the Kingdome of England.*"[90] He reminded his readers of his punishment: time in the bilboes, the confiscation of his property, and the burning of his house. But he added a crucial detail. Some of the indigenous came to watch the proceedings and, as Morton put it, "did reproove these Eliphants of witt, for their inhumane deede." He likened these Algonquians to Balaam's ass, which in the book of Numbers (chapter 22) had shown great wisdom.[91] Like the ass, which had seen an angel and warned its owner to obey God's dictates, so these Ninnimissinuok informed the Pilgrims "that god would not love them, that burned this good mans howse."[92] This act of violence enabled Morton to revel in his own exile. His house lay in ashes unless it could imitate the phoenix and rise to "be new againe, (to the immortall glory and renowne, of this fertile Canaan the new,[)] the stumpes and postes in their black liveries will mourne, and piety it selfe will add a voyce to the bare remnant of that Monument, and make it cry for recompence, (or else revenge) against the Sect of cruell Schismaticks," he declared, invoking the language of the established church against the dissenters' original sin.[93]

Morton emphasized two religious ideas. First, he criticized twelve "unwarrantable" tenets of the Puritans' faith. These included the fact that magistrates, not ministers, had the legal authority to conduct a marriage, and further, that the use of a ring in the ceremony was "a relique of popery" since this was "a diabolicall circle for the Divell to daunce in."

Morton chastised the dissenters for claiming that the Book of Common Prayer was "an idol: and all that use it, Idolaters." He even found fault in the way that they prayed with their eyes closed because, he wrote, "they thinke themselves so perfect in the highe way to heaven, that they can find it blindfould: so doe not I."[94]

Morton's other religious observation was more personal. He saw his banishment via a ship sent to England as a reenactment of the story of Jonah, in which he played the starring role and the ship that hauled him eastward became the whale. The ship, he complained, was ill stocked, and it barely made it to the Azores with enough provisions to keep the prisoner and the others alive. But, like Jonah, he survived.[95]

Disgorged from the belly of the beast, Morton claimed that he had not troubled the Puritans except "at the Counsell table," a reference to his work with Gorges to undermine the patent of the New England settlers. He understood that he was "a Separatist amongst the Separatists," a moment of self-awareness that led him to emphasize the Puritans' distance from acceptable practice. "Repent you cruell Schismaticks, repent," he argued, one of four times he cried for their repentance in the final paragraph of his text. The "Charter and the Kingdome of the Separatists" would soon come to an end, he wrote. They had better be prepared for the next chapter.[96]

Morton's recounting of religious errors to be found in the Pilgrims' and Puritans' practice must have seemed especially galling to those who saw their migration as the best hope for Reformed Christianity. He understood, as well as anyone in his time, the power of a book to achieve political ends. He knew by 1637 that there was nothing more to contribute to the quo warranto case and likely little he could do to influence policy makers or courts in London. Morton published the book because he believed that the Ninnimissinuok and English might still be able to coexist if only the English-reading world would see the charade of the self-righteous dissenters for what he believed it was: a cover, imperfectly deployed, to justify their seizure of property that belonged in the hands of the Ninnimissinuok or of Gorges. In either case, Morton stood to profit.

Morton's most revealing moment focused on the epidemic of 1616 to 1619. By the time *New English Canaan* appeared, news of the devastation was widespread and many colonists had no doubt accepted the logic, put forward by multiple sources, that the sickness had been a divine act of the Christian god intending to smooth the way for those bearing the Word to a distant land. Morton did not depart from the idea that the "hand of God fell heavily" on the Ninnimissinuok "with such a mortall stroake, that they died on heapes, as they lay in their houses and the living: that were able to shift for themselves would runne away & let them dy, and let there Carkases ly above the ground without buriall." There were few survivors of this once well-peopled region. The "bones and skulls upon the severall places of their habitations, made such a spectacle . . . as I travailed in that Forrest, nere the Massachusetts," he recalled, that "it seemed to mee a new found Golgatha."[97]

Here was a place of suffering. By likening the unburied victims of this unknown plague to Calvary, Morton did not isolate the Natives in their misery. Instead, this tragedy marked a shared moment in the painful human past, just as Christ's crucifixion had symbolized a universal agony. Unlike his contemporaries, Morton saw the devastation for what it was—a sign not of the impending victory of the invaders but instead a cruel marker of a world being destroyed. Little could he have known that, just as his book was being published, another event would alter the fate of southern New England.

CHAPTER FIVE

Acomenticus

S OMETIME late in the autumn of 1643, Thomas Morton returned to New England. Winthrop, all too aware of the contents of *New English Canaan*, marked Morton's reappearance in his journal, noting the return of "our professed old adversary, who had set forth a book against us, and written reproachful and menacing letters to some of us."[1] Winthrop resented the way that Morton had rehearsed the history of the region. The off-and-on governor of Massachusetts was of course depicted as a liar and Morton cast himself as the long-suffering hero who endured trial after trial in pursuit of his goals. The Puritans of Massachusetts Bay had exiled Morton over a decade earlier because they viewed him as a threat, specifically by trading weapons to Natives and encroaching on the fur trade. Morton's first exile had followed the farcical arrest at Ma-re Mount, his second after his alleged defrauding of local Algonquians. But the landscape that Morton found upon his return in 1643 looked very different from the one he had left earlier.

By the time he got back, the Ninnimissinuok no longer had the authority they had during Morton's time there earlier. Indigenous still outnumbered colonists in southern New England, but they had experienced a radical disruption in Morton's absence. In the minds of Bradford and Winthrop, this change marked a moment of triumph. For Morton, it represented the second great tragedy to befall the Native peoples he admired.

While Morton was perhaps waiting in England for early copies of *New English Canaan* to arrive, relations between the Ninnimissinuok and the English had deteriorated. In September 1636 John Winthrop wrote in his journal that he had heard that the Narragansetts had made a truce with the Pequots, who had been telling the Narragansetts that "the Englishe were minded to destroye all Indians."[2] When the Narragansett headman Canonicus sent a message to the Puritans that Pequots had killed some colonists at Saybrook (and possibly also on Block Island), Winthrop sent for the Narragansett sachem Miantonomo, who arrived in Roxbury around noon on October 21. Twenty armed guards escorted the headman to Boston, where the governor had already assembled most of the colony's ministers and magistrates to find a way forward to prevent further troubles.[3]

After dinner that evening, Miantonomo tried to reassure the colonists of the Narragansetts' loyalty. He claimed, Winthrop reported, that they "had always loved the English, and desired firm peace with us," and that they stood ready to oppose the Pequots. The next morning the two sides signed an agreement, whose terms Winthrop summarized in his journal. The allies hoped to preserve trade and promised that neither would "make peace with the Pequots without the other's consent." To minimize tensions, the Narragansetts agreed not to approach colonial settlements during time of war with the Pequots "without some Englishman or known Indian." The Natives would also return runaway servants who had come to live with them. Because the English were concerned that the Narragansetts might not have understood exactly what was written in the agreement, they arranged to make a copy for Roger Williams, who had been banished from Massachusetts less than a year earlier but whom Puritan officials trusted as a colonist who had the respect of the Natives and knew their language. Winthrop knew that Williams could interpret the agreement for the Narragansetts.[4]

Whatever hopes the English had for peace soon faded. In late January 1637 Winthrop wrote in his journal that Lion Gardiner of Saybrook, a military veteran who had traveled to New England in 1635 to help defend English immigrants, had been out with nine armed colonists near the mouth of the Connecticut River when they came up on three Ninnimissinuok, who fled. The colonists gave chase—right into what Winthrop saw as an ambush by fifty Natives. Before long four of the English lay dead and all would have perished "had they not drawn their swords and retired."[5]

A month later, the churches in Massachusetts Bay participated in a general fast, a communal day of prayer to seek God's protection. Much was on the colonists' minds. The English in Massachusetts heard one story after another of the persecution that Puritans kept experiencing at the hands of the Church of England. They worried too about a downturn in their own economic prospects. Colonists in Connecticut and Massachusetts faced dissension within their own congregations, in part because of intense religious debates relating to the doctrines of justification and sanctification.[6] As Winthrop saw the situation, "it began to be as common here to distinguish between men, by being under a covenant of grace or a covenant of works, as in other countries between Protestants and Papists."[7] The religious debate spilled over into politics. In March the members of the General Court declared that none of its sitting members "ought to be publicly questioned by a church for any speech in the court, without the license of the court." The politics of sin were real, but the politicians in the General Court needed to find ways to operate in an imperfect world.[8]

Just as they feared divisions among their own relating to doctrine and practice, so the Puritans grew ever more nervous about their indigenous neighbors. In March Miantonomo, in an effort to retain positive relations, sent forty fathoms of wampum to the English. The Natives also sent the hand of a Pequot. The colonists sent gifts back, presumably pleased to see that tensions divided one group of Ninnimissinuok from another.[9]

Nonetheless, fear of the Pequots grew during the spring. Colonists became convinced that the antagonism would increase and that it would be best to defeat the Pequots soon. As the chronicler Edward Winslow put it, "Otherwise the natives we feare will grow into a stronger confederacy to the further prejudice of the whole English."[10] Stories of Pequot attacks on

English migrants spread through the colonies. Though officials in Plymouth and Massachusetts at times disagreed on events, they came to agree that they should form an alliance for their mutual protection.[11]

In mid-May Winthrop was reelected governor in an election marked by "fierce speeches" and "great danger of tumult" resulting from doctrinal disputes.[12] Tensions with the Pequots and the need to maintain an alliance with the Narragansetts remained on his mind. Roger Williams had written two letters detailing Miantonomo's suggestions of how best to attack the Pequots, with a caveat that "it would be pleasing to all natives, that women and children be spared, etc." He reminded the governor that tensions between the English and the locals were of long standing, and that when he had first arrived, Canonicus had "accused the English and myself for sending the plague amongst them, threatening to kill him especially." Williams believed that the local headman had gotten this notion from some of his followers who wanted the colonists to leave. Williams responded to the accusation by asserting that "the plague and other sicknesses were alone in the hand of the one God, who made him and us, who being displeased with the English for lying, stealing, idleness and uncleanness, (the natives' epidemical sins,) smote many thousands of us ourselves with general and late mortalities."[13]

Sometime in mid- to late May, Winthrop noted in his journal that the colonists had received a message from Miantonomo that the Pequots had sent away forty women and children "to an island for their safety." Sensing rising danger, the Puritans dispatched forty men to the Narragansetts. Miantonomo augmented that force with sixteen of his own men. Then the Puritans decided to enlist another 160 men "to prosecute the war." Soon after, English colonists killed eight Pequots along the Connecticut River and took seven women captive, with the idea that they would trade them for two young English women whom the Pequots had recently taken.[14]

That same day Winslow wrote to Winthrop, informing him that he had heard that the Pequots "follow their fishing and planting as if they had no enemies" and that they had sent off women and children to Long Island. The Pequots, Winslow wrote, "professe there you shall find them, and as they were there borne and bred there their bones shall be buried and rott in despight of the English." Despite such boasts, Winslow believed that the English would prevail in any conflict.[15] While domestic tensions continued to flare in Massachusetts, the Narragansetts and an armed English guard from Connecticut, which had become a colony when migrants from the Bay Colony established a church in Hartford in 1636, readied for action.

Morton could not have had personal knowledge of the events taking place during the late spring and summer of 1637 among the Ninnimissinuok, but by year's end word of astonishing violence reached England. One brief history of the conflict, written by a man named Paul Vincent, closely resembled the accounts in Winthrop's journal.[16] His account spared no details, offering a moment-by-moment narrative of the primary assault against a Pequot settlement on the Mystic River, including the burning of the town. Once the village was set alight, the fire "so raged," Vincent wrote, that the flames and the liberal use of weapons led "in little more than an houre," to three to four hundred being killed." He later added that the colonists knew these houses contained women and children.[17]

The tone of Vincent's narrative suggests that Morton's hope for peaceful coexistence had now disappeared. By the time the fighting ceased, his narrative reported, the English claimed they had killed or captured at least seven hundred Pequots and suffered only sixteen casualties themselves. "I have done with this tragick scene," Vincent wrote, "whose catastrophe ended in a triumph."[18]

While Vincent acknowledged that the entire episode was a tragedy, he still believed it necessary. Prior to this, he wrote, the English had been too patient with the Natives in North America, with devastating consequences. "The long forbearance, and too much leniency of the English toward the Virginian Salvages," he wrote, "had like to have been the destruction of the whole Plantation. These Barbarians (ever treacherous) abuse the goodnesse of those that condescend to their rudeness and imperfections."[19]

This was a stunning admission. In Vincent's mind, and likely in the thoughts of many New England colonists, the Ninnimissinuok were no different from the Powhatans who had risen up against the English along the shores of the Chesapeake in 1622. According to such logic, indigenous Americans were the enemy wherever they were found. If the English were to succeed with the colonization of North America, then they needed to vanquish Native enemies, as they did in Virginia in the aftermath of the assault of 1622 and again in the sustained campaign against the Pequots in 1637. At least one English chronicler justified the slaughter of women and children who cried out for mercy by arguing that the English could not provide it since "some of the Soudliers think the Devil was in them."[20]

Within a year a more comprehensive account of the conflict with the Pequots appeared, written by Captain John Underhill, who had played a significant commanding role in the campaign. There was no ambiguity in his description of the need for war against "that insolent and barbarous Nation, called the Pequeats, whom by the sword of the Lord and a few feeble instruments" had to be vanquished. Their deaths needed no justification.[21]

Underhill understood that some of his readers would demand an explanation for the apparent cruelty of the English. "Why should you be so furious (as some have said)," he asked, "should not Christians have more mercy and compassion?" "I would referre you to *Davids* warre," he wrote, "when a people is growne to such a height of bloud, and sinne against God and man, and all confederates in the action, there hee hath no respect to persons, but harrowes them, and sawes them, and puts them to the sword, and the most terriblest death that may be." This death of innocents was unfortunate, but "sometimes the Scripture declareth women and children must perish with their parents." The time had passed to challenge what had happened. "We had," he concluded, "sufficient light from the word of God for our proceedings."[22]

To emphasize his point, Underhill included a diagram depicting the assault on the Pequots living at Mystic. "The figure of the Indians fort or Palizado in New England," the caption read, "and the maner of the destroying it by Captayne

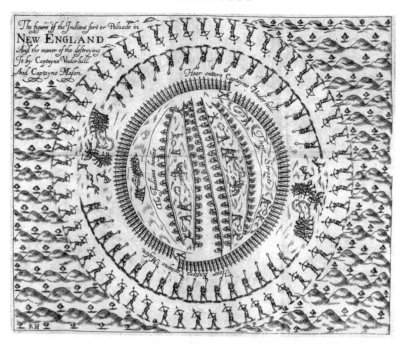

"The figure of the Indians Fort or Palizado in New England,"
from John Underhill, *Newes from America* (London, 1638).
(The Huntington Library, San Marino, California.)

Underhill and Captayne Mason." If ever there was an orderly
depiction of slaughter, this was it.

All told, Underhill claimed, the colonists had killed fifteen hundred Pequots in two months, "so as their Countrey
is fully subdued and fallen into the hands of the English."[23]
On June 15 Winthrop reported that the colonists had "a day
of thanksgiving" in their churches "for the victory obtained
against the Pequods, and for other mercies."[24] But the war

was not yet over. Roger Williams heard a rumor that surviving Pequots would have attacked the Narragansetts if they had the chance—a mist prevented them—and used the incident to warn Winthrop that colonial officials should treat any remaining Pequots "kindly" so they would not "turne wilde Irish," a reference to the long-standing resistance that the English invaders had encountered since Norman times in Ireland.[25] Rumors swirled all summer about alleged Pequot threats.[26] Such fears motivated the murder in late June of twenty-two Pequot men by the colonist Israel Staughton and his men, though the soldiers spared two of the men and the eighty-one women and children with them.[27]

Still, that summer brought welcome news to Winthrop. On June 26 he heard that Gorges had received permission to govern a colony to be called New Somersetshire, which was to extend from Cape Elizabeth to Sagadahoc. It would not include territory farther south. The previous September cattle and colonists had arrived at Piscataqua, bound for Gorges's nascent settlement at Acomenticus (or Agamenticus), the site of modern York, Maine. The Puritans' fears that Gorges would undermine the Massachusetts Bay Colony could perhaps be put to rest.[28]

The war's end brought two related developments. In southern New England, colonial officials authorized the sale of Pequot captives into slavery—some were taken as far as the Puritan colony of Providence Island off the coast of Nicaragua, where one local record referred to them as "the Cannibal Negroes brought from New England."[29] If some of the colony's founders had rebuked Thomas Hunt two decades earlier for his slave-trading activities, by the summer of 1637 colonial officials apparently thought that the Pequots had surrendered any right to be free.[30] This did not represent a condemnation of all Natives. In August 1638, well after the war, Massachusetts authorities heard about the murder of an Algonquian in Providence by four runaway servants from Plymouth. The officials prosecuted the three they could find and executed them.[31]

The other legacy could be found in the dissenters' writings. In his account, Bradford collapsed much of the violence of the war into the assault on the banks of the Mystic, which he described in brief but searing detail. "It was conceived they thus destroyed about 400 at this time," he wrote in reference to the colonists' assault. "It was a fearful sight to see them thus frying in the fire and the streams of blood quenching the same," he continued, "and horrible was the stink and scent thereof; but the victory seemed a sweet sacrifice"—a line he borrowed from Leviticus—"and they gave the praise thereof to God, who had wrought so wonderfully for them, thus to enclose their enemies in their hands and give them so speedy a victory over so proud and insulting an enemy."[32]

Such sanctifying rhetoric appeared time and again. John Mason, one of the leaders of the assault, believed that God had brought the English to North America and helped them vanquish those who stood in their way. After the fire at the fort had begun, he wrote, it spread quickly, "to the extream Amazement of the Enemy, and great Rejoycing of our selves." The Pequots had once "exalted themselves in their great Pride," he wrote, "threatening and resolving the utter Ruin and Destruction of all the English, Exulting and Rejoycing with Songs and Dances." But that time had come to an end. "God was above them," Mason boasted, "who laughed [at] his Enemies and the Enemies of his People to Scorn, making them as a fiery oven." Their boastfulness had been repaid with an attack so fast and fierce that they could not even arm themselves in time. "Thus did the LORD judge among the Heathen," Mason concluded, "filling the place with dead Bodies!"[33]

In May 1636, before the spiraling of events that led to the horrors on the Mystic, Winthrop had written in his journal about the death of the other John Mason, one of Gorges's partners in the efforts to undermine the colony. Winthrop labeled Mason "the chiefe mover in all attemptes against us."[34] In late July 1640, three years after the war against the Pequots, he wrote about him again: "Capt. Mason of London, a man in favor at court, and a professed enemy to us."[35]

Mason had owned land at Piscataqua, where he hoped to make a good profit by setting up a sawmill, the kind of venture that one would expect to prosper with the expansion of the colonial population. But his business did not thrive. Rather than solve his own problems, he instead decided to turn against the Massachusetts Bay Company. He hired Gardiner and Thomas Morton, among others, Winthrop wrote, "to prosecute against us at council table, and by a quo warranto, etc.," challenge the legitimacy of the colony's charter. Morton proved an eager assistant in the task. He "wrote divers letters to his friends here," Winthrop complained, "insulting against us, and assuring them of our speedy ruin." But the plan went nowhere. Mason, he claimed, regretted his earlier work for Morton and promised on his deathbed that he would "be as great a friend of New England as he formerly been an enemy" if he recovered.[36]

That reference to the quo warranto that Gorges had hired Morton to argue for him burned in Winthrop's memory because he understood that it posed as great a threat to the Massachusetts colony as the Pequots. In July 1640 he wrote in his journal that Gorges "also had sided with our adversaries against us, but underhand, pretending by his letters and speeches to seek our welfare." But, he continued, Gorges failed. "He attempted great matters," Winthrop continued, "and was at large expenses about his province here, but he lost all."[37]

Morton must have known that Massachusetts authorities never surrendered the charter. But still he returned, perhaps believing that his prospects in New England were brighter than in a war-torn England dominated by a Puritan Parliament. If so, he miscalculated. In June 1644 Massachusetts authorities arrested him in Ipswich, charging him with undermining their charter with the council in London. They immediately locked him up.[38] On September 9 they put him on trial so "that the country," as Winthrop put it, "might be satisfied of the justice of our proceeding against him." Initially Morton denied the charge against him. But then the officials pulled out the letter Morton had written to Gardiner that they had saved since opening it over a decade earlier. That letter, the court reminded Morton, had charged the colonists "with treason, rebellion, etc.," and noted that he had announced himself as a witness. Morton replied that he was not the author of any charges but simply a witness to them.[39]

The court did not accept this reasoning. Instead, as Winthrop wrote, the Massachusetts authorities laid out a threefold argument. First, they asserted that "Gardiner had no occasion to complain against us, for he was kindly used, and dismissed in peace, professing much engagement for the great courtesy he found here." Second, Morton had "set forth a book against us, and had threatened us, and had prosecuted a quo warranto against us, which he did not deny." And finally, the court then produced the letter Morton had written on May 1, 1634, to William Jeffrey, which had been intercepted by the colonial authorities in August of that year. This was the damning evidence about Morton's actions—essentially the dress rehearsal for the drafting of *New English Canaan*—after his second exile.[40]

The letter in the hands of Morton's greatest enemies was incriminating enough. But his adversaries, wanting as much proof of Morton's treachery as they could find, sent an emissary to London to seek further cause.[41] During that time they kept Morton confined. About a year after his initial arrest they brought him back to court, "and after some debate what to do with him," Winthrop wrote, "he was fined 100 pounds, and set at liberty." They could have beaten him to satisfy the judgment against him but, as Winthrop wrote, "we thought not fit to inflict corporal punishment upon him, being old and crazy." Worse still, he was destitute and so became "a charge to the country, for he had nothing." Edward Winslow agreed with that assessment. Morton, he claimed, lacked resources to survive, and Winslow was eager for "this serpent," who was "the odium of our people," to be sent away before he convinced less sophisticated colonists that they would get the land he promised to give them "about New haven, Narrohiganset, etc." Morton was unable to pay the fine. As a result, Massachusetts authorities banished him once more, but they let him remain until the end of winter.[42]

And so, for the third time, Morton was an exile, headed to Gorges's plantation at Acomenticus. He would never see Massachusetts again.

By the time Morton arrived in 1644, Acomenticus had already begun to earn a reputation. It was, John Underhill had written, "a place of good accommodation," only five miles from the Piscataqua River. As early as 1636 Gorges had begun to stock his plantation there with cattle and colonists from Bristol. Underhill thought the region was "worthy to bee inhabited," with rich soil that could produce corn, flax, hemp, and any other produce that New England could support.[43]

In 1641, two years before his return to New England, Morton had served as a witness when Gorges wrote the town's charter.[44] He was perhaps supposed to bring a copy to the region later that year. But as Thomas Gorges wrote to his cousin Ferdinando that autumn, Morton had not arrived, though he had seen a letter in which Morton demanded funds to cover "his great payns & travel." The younger Gorges, who served as deputy governor of Maine from 1640 to 1643, acknowledged that Morton might be "an able man," but he wondered whether it was a good idea for "a Lord of a province in N. Ing."—a reference to the older Gorges—"to countenance him that hath declared himself an enemy to the land."[45]

Morton's relationship to George Cleeve, a onetime associate of Gorges's, raised further suspicion that he had broken with his longtime partner. In 1636 Gorges had sold Cleeve

and his partner Richard Tucker a coastal parcel in Maine estimated to be fifteen hundred acres near Hogg Island.[46] But
soon Cleeve pursued his own interests in New England and
apparently hired Morton to be his lawyer, an action that led
Gorges in 1637 to claim that from that point forward Morton was "wholely cashiered from intermedlinge" with any
of Gorges's business.[47] Morton was also present to witness
Cleeve's purchase of additional land in Maine.[48] In the years
that followed, Cleeve's aspirations grew from establishing a
trade station in 1637 to founding the separate colony of Lygonia, a large part of Gorges's Maine lands—perhaps sixteen hundred square miles—that the putative proprietor had
named after his mother. But the timing of the plan proved
inauspicious. The English Civil War had begun in 1642 and
almost overnight English migration to New England declined
to a trickle of what it had been. Gorges, loyal to the Crown,
hoped the dispute would end soon, a sentiment that Cleeve,
sympathetic to the Puritans of Massachusetts, shared. Both
believed that the success of their Maine ventures depended
on English migrants. But the flow of travelers never returned
to prewar levels. Realizing that the situation was not going to

---

(*opposite*) This map from Wood's *New England's Prospect*, engraved
only four years after the founding of the Massachusetts Bay
Colony, reveals that even then the new colony had already
spawned more towns than New Plymouth, whose residents
had barely moved beyond their initial settlement of 1620.
The map identified the locations of Mount Wollaston near
Wessaguset as well as the Isles of Shoals and Acomenticus.
(The Huntington Library, San Marino, California.)

The South part of New-England, as it is Planted this yeare, 1634.

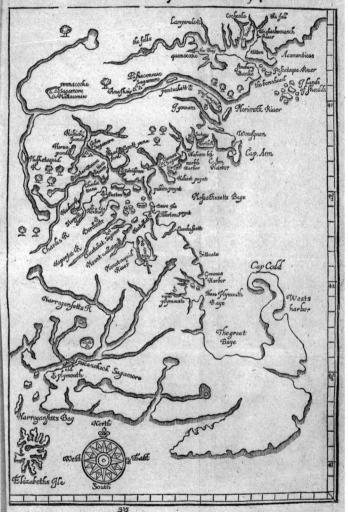

change, the colonists who had gone to Lygonia voted in the 1650s to accept the authority of the Massachusetts government.[49]

Whatever tension threatened the relationship between Morton and Gorges apparently faded quickly. In 1641 Morton served as a witness when Gorges, in his capacity as "Lord of the Province of Maine," established the charter for Acomenticus.[50] In 1645, now settled among the small cluster of English migrants huddled near the Atlantic, Morton petitioned the Massachusetts General Court to redress what he saw as the illegal treatment he had received in the colony. He rehearsed all that he had suffered, with the exactitude that one might expect from a lawyer. First, he informed the court, his house had been burned and his goods confiscated. Second, he had been "clapt into Irons, & sent home in a desp[er]ate ship unvittelled as if he had been a man worthy of death." Third, he asked the court to consider whether his recent actions had been "serviceable to some gentlemen in the Country," which he believed, but in a moment of false modesty, he added that he would not "praise my selfe" for such an action. Fourth, he had returned to New England "on godly gentlemens imploym[en]tes" only to encounter those bearing "form[er] Jelosy" of him as well as "a late untrue intelligence," a reference presumably to the letter Winthrop claimed to have saved for a decade. He had been imprisoned for months, he added, and "laid in Irons to the decaying of his limbes." The time had come, he pled, to put the past aside so that he could do service for the colony "as god shall inable him."[51]

With the document in hand, the deputies asked the magistrates to explain why Morton's petition had not been made available during his trial. According to Thomas Dudley, who was then serving another term as governor, the text had not been introduced because the court was waiting for additional evidence against Morton, which they expected to arrive on the next ship.[52] That evidence never appeared, nor is there any indication that Morton received a favorable response to his request, unless his banishment without additional physical punishment or fine can be taken as a sign of the court's willingness to accept the legitimacy of at least some of what Morton alleged.

Before he left on his third journey across the ocean, Morton had written his will. He identified himself as a gentleman of Clifford's Inn in London, one sign among others that he never returned to Swallowfield after he left there two decades earlier. He left all of his possessions to a cousin named Tobias Milles and a widowed niece, Sara Bruce. The estate consisted, he claimed, of extensive holdings in New England: five thousand acres on the east side of the Quillepiock River in the province of Carlile, which included four miles along the side of the river itself; another five thousand acres on the opposite bank of the river; two thousand acres in Lygonia adjacent to the River Pesumkegg, a tributary of Casco Bay; two islands in Casco Bay near the river, known as the Clapboard Islands, a name presumably derived from the availability of timber for houses; and all of the island of Martha's Vineyard. He never mentioned owning any land in Acomenticus, perhaps because he did not anticipate ending up there.[53]

Morton died in Acomenticus—"poor and despised," if Winthrop is to be believed—sometime around 1646.[54] There is no marker for his grave, but he was presumably buried in a cemetery along the banks of the Agamenticus River. "He lies unhonored," one local scholar, imbued with the anti-Puritanical fervor of many of Maine's earlier historians, has written, "but not unsung among the town's distinguished dead."[55] Morton might have been seventy years old when he died, a relatively rare long life for a man in England at the time, but less impressive by the standards of New England.[56]

Morton's death in the mid-1640s did not signal a decisive turning point in New England's history. That time had already passed. The epidemic of the late 1610s had altered the population of the region and facilitated English colonization. The war against the Pequots almost twenty years later solidified the English colonial position: any Natives who blocked the way to prosperity needed to be vanquished. In years to come, that mentality would drive further violence, fueling both the destruction of indigenous communities and the enslavement of captives. New England was no Canaan for its indigenous peoples or English adventurers like Morton and Gorges, who hoped for a different kind of colonial enterprise.

Bradford and Winthrop, the representatives of the dissenters who had sailed across the Atlantic to create their own vision of a new society, needed to exile Morton because his dream threatened theirs. They were right. The twin tragedies of the early seventeenth century solidified the Pilgrims' and Puritans' hold on southern New England, the homeland of the Ninnimissinuok. The epidemic of 1616 to 1619, which concluded on the eve of the Pilgrims' arrival, smoothed the way for the newcomers by reducing their competitors for the prime lands along the Atlantic, necessary for fishing villages, and the interior, needed for English-style farms. The resolution of the Pequot War of 1637 solidified the dissenters' still-tenuous hold on the region by revealing to all, on both sides of the Atlantic, the ruthless ways that these English would treat any indigenous group that stood in their way.

Those achievements on the ground figured prominently in the dissenters' ideology as well. The epidemic, as many of them explained, represented a divine action, a clearing of the land by the Christian god. The Pilgrims and Puritans built that notion into their rhetorical arsenal. The cataclysm along the banks of the Mystic River similarly figured in the stories that dissenters told about themselves to the larger world. If all events signaled the unfolding of a divine plan, as Bradford wrote more explicitly than anyone else, then victory over these haughty enemies needed to be celebrated in narratives.[57] This is what happened in the tracts produced by Bradford, Vincent, Underhill, and Nathaniel Morton, among others. The Pequots' death in that burning village represented the triumph of the Pilgrims' and Puritans' god.

Thomas Morton posed a danger because the Pilgrims' and Puritans' success was, contrary to the dissenters' explanations, precarious. Leaders like Winthrop feared the publication of Morton's book not only because it made the dissenters look awful, which it did, but because they worried that it could be used alongside a case like the quo warranto that Gorges and Morton presented. The book was an attack on them similar to the legal assault. Morton, the lawyer with so much personal experience in court, knew how to argue a case in front of a judge—or the king's Privy Council. That third exile, when even Winthrop admitted that Morton no longer constituted any real threat, reflected the Puritans' anxiety. Colonial authorities understood the fragility of their achievement. They told the world that their god planned everything that happened. But unable to read the mind of the almighty, they could not accept that Morton could live with them. Read through their ideology, his presence signaled a challenge put in place by their god to test their fortitude. Exiling him showed their commitment to an unwavering and divinely sanctioned standard.

Morton proposed a different way to live: the Puritans and Pilgrims should lose their claim because they had exceeded the authority of their original charter, and he and others would create new communities, possibly with Gorges presiding over an immense territory where he would possess vast rights as the "absolute lord" of New England, as his nineteenth-century biographer put it. Gorges realized the profits to be made from the fur trade and hoped to establish a station on the Piscataqua River. In his last years he laid out plans for the division of much of modern Maine, in territory that stretched between the Piscataqua at the southern end and Sagadahoc to the north, reaching 120 miles into the interior. Beyond naming one part of this territory Lygonia, he proposed changing the name of Acomenticus to Gorgeana. He

---

(*opposite*) Ferdinando Gorges's claim to Maine, which included the later planned colony of Lygonia, was based on a charter that the Council for New England received from King James I. This map, drawn by Rebecca Wrenn, is based on one created by James P. Baxter in 1885, in the collections of the Maine Historical Society.

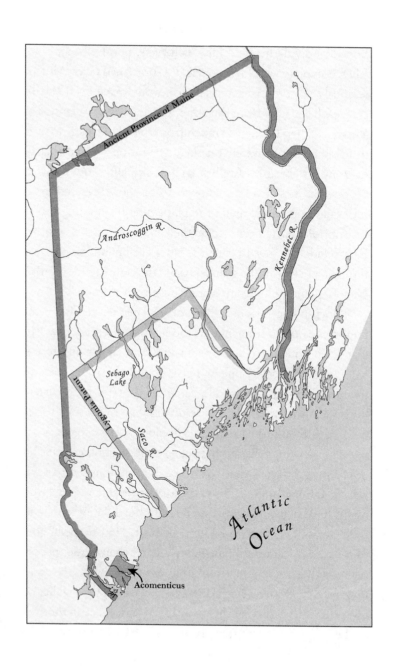

Ancient Province of Maine

Androscoggin R.

Kennebec R.

Sebago
Lake

Lygonia Patent

Saco R.

Atlantic
Ocean

Acomenticus

hoped to divide his land into bailiwicks, hundreds, and parishes, complete with local courts. If Gorges had taken Morton seriously, Algonquians and English would have lived side by side, each learning from the other, a fitting society planned by a man who had learned so much from the Abenakis who lived in his house in London. Yet the distribution of land that he oversaw rewarded his English friends and allies, not Natives. Gorges did not live long enough to see how these communities developed. He died in 1647, passing his holdings on to his son John, who then bequeathed them to his son, another Ferdinando Gorges. In what the older Ferdinando might have thought a betrayal, the grandson sold the rights to his family's New England holdings to Massachusetts in 1677.[58]

Morton's actions and those of his enemies reinforce the importance of contingency in the history of early New England. He sought to create a new biblical Canaan and to coexist with the locals, but he never found the right allies to put his plan into action. He came up short at each turn—his book initially banned, his letter arriving in Massachusetts before his final return there, his dreams of coexistence shattered by growing tensions between colonists and Pequots and devastating diseases that weakened Ninnimissinuok, a civil war in England halting migration of men and women who might have helped Lygonia thrive. Bradford, Winthrop, and their associates disdained Morton's plan. Had he been able to execute it, he would have undermined their trade, necessary for their economic livelihood, put their communities at risk from Natives bearing guns, and threatened the legality of their charter, needed for their continued legitimacy in the eyes of the English. Losing that claim would have meant that English authorities could send new colonists with a new charter to replace them. This Lord of Misrule would have to be banished three times before he understood that his dream was but a hallucination, a vision of harmony fading into the gloaming of a New England dusk.

CHAPTER SIX

Legacies

B Y the latter decades of the seventeenth century, scores of observers had offered opinions about the colonial enterprise in New England. Ministers retraced elements of the history of Plymouth and Massachusetts Bay. Letters traveled regularly back and forth across the Atlantic. Some sat down to write works of history, aiming to capture the development of the colonies while events were still fresh. Among the topics that appeared in these works were the trials of Thomas Morton. Later, after Morton's book had begun to circulate again in the nineteenth century, he became a character in works of history and fiction for generations, eventually becoming more the hero and less the villain, an object of admiration and courage rather than scorn. The story of Morton and of *New English Canaan* helped to establish a vein of countercultural thinking that moved into the mainstream in the works of authors who became part of the American literary canon.

He left, then, intertwined literary and political legacies—including English colonies more secure in their sense of mission and independence from the Crown than they might have been had Morton not posed such a challenge to them.

Appreciation of Morton's story could not have been expected earlier. Before the American Revolution, he remained a figure of contempt. In the middle decades of the seventeenth century, Bradford's nephew Nathaniel Morton drew on his uncle's manuscript in *New-England's Memoriall,* published in Cambridge in 1669. Though he did not copy all of Bradford's history, he did include the siege of Ma-re Mount, thereby bringing that part of Thomas Morton's saga to a wider public.[1] In the years that followed, others too had access to Bradford's manuscript, including the clerics Increase and Cotton Mather and the historians William Hubbard and Thomas Prince; the latter referred repeatedly to Bradford's manuscript in his notes and drew directly on that text for his description of Morton.[2] The minister John Hancock, delivering a sermon at Braintree on September 16, 1739, to mark the centenary of the first gathering of the church there, drew on *New-England's Memoriall* to ascribe Morton's first exile to "his wicked and insufferable Behavior."[3] As John Adams wrote in his unpublished history, Thomas Hutchinson, the last royal governor of Massachusetts, briefly retold the story of Morton's separation from the Pilgrims and how he established himself as the master of Ma-re Mount by liberating servants and putting up a maypole. "At length," Hutchinson noted, "he made himself so obnoxious to the planters in all parts, that, at their general desire, the people of New-Plymouth seized him by an armed force, and confined him, until they had an opportunity of sending him to England." Even from there he remained a threat to colonists, especially when he worked with others to prosecute the quo warranto of 1635 and hence undermine the legitimacy of the charter of the Massachusetts Bay Company, a point Hutchinson made in his history of New England, published in 1764, a decade before he sailed to London as perhaps the most despised British official in North America.[4]

To be sure, observers' views of Morton depended on their political orientation, especially their thoughts about whether the Pilgrims and Puritans had behaved properly when they created their colonies. The Puritan historian Edward Johnson viewed Morton as one of the great adversaries of Massachusetts Bay. In 1654 he acknowledged that Morton "wanted not malice, could he possibl[y] have attained the meanes to effect" his goals without it. But divine intervention prevented the fulfillment of his plans. "The *Lord Christ* prevented both him and his Masters, whom with flattery he sought to please with scurrilous deriding the servants of *Christ*, to bring them into contempt," Johnson wrote, "yet the Lord prevented all, and delivered this wretched fellow into his peoples hands againe after all this who dealt as favourably with him as *David* did with *Shimmes*."[5]

But not everyone agreed with such an assessment. Samuel Maverick, who migrated to New England at around the same time as Morton and was also a member of the Council for New England, shared some of Morton's attitudes toward the Natives. An ally of Gorges, Maverick in 1633 had been one of the few colonists who had gone to attend local Algonquians during a smallpox epidemic. With his wife and servants, Maverick had ministered to the ill and buried the dead, something Winthrop believed was "worthy of a perpetuall remembrance." Years later, in an unpublished book-length manuscript, Maverick noted that he had read *New English Canaan*, which he described as "the truest description of New England as then it was that ever I saw." He saw Morton's persecution at the hands of the authorities in Plymouth and Massachusetts as unjust and his exile as punishment for what he had written in his book. Given the fact that these same authorities had overstepped their bounds from the start by demanding that only church members could be freemen, Maverick added, their treatment of Morton was hardly surprising.[6]

Despite the paucity of copies of his book, details about Morton's life continued to appear in writing. At least one copy of *New English Canaan* was available in Pennsylvania in 1755 when it arrived at the Library Company of Philadelphia, where it could have been read, along with other early histories of the colonies, by the institution's subscribers.[7] Winthrop's journal, like Bradford's history, had circulated in manuscript since the seventeenth century and had been used by New England's earliest historians, Increase Mather, William Hubbard, and Thomas Prince, but it remained available only in a copy in the possession of one branch of the Winthrop family until the period of the Revolution, when Connecticut's governor John Trumbull worked with an assistant to transcribe much of it. After Trumbull's death in 1785, his secretary prepared an edition, published in Hartford in 1790 with the title *A Journal of the Transactions and Occurrences in the Settlement of Massachusetts and the Other New-England Colonies.* That edition, and one that followed, preserved details of Winthrop's relationship with Morton, including the long incriminating letter that Morton had written in 1634 that Winthrop had used as evidence in the proceedings that led to Morton's final banishment from Massachusetts.[8] The original remained in circulation too, available for John Adams, among others.[9]

In the early years of the nineteenth century Morton's ideas continued to circulate despite the rarity of *New English Canaan* in the United States. In 1810 the *Monthly Anthology and Boston Review*, a literary magazine, ran a two-part synopsis of the book, including long sections of the text. The unnamed editor of these pieces, now long separated in time from the founding of New England, pointed to the self-serving narratives of the region's earliest historians — Bradford, Winthrop, Nathaniel Morton, Mather, Hubbard. From their writings one could "suppose the first planters of Plymouth to be men of whom the world was not worthy; that their conduct was so pure and excellent, as to need not even the mantle of charity to cover their failings." Morton, by contrast, was among those "who took pains to depreciate their worth, and make them appear to every disadvantage." The anonymous editor, who might have been John Quincy Adams, believed that the early English settlers "were the dupes of puritanick cant, sour, tasteless asceticks, bigoted in their sentiments, and sordid in their manners, desirous of anarchy at home, and practisers of intolerance abroad." The editor recognized Morton as a sarcastic commentator who employed satire to puncture the sanctimonious, understanding as well that Morton at least saw the dangers of a place where religious fanaticism prevailed. "Notwithstanding the many excellences of those men who came over to New Plymouth," the editor concluded near the end of the second installment, "we must allow some blame for this kind of bigotry, and as large a share for the encouragement they gave to fanatical exhorters. Even if men have gifts, and are useful at religious conferences, they ought not to invade the pastoral office."[10]

Within a decade elements of Morton's tale began to reach a wider audience.[11] Washington Irving drew on Morton's version of the desecration of Cheecatawback's mother's grave in "Traits of Indian Character," one of the stories in *The Sketch Book of Geoffrey Crayon, Gent,* published serially in 1819 and 1820.[12] In June 1821, the *New-England Galaxy and United States Literary Advertiser* ran a short version of Morton's history in Plymouth, perhaps to mark the two hundredth anniversary of the founding of the colony.[13] Lydia Maria Child provided a caricature of Morton in *Hobomok* (published in 1824), having one of her characters warn another to avoid "the flesh-pots of Egypt," resist "French frippery," and not become an "idle follower of Morton, who was drowned in yonder bay" and had been "inwardly given to the vain forms of the church of England," which was the reason "his God left him, and Satan became his envoy."[14] In *Hope Leslie,* published in 1827, Catherine Maria Sedgwick has one character receive a letter from Morton inviting him to Ma-re Mount, only to discover upon arrival that Morton was "in jail, and in honest opinion, is reputed crazy—as, doubtless, he is!" The character nonetheless took Morton's advice that he disguise himself as one of the Pilgrims "till we were quite independent of the favour of the saints."[15]

In November 1830 Samuel Gardener Drake, a historian who in 1828 had opened the first antiquarian bookshop in Boston and would later in his life be a founder of the New England Historical and Genealogical Society, discovered Morton. He had read about *New English Canaan* in the 1810 issues of the *Monthly Anthology* and then borrowed the book from John Quincy Adams. Recognizing its value and frustrated that there were so few copies of the book in the nation, he sat down and transcribed the contents. In a brief note he wrote that it had rained for eleven days since he had borrowed the book and so he had the time to tend to his regular business and still complete the copying. To make sure he got everything correct, he had his wife read the printed version while he read his transcription out loud before he sent the book back to the former president. Later in the century, the Reverend William S. Bartlet, who was also a historian of Protestant religion in America, similarly copied the book so he could have it at hand. He, too, likely used the copy obtained by John Quincy Adams.[16]

Morton gained wider fame when Nathaniel Hawthorne took up his story, notably with "The May-pole of Merry Mount," which was reprinted after its initial 1836 appearance in his *Twice-Told Tales* in 1837.[17] Hawthorne here drew on earlier historical writing that retold the story of the most famous incident in Morton's life. Specifically, he likely read the work of Hubbard, Hutchinson, and Nathaniel Morton as well as other annalists of early New England whose works had been reprinted in the 1820s.[18] With that research in hand, Hawthorne, in a frequently cited sentence, wrote, "Jollity and gloom were contending for an empire." But despite claiming that this little "philosophic romance" had been drawn on "the facts, recorded on the grave pages of our New England annalists," the story was not about Morton. Instead,

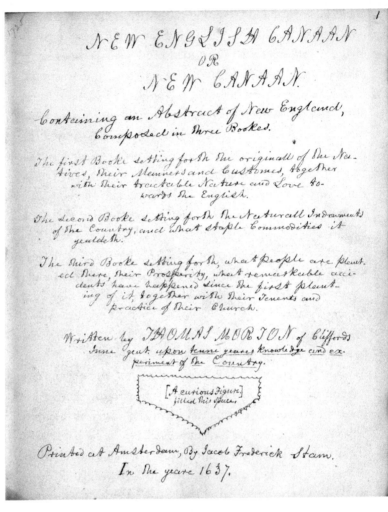

A prolonged period without sunshine in November 1830 was, the
Boston merchant and antiquarian Samuel Drake wrote, "favorable
to the undertaking" of making a copy of Morton's book.
(William L. Clements Library, University of Michigan.)

it was "a sort of allegory," as he noted, adding that "the future complexion of New England was involved in this important quarrel." The fate of the region hinged, in this short story, on what would happen with the maypole. The "darksome figures" of the Puritans became "intermixed with the wild shapes of their foes, and made the scene a picture of the moment, when waking thoughts start up amid the scattered fantasies of a dream." Hawthorne emphasized the stakes of the contest. "Should the grisly saints establish their jurisdiction over the gay sinners, then would their spirits darken all the clime, and make it a land of clouded visages, of hard toil, of sermon and psalm, forever," he wrote. "But should the banner-staff of Merry Mount be fortunate, sunshine would break upon the hills, and flowers would beautify the forest, and late posterity do homage to the May-Pole!" The central figure was John Endecott, "the severest Puritan of all who laid the rock-foundation of New England," the "Puritan of Puritans," an "immitigable zealot" who with his own sword cut down the maypole.[19]

But Hawthorne was not done with Morton. In 1848 he published "Main Street," in which an unnamed narrator recounts the history of the first hundred years of New England, with a particular focus on Salem and, more generally, Massachusetts. Here the author used words to paint a vivid portrait of Morton out of thin air. Walking among "these Puritans and Roundheads" was "the very model of a cavalier, with the curling lovelock, the fantastically trimmed beard, the embroidery, the ornamented rapier, the gilded dagger, and all other foppishness that distinguished the wild gallants who rode headlong to their overthrow of King Charles. This is Morton of

Merry Mount," he added, "who has come hither to hold a council with Endicott, but will shortly be his prisoner." Soon Anne Hutchinson, another famous exile from Massachusetts, joins Morton as a character in the elaborate yarn spun by a figure labeled "the showman." Hawthorne knew that the two did not meet, but recognized that he could use the poor treatment of each at the hands of the Pilgrims and Puritans as a cudgel against New England's founders. Three years later he included the story in his collection *The Snow-Image, and Other Tales.*[20]

By then John L. Motley, who would later write a three-volume history of the Dutch republic, had published a two-volume romance novel, which ran to a total of 470 pages, entitled *Merry-Mount.* The physical description he offered of Morton bore a resemblance to Hawthorne's character, a sign not of plagiarism but of an antebellum American vision of a man who stood up against the Puritans.[21] In 1880 the poet Henry Wadsworth Longfellow immortalized Morton's relationship with Christopher Gardiner, though in verse that was less paean than critique. Gardiner, he wrote,

> passed his idle hours . . .
> With roystering Morton of Merry Mount,
> That pettifogger from Furnival's Inn,
> Lord of misrule and riot and sin,
> Who looked on the wine when it was red.[22]

During the nineteenth century, one after another edition of *Twice-Told Tales* appeared, circulating anew Hawthorne's take on Merry Mount.[23] Some of those copies included an engraving of Morton's maypole. Illustrations of the maypole appeared in popular histories as well, establishing a visual motif that would last into the twenty-first century. The story has circulated ever since, in reprintings of Hawthorne's short stories and in editions of his complete works.[24] The writer Wallace Stegner, introducing an edition of *Twice-Told Tales* in 1966, recognized the eternal questions that the story posed. Hawthorne's story, he wrote, "chronicles more than a brush between Plymouth Colony and Mount Wollaston, Puritans and playboys, gloom and jollity: it reports an expulsion from an Eden—an Eden less innocent than the original—by an omnipotent authority whose righteousness is close to self-righteousness." In Stegner's view, "There is no light and no dark, there are only shadows. That Fall is as ruefully mixed as it could well be; it poses questions, not answers, but the questions are incorrigibly moral."[25]

Morton the person, as opposed to the fictionalized version of him in Hawthorne's work, continued to figure in historians' accounts of early New England. In 1855 Drake, having done his transcript of *New English Canaan* years before, produced a lengthy history of Boston based on materials gathered over a quarter century. He listed Morton (and a Thomas Morton Jr.) among those who had arrived in Plymouth by 1623, an affirmation of Morton's claim about his first quick trip to the region. Time and again Drake praised Morton's commitment to creating a new society as well as his intelligence. True, he had provided an unfavorable treatment of the Puritans in his book. As Drake recognized, "though they may not have done him justice in every particular, he has certainly not erred in over justice to them." His book, Drake continued, revealed

Book illustration flourished in the United States in the
nineteenth century, including in works of history that told the
story of Morton, Bradford, Endecott, and the maypole. These
examples, from William Cullen Bryant's *Popular History of the*

United States (1876–81) and Walter Montgomery's *American
Art and American Art Collections* (1889), typified nineteenth-
century Americans' interest in Morton and the maypole.
(The Huntington Library, San Marino, California.)

In 1966 the illustrator Valenti Angelo juxtaposed the
maypole and a church in a benign image that appeared
in an edition of Hawthorne's *Twice-Told Tales* produced
for the members of the Limited Editions Club.
(© MBI, Inc.)

"a good deal of talent as well as learning; shrewdness of observation, as well as much graphic description. He was deeply
in love with New England," just as John Smith had been.[26]

Drake argued that Morton's place in the region's history
had been overshadowed by the venom of his antagonists, who
focused on what they saw as the shenanigans around the maypole. "Great offence was taken by the Pilgrims at their impiety," he wrote, "as they viewed their conduct to be impious,
and Morton and his friends derided [the Pilgrims] for their
overmuch piety and austere manners." This religion-fueled

dislike prompted his first exile. Drake surmised that Morton did not realize the lasting power of his antagonists' accusations. "Had he ever imagined that it would become matter of serious history, he would doubtless have left us a very different and more circumstantial account." Instead, it was Nathaniel Morton and those who read his book who defined Thomas Morton's legacy, at least until the nineteenth century, a point Drake made by citing other authorities who had used *New-England's Memoriall* to rehearse the story of Mare Mount.[27] Similarly, Drake's account of Morton's second exile cast doubts on the Puritans' claims that he had acted in ways against the interest of local Natives. "That Morton was greatly misrepresented there is not much room to doubt," he wrote in a footnote, "while there may be no doubt that he was a reckless and misguided man." Drake inserted a small illustration of a forlorn man sitting on a log with his legs confined in bilboes in one footnote and in another referred to him as "Morton the Disturber," a bit of sarcasm to suggest that Winthrop and his allies tended to be more overwrought than might be reasonable.[28]

By the time Drake's history circulated, *New English Canaan* was back in print, this time as part of a collection of documents edited by the book collector and politician Peter Force. At the time, Force was also the mayor of Washington, D.C. John Quincy Adams visited his office just as Force was organizing his project. "He is preparing a vast collection of ancient documents, relating to the history of this country," the former president wrote in his diary on September 16, 1837, "and has a very great and curious collection of his own." In the end, Force produced four volumes, one of which included

New English Canaan, which he believed had been published in London in 1632.[29]

About four decades after Force's efforts, Charles Francis Adams Jr., who had been born in 1835, took out the family copy of *New English Canaan* and produced a modern edition of the text for the members of the Prince Society, which had been founded in Boston in 1858 "for the purpose," the act of incorporation of March 18, 1874, notes, "of preserving and extending the knowledge of American History, by editing and publishing such manuscripts, rare tracts, and volumes as are mostly confined in their use to historical students and public libraries."[30] As it happened, the society's first book was an edition of William Wood's *New England's Prospect*.[31] Society members would have to wait until 1883 for a chance to read Adams's version of Morton's account, though he had by then already revealed much of what he had to say in the *Atlantic* in 1877.[32] Before Adams published his edition of Morton's book, he had already written a two-volume biography of the famed explorer Richard Henry Dana, author of *Two Years before the Mast* (first printed in New York in 1840), a two-volume history of Massachusetts Bay with the rather modest title *Three Episodes of Massachusetts History*, and a study entitled *Massachusetts: Its Historians and Its History*.[33]

Yet while this Adams's intellectual abilities, like those of others in his family, were expansive, he realized that he had a problem with Morton's book. In the first place, he had never edited such a text before, and now he had in his hands what he candidly called "a singular book" remarkable for "the extent of ground it covers." The book, he continued, was "full of obscure references to incidents in early New England history," but it also dealt "directly with the aborigines, the trees, the animals, fish, birds and geology of the region; besides having constant incidental allusions to literature — both classic and of the author's time, — to geography, and to then current events." How could anyone take on the Herculean task of figuring out what those old pages meant? "No one person can possess the knowledge necessary to thoroughly cover so large a field," he concluded. The only way forward was to consult "specialists."[34]

By the time Adams sat down to decipher Morton's words, collecting and publishing historical documents had become a vibrant pursuit across the Anglophone world. The Massachusetts Historical Society had been publishing such works since 1792. In 1843 the Worcester-based American Antiquarian Society, which had been founded in 1812, began to issue its *Proceedings*, which often included circulation of older documents. Scholarly editing had become more sophisticated by the middle of the nineteenth century, as was evident in the glosses and notes in the books produced by the London-based Hakluyt Society, established in 1846.

While historical research could be conducted in a number of cities in the United States by the late nineteenth century, perhaps none could offer the resources available in Boston and Cambridge, the home to the Prince Society, the Colonial Society of Massachusetts, the Massachusetts Historical Society, and Harvard College, the oldest and richest educational institution in the United States, where this Adams was a member of the graduating class in 1856. Within this intellectual milieu, Adams would have known that his edition had to be exemplary, with every obscure reference explained so that the reader could understand the full meaning of words originally published 250 years earlier.

But if being in Boston put pressure on an editor to get the details right, it also offered an intrepid scholar a community of the like-minded, many gathered in and around Harvard or in the city's own citadels of learning, such as the Boston Public Library, which had opened in 1854. Like many of the scholars to be found in the Bay State, Adams had served as an officer during the Civil War, including as a captain in the Union forces at Gettysburg in 1862 and later colonel of the squadron known as the Fifth Massachusetts Colored Cavalry. After the war, he wrote a history of railroads, and eventually became the president of the Union Pacific Railroad, a post he held from 1884 to 1890. In 1883, the same year that he published his edition of Morton's book, he became the president of the Massachusetts Parks Commission. Though he wrestled with financial problems, he was a near-perfect product of a city that thought of itself as the Athens of America.

For his edition of *New English Canaan*, Adams took advantage of the region's abundant scholarly talent. He turned first to Charles Deane, one of the leading experts on New England history and the editor of the first printed edition of Bradford's history of Plymouth, which was published in 1856 in the *Collections* of the Massachusetts Historical Society. He also reached out to Justin Winsor, who was then the president of the American Library Association and had already begun to publish his *Narrative and Critical History of America*, which appeared in eight massive volumes from 1884 to 1889. He corresponded with George Edward Ellis, a widower who had turned to historical research after the death of his wife and only child. Ellis, who had served as the vice president of the Massachusetts Historical Society from 1877 to 1885, was a prolific author whose theological works and published sermons ranged from temperance and church music to redemption and sanctification, and whose historical writings included books on the battle of Bunker Hill and biographies of Anne Hutchinson and William Penn. In 1888 he would publish *The Puritan Age and Rule in the Colony of Massachusetts Bay, 1629–1685*, cementing—as if anyone would have doubted it—his position as an authority of the early history of the colony.

But understanding the historical context of early New England was, as Adams knew, only one part of the intellectual problem. There were so many classical allusions in *New English Canaan* that Adams turned to four trusted authorities: George Martin Lane, a professor of Latin at Harvard; William Whitwell Greenough, the president of the board of trustees at the Boston Public Library; William Everett, who had studied Latin and then taught it at Harvard during much of the 1870s; and Thomas Wentworth Higginson, who had enrolled at Harvard when he was thirteen years old, eventually studied for the ministry, and went on to a career advocating abolitionism well before the Civil War and equal rights for women and for African Americans afterward. For assistance with the scriptural allusions Adams consulted with Charles Eliot Norton, a fellow member of the Prince Society who became one of the nation's leading art critics as well as the founder, in 1879, of the Archaeological Institute of America. John Chipman Gray, remembered today as the co-founder of the Boston law firm Ropes and Gray and a prominent professor at Harvard Law School with particular expertise in the law of property, managed to trace five hundred years of legal precedent for Adams's edition. Adams noted that he also relied on Lindsay Swift, then a recent graduate of Harvard soon to take up a position as a bibliographer and editor at the Boston Public Library, who "has explained archaic expressions," Adams wrote, "to the meaning of which I could get no clew." According to his obituary in the *Cambridge Tribune* in 1921, Swift was an editor of the library's quarterly bulletins and a regular contributor to the *Saturday Evening Post*, the *Nation*, and the *Boston Evening Transcript*.[35]

Morton had included enough references to the natural environment that Adams felt compelled to recruit a team of leading scientists to guide him. For geological details he turned to Josiah Dwight Whitney, an expert on American ores from his experience as a field geologist with the Isle Royale Copper Company in Michigan, who had become the first Sturgis-Hooper Professor of Geology at Harvard in 1865, a position he held until he died thirty-one years later. He also consulted with Nathanial Shaler, who joined the faculty at Harvard soon after he graduated and taught paleontology there from 1869 to 1888. Adams relied on two experts for the plants described by Morton. The first was Asa Gray, the leading botanist in the United States in the nineteenth century, who had taken up a professorship at Harvard in 1842, was among the initial fifty scholars who founded the National Academy of Sciences in 1863, and was a close friend and frequent correspondent of Charles Darwin. The other was Charles Sprague Sargent, who studied biology as an undergraduate at Harvard and then turned to botany after three years' service for the Union during the Civil War. As the first professor of arboriculture at Harvard, he had responsibility for the new Arnold Arboretum. A light teaching load allowed him to collaborate with the landscape architect Frederick Law Olmstead, who was in the late nineteenth century planning Boston's "emerald necklace," the linked series of green spaces that continue to define much of the city's character.

William Brewster, who had been the keeper of the mammal and bird collections at the Boston Society of Natural History since 1879, provided guidance for the ornithological references, while an ill Mr. Allen—quite possibly William Henry Allen, the president of Bowdoin College, who died in 1882—assisted with the material about animals. Adams mentioned that he relied on Agassiz and Lyman to understand the references to fish. The former was likely Alexander Agassiz, son of the world-renowned Louis Agassiz (who had been Shaler's teacher at Harvard), a well-known marine ichthyologist with particular expertise in starfish, coral reefs, and echini (sea urchins). The other was Agassiz's brother-in-law, Theodore Lyman, who published six papers on the marine invertebrates known as serpent stars from 1859 to 1865 and later served on the board of trustees at Harvard's Museum of Comparative Zoology. For the birds he turned to Frederic Ward Putnam, a onetime ornithological prodigy—he was the curator of ornithology at the Essex Institute in Salem when he was only seventeen years old—who had come to Louis Agassiz's attention and then studied under him at Harvard. By the time Adams sought his expertise, Putnam was the curator of the Peabody Museum of Archaeology and Ethnology at Harvard.[36]

Finally, Adams needed a bit of guidance for the non-English people who appeared in *New English Canaan*. "I met some allusions to early French and other explorers," Adams added, "and naturally had recourse to Messrs. Parkman and Slafter." The former was Francis Parkman, another member of the Prince Society who was in the midst of writing his nine-volume masterpiece, *France and England in North America*, which began to appear in print in 1865 and concluded in 1892. The latter was the Reverend Dr. Edmund F. Slafter, who was then the president of the Prince Society as well as the secretary of the New England Historical and Genealogical Society. Slafter had added a long "memoir" to the 1880 Prince Society edition of the *Voyages* of Samuel de Champlain, who was of course the first European to describe the region where the English built New Plymouth.[37]

The last expert Adams named was J. (James) Hammond Trumbull, who could explain what the Native words in the text meant since he "recognized to the fullest extent the public obligation which a mastery of a special subject imposes on him who masters it."[38] Trumbull, one of the rare scholars Adams consulted who had not attended Harvard (he had gone to Yale), had published an edition of Roger Williams's *A Key into the Language of America* in 1866, and had emerged as the leading authority on Massachusett; his *Natick Dictionary* was published by the Smithsonian's Bureau of American Ethnology in 1903.[39] Mastering this language was no simple achievement. As Adams and others of his generation had concluded, in the words of one librarian, Massachusett was then an "obsolete language of the aborigines of North America."[40] They were correct if they were referring to Massachusett as a spoken language. But by then there were written texts, including Massachusett records of real estate transactions through the seventeenth century and even a political protest from a group of Christian Mashpees in Barnstable County in 1752.[41]

Trumbull and Adams might have thought that the language was no longer spoken because they probably believed that its speakers had disappeared. But they were likely wrong. The idea that indigenous residents had left the region was the product of a historical consciousness developed by nineteenth-century local historians who could have had political motivations for marking the end of one or another group's existence.[42] Others had economic incentives for trying to make New England's indigenous peoples disappear.[43] But the Massachusett manuscripts reveal how Native peoples preserved their culture in part by accepting an English notion of literacy. Their writings demonstrate continual presence in the region long after many nonindigenous observers believed they were gone.[44] Further, the adoption of written language did not signal the end of oral history traditions.[45] After becoming rare for perhaps six generations, the language is again spoken, though it is now known as Wôpanâak.[46]

Adams was right that it took a village of the learned to explicate the writings of Thomas Morton, the thrice-exiled tormenter of William Bradford and John Winthrop. But the effort was worth it. He and his collaborators guaranteed that Morton's book, with all of its complexities, remained available for later generations of readers. In the process, he helped realize the vision of his father, who as a teenager had recognized that the book's "learning and satirical wit and feelings . . . may have become part of the soil" of the old Adams homestead.

By the early years of the twentieth century, Morton had gained a following as a precursor of an alternative America — a free-spirited, nature-loving soul, more at home in the company of Native Americans than English colonists. As editors of one anthology of early American writing published almost fifty years ago put it, Ma-re Mount could have been a "beatnik colony in the seventeenth-century New England woods, presided over by university Bohemians — full of classical quotations, rum and deviltry." To be sure, not everyone praised such behavior. The historian Charles McLean Andrews, writing in the 1930s, saw the value of Morton to enliven "the encircling gloom of the Pilgrim and the Puritan," but added that he had "no moral standards of thought or conduct." Another historian noted that Morton had become "an irresponsible libertine, attempting to create a fanciful version of some classical pagan paradise." One saw the struggle as a clash "between repressive Puritan Elizabethan lifestyles."[47] Still another recognized his role in the emergence of Wicca and paganism, an "eco-warrior" who some adherents identified as a "prototypical American Pagan."[48] At some point in the latter decades of the twentieth century, the Thomas Morton Alliance, a pagan-leaning countercultural group, produced a pin that depicted the roots of a tree and the trunk rising from the ground as a raised fist. Morris dancers celebrated around a new maypole in Quincy during the first years of the twenty-first century.[49] In 2011 Deval Patrick, a governor of Massachusetts willing to move far from the actions of his predecessor John Winthrop, proclaimed May 1 of that year to be Thomas Morton Day, citing the English migrant's "respectful relations with Native Americans," his "intrepid explorations of Massachusetts," and the fact that *New English Canaan* "represents an invaluable 'first chapter' of Massachusetts history."[50]

But it was not just the Morton of the maypole story who reemerged in the twentieth century. He was also trotted onto the stage when an author wanted to make a point about political as well as cultural resistance, or perhaps to make a profit. In 1930 the *New York Times* ran a long article tracing the rise and fall of New England. "The Elizabethan tradition in New England died with Morton," Helen Augur wrote on the three hundredth anniversary of the founding of the Massachusetts Bay Colony, "and gave way to Puritan straitness and severity."[51] That same year a British Harvard graduate named Henry Ainsworth, asserting he was one of Morton's descendants, laid claim to perhaps one-half of the city of Quincy. He gave up the quest within a few days, informing the city council that he needed to return to England on unspecified urgent business. By then, the *Boston Globe* had written six articles on his claim, with the last noting that Ainsworth would miss the upcoming celebration of the tercentenary anniversary.[52] Three years later the poet and essayist William Carlos Williams found inspiration in Morton's story. In 1933, with his eye trained on the stories of Morton's first exile, he wrote that the "gambol on the green" at the maypole "brought matters to a head with a vengeance." Williams believed the Pilgrims revealed their worst at this moment: "Trustless of humane experience, not knowing what to think, they went mad, lost all direction."[53] Four years later Morton made a cameo appearance in Stephen Vincent Benét's *The Devil and Daniel Webster* as one of the infamous Americans who takes a seat on a jury in hell to judge the novella's protagonist, who has sold his soul to the devil and is being defended by the famous New England lawyer.[54]

In 1965 the poet Robert Lowell wrote three one-act plays grouped together as *The Old Glory*. The first, *Endecott and the Red Cross*, dramatized fictional conversations between Morton and John Endecott, the colonial official who ordered the chopping down of the maypole. Lowell listed his sources as Hawthorne's short stories and Morton's *New English Canaan*. Here, as in other twentieth-century texts, Morton comes off less as reckless and more as a reasonable man standing as a foil to a zealous Puritan leader. More to the point, Morton becomes an American archetype, defying English soldiers who despise their posting. Those troops hate the Puritan overlords—notably Endecott—who in the play are so consumed with self-righteous fury that they are as eager to defy the king as to murder Natives. Morton, by contrast, defines the moral center: "Oh, America is God's land. Even the blue-assed Puritans can't change that!"[55]

(*opposite*) One can only wonder what Governor John Winthrop would have thought if he had known that almost three hundred years after the founding of the colony Governor Deval Patrick would declare Thomas Morton Day in the Commonwealth.
(GO60.03/series 2763. Office of Constituent Services proclamation files, Thomas Morton Day Proclamation, dated March 9, 2011. Massachusetts Archives. Boston, Massachusetts.)

Commonwealth  of Massachusetts

A Proclamation

His Excellency Governor Deval L. Patrick

Whereas Thomas Morton was born in Devon, England, around 1576, and became the first English person to settle and build a plantation (at "Mount Wollaston" in Quincy) on Massachusetts Bay in 1624; and

Whereas Thomas Morton's respectful relationships with Native Americans made his plantation, called "Ma-Re Mount" or Merrymount, the most prosperous trading-post of its time and place; and

Thomas Morton's intrepid explorations of Massachusetts and "New England" produced a detailed portrait of Native American cultures, and of America's rich and beautiful natural endowments; and

Whereas Thomas Morton, his company and "all comers" erected a Maypole on May Day, 1627, at Merrymount to celebrate their intercultural prosperity with a traditional English "Revel"; and

Whereas Thomas Morton wrote and affixed his "Poem" and "Song" to the Maypole to propose annual Revels that would facilitate respect, cooperation and prosperity on the New England frontier and therefore some believe he may be America's first poet in English; and

Whereas The 1637 book about his observations and experiences---*New English Canaan*---represents an invaluable "first chapter" of Massachusetts history,

Now, Therefore, I, Deval L. Patrick, Governor of the Commonwealth of Massachusetts, do hereby proclaim March 1st, 2011, to be

THOMAS MORTON DAY

And urge all the citizens of the Commonwealth to take cognizance of this event
and participate fittingly in its observance.

Given at the Executive Chamber in Boston, this ninth day of March, in the year two thousand and eleven, and of the Independence of the United States of America, the two hundred and thirty-fourth.

By His Excellency

DEVAL L. PATRICK
GOVERNOR OF THE COMMONWEALTH

WILLIAM FRANCIS GALVIN
SECRETARY OF THE COMMONWEALTH

God Save the Commonwealth of Massachusetts

This scene from E. J. Barnes's "Thomas Morton, Merry
Mount's Lord of Misrule," which appeared in *Colonial
Comics: New England, 1620–1750* in 2014, captures the sense
of Bacchanalian excess that terrified the Pilgrims.
(© E. J. Barnes, 2014.)

Philip Roth, through his protagonist David Kapesh in *The
Dying Animal* of 2001, picked up the same themes. Kapesh
is an aging late twentieth-century libertine, a part-time professor who has frequent affairs with his students and is sufficiently semi-famous as a scholar that one of his lovers fears
being seen with him in public lest news of their encounter end
up in a tabloid newspaper. In the midst of the narrative, Roth
has Kapesh describe Morton, who comes across as strident
but unthreatening, and the Pilgrims and Puritans, whom he
cast as tightly wound persecutors. To Roth, Morton exempli-

fied perpetual types. "He's a kind of forest creature out of *As You Like It*," Kapesh reports, "a wild demon out of *A Midsummer Night's Dream*. . . . Shakespeare is Morton's rock-and-roll." Roth, like Lowell, picked up on the eager transgressive sexuality of Ma-re Mount. "Age-old American story," as Roth put it: "save the young from sex. Yet it's always too late. Too late because they've already been born."[56]

For Roth's character, Morton had initiated an anti-authoritarian strain in American popular culture that would not resurface until Henry Miller. "The clash between Plymouth and Merry Mount, between Bradford and Morton, between rule and misrule," Kapesh announces as he depicts the cultural tsunami that convulsed the nation in the 1960s — "the colonial harbinger of the national upheaval three hundred and thirty-odd years later when Morton's America was born at last, miscegenation and all." Kapesh believes that Morton's likeness should be carved onto Mount Rushmore because his seventeenth-century hero laid the foundations for a sexual revolution that enabled a serial predator like him to sleep with students as long as he never broke his own rule that they could not consummate their relationship until he had recorded their grade for the semester.[57]

Bradford and Winthrop had hoped that the Pilgrims and Puritans would create model colonies that fit divinely sanctioned goals. But as later critics realized, their actions — including their persecution of Morton — illuminated the limit of their visions. Hawthorne's version depicted Ma-re Mount as a place caught between competing agendas and could be read as allegory or farce. Morton's *New English Canaan*, though shot through with satiric references to his tormenters, was unflinching in its dissent against the dissenters and so read as tragedy or as evidence that could be offered in a legal pleading. The threat Morton posed to the Pilgrims and Puritans lay not in drinking, dancing, and cohabitating with and selling guns to the Ninnimissinuok. Nor was he a menace because his model of a village proved attractive. There were likely at least twenty times more Pilgrims, not to count other English, in New Plymouth in 1628, and by the mid-1630s Massachusetts Bay had drawn thousands more migrants from England than New Plymouth ever managed. Morton had seven allies when colonial authorities first exiled him, and perhaps none at all the two times Massachusetts authorities sent him away. By any measure he was a failure as a would-be colony builder. The threat he did present came from his skills as a lawyer and a writer. Morton posed a danger because he worked to undermine the legitimacy of the legal claim that gave colonists the authority from their monarch to establish and maintain villages on the homelands of others.

New English Canaan was Morton's effort to reorient one part of the English colonial project. He believed there was still time to find a way toward a new kind of Canaan—a promised land like that his god had given to the ancient Israelites without the slaughter of many of its inhabitants described in the book of Joshua. Perhaps he chose Canaan for his title because he knew that the Puritans, in England and New England, were obsessed with that biblical story, placing themselves in the role of the Hebrews who wandered in the wilderness until their god showed them where to go. The scriptural history of Canaan explained both their present condition as their Lord's chosen and their future destiny as the creators of a New Jerusalem.[58] Morton saw the flaws of the Pilgrims' and Puritans' actions but recognized the rhetorical utility of exegetical argumentation. Maybe this Jonah could point the way toward a kinder future.

The colonists who thrust Morton out of New Plymouth and Massachusetts wanted to silence him. They had good reason to erase the influence of this potent antagonist whose actions defied their authority time and again. Perhaps they saw his actions as a test—a trial for them to prove to their god that they were worthy. More mundane concerns no doubt mattered too. In the 1630s, after Morton's second exile, some of the Pilgrims and Puritans might have recognized that Morton could make a powerful argument that the migrants were not living up to their initial plans. After all, the Massachusetts Bay Charter of 1629—the document they refused to send back to England—specified that the "principall ende of this planta[ti]on" was to create a model society where the actions of the colonists would "incite the natives of the country to the knowledge and obedience of the onlie true God and Savior of mankind, and the Christian faith."[59] The ashes of the Pequot community on the Mystic could be used as proof of their failure.

To the Puritans' benefit, the quo warranto judgment could not be enforced. The action of the General Court in this case, though none could have seen it at the time, constituted the colony's first declaration of its independence, providing a lesson that resistance to a monarch's decision could be the best way forward for those on the ground in North America. But there is another legacy too. The events of the 1630s—the time from Morton's second exile to the abandonment of the quo warranto and the assault on the Pequot settlement—remind us that colonial goals, no matter how aspirational to those who proposed them, could also justify violence and dispossession. This was Morton's insight, and one reason why his story continues to resonate.

Timeline

c. 1575/1576
- Thomas Morton born, likely in West Country of England.

March 24, 1603
- Queen Elizabeth I dies; King James VI of Scotland becomes King James I of England.

1605
- Maneddo, Skicowaros, and Sassocomoit, three Eastern Abenakis who had traveled to England with the English sea captain George Waymouth, take up residence in Sir Ferdinando Gorges's house.

March 1616
- George Miller Sr. dies in Swallowfield.

1620
- Alice Miller marries Thomas Morton, who had been her lawyer.

September 6, 1620
- The *Mayflower* departs Southampton; it arrives off Cape Cod two months later.

November 3, 1620
- Sir Ferdinando Gorges petitions to reestablish the Council for New England's claim to North America between 40 and 45 degrees north latitude.

May 24, 1622
- Morton appears for the first time in the Chancery Court in Westminster to press Alice's case.

June 3, 1622
- The dispute between George Miller Jr. and Morton reaches the Star Chamber.

1622
- Morton likely makes his first journey to New England.

c. 1624
- Morton crosses the Atlantic and takes up the land previously held by Captain Wollaston at Wessaguset.

1627
- John Winthrop records allegations that Morton had committed murder in England.

1628
- Pilgrims arrest Morton and exile him to England.

1629
- Morton returns, first to Plymouth and then back to his old house at Ma-re Mount.

1631
- Puritans exile Morton to England and believe he will serve time in jail.

1632/1633
- English printer Charles Greene reports that agents working for the new colonies in New England are suppressing his attempt to publish Morton's *New English Canaan*.

1635–37
- Morton and Sir Ferdinando Gorges bring quo warranto charges against the Massachusetts Bay Company.

1637
- The Dutch printer Jacob Frederic Stam publishes *New English Canaan* in Amsterdam.

1638
- The Massachusetts General Court sends a petition to London relating to its refusal to return its charter.

1639
- Gorges receives patent to territory in modern Maine.

TIMELINE

1643
- Morton returns to Massachusetts Bay and is soon jailed.

1644
- Massachusetts authorities release Morton and exile him to Maine.

1646/1647
- Morton dies in Acomenticus.

1669
- Nathaniel Morton publishes *New-England's Memoriall*, the first printed version of the story of Morton and the maypole at the place the Pilgrims call Merrymount.

1755
- A copy of *New English Canaan* arrives at the Library Company of Philadelphia.

1798/1799
- John Quincy Adams purchases a copy of *New English Canaan* bound with other books at an auction in Berlin.

1802
- John Adams writes "Scraps of the History of Mount Wollaston."

1812
- John Adams and Thomas Jefferson exchange letters about *New English Canaan*.

1838
- The antiquarian and politician Peter Force publishes a copy of *New English Canaan* in a collection of political writings about early America, the first time the book has been reprinted since 1637.

1883
- Charles Francis Adams Jr. edits and publishes an edition of *New English Canaan* for the Prince Society in Boston.

May 1, 2011
- Governor Deval Patrick issues a proclamation declaring Thomas Morton Day.

Note on Sources

Charles Francis Adams Jr. understood that Thomas Morton was, among other things, a historian. *New English Canaan* stands, one could argue, as the second most important historical narrative of early seventeenth-century New England. To be sure, it lacks the monumentality and precise attention to chronological detail to be found in William Bradford's *Of Plymouth Plantation*. Further, Morton of course had a political argument to make in his history. But recognizing this does not render Morton's book less revealing as a source. Bradford's work, after all, was just as imbued with a political mission. In his telling, the people of New Plymouth, deeply devout in their commitment to Reformed Christianity, risked everything by moving from the relative comforts of Leiden to what he and other English referred to as a "wilderness." There they endured despite the many tests that their god had placed before them—errant adventurers like Thomas Weston who ignored the Separatists' teachings, indigenous enemies like the Pequots who strove to undermine the newcomers' economy, migrants like John Oldham and John Lyford who challenged the Pilgrims' authority, and a natural world that could bombard them with winter storms and block their access to England. Bradford wept at the loss of the Pilgrim Fathers who had led the migration and reported on the execution of a teenager named Thomas Granger for bestiality. While historians use his history because of the details it provides about New England before 1650, it needs to be read as just as politically motivated as Morton's three-part exegesis of what he hoped could be a new promised land.

Precious few details about Morton's life survive. There are no known portraits, no archive of his papers, and his gravesite, if it exists, bears no marker. (The oldest church graveyard in York, Maine, does not include the earliest colonial residents of the town, though it contains many later seventeenth-century tombstones.) But in recent years many scholars have come to appreciate Morton as a historian and to use *New English Canaan* as a primary text for understanding what the region was like before the newcomers became ever more effective at reducing and removing many of its Natives. William Cronon and Neal Salisbury, two pathbreaking scholars of early New England, used *New English Canaan* as a primary source — for relations between Natives and newcomers (in Salisbury's *Manitou and Providence: Indians, Europeans, and the Making of New England, 1500–1643* [New York, 1982]) and to understand both the environment and Ninnimissinuok ways of shaping it to meet their needs (in Cronon's *Changes in the Land: Indians, Colonists, and the Ecology of New England* [New York, 1983]).

Morton's book works as a primary source because it reveals one persistent observer's mind in a way that has caught attention despite what many have seen as the failures of the text itself. In other words, what Morton reported remains of enormous importance even if his book, as the literary scholar William Heath put it in a superb essay, "is the work of a dabbler and dilettante — marred by slap-dash composition, convoluted argumentation, and a plethora of classical allusions"; nonetheless, "as natural history, anthropology, comic romp, pastoral interlude, and exposé of hypocritical bigotry, *New English Canaan* is a step in the right direction." See Heath, "Thomas Morton: From Merry Old England to New England," *Journal of American Studies* 41 (2007): 135–68, quotation at 164. The literary scholar Daniel Shea noted that the Puritans and their literary heirs tried to erase Morton from the canon. "From the point of view of literary history," he wrote, "Morton's book is admittedly an evolutionary relic and dead end, clumsy-winged, perverse even in its flights." But that effort failed since Morton has remained part of the cul-

NOTE ON SOURCES

tural legacy of the era. See Shea, "'Our Professed Old Adversary': Thomas Morton and the Naming of New England," *Early American Literature* 23 (1988): 52–69, quotation at 53. John P. McWilliams Jr. shrewdly analyzed the ways that Morton figured in creative works into the early decades of the twentieth century in "Fictions of Merry Mount," *American Quarterly* 29 (1977): 3–30. In an essay that moved from then contemporary politics backward to Morton and the maypole, with a great deal on the zealotry of John Endecott, the historian Richard Drinnon traced the doomed "campaign to silence Morton" and saw the emergence of the Lord of Misrule across the American experience. As he wrote, "Not even all the afflicted Saints could stop the formation of a countertradition, a tradition fittingly rooted in the emotions driven underground and surfacing periodically as invasions of Merry Mounters, familists, Ranters, millenarians, anarchists, Flower Children, and others from the remote recesses said to be the lurking places of nymphs and fauns." See Drinnon, "The Maypole of Merry Mount: Thomas Morton & the Puritan Patriarchs," *Massachusetts Review* 21 (1980): 382–410, quotations at 389 and 410.

No scholar has done a better job of getting at the core meaning of *New English Canaan* than John Demos in "The Maypole of Merry Mount," which appeared in *American Heritage* 37: 6 (October 1986): 82–87. The clash between Ma-re Mount and the Puritans, Demos wrote, "is a prototype of much that came later in American history: the conquest of frontiers and their native populations, the massive development of environmental bounty, the whole go-ahead spirit." Morton offered a different vision in his book—"what might have been but wasn't," as Demos put it, including "an instinct for compromise between human need and environmental constraint."

But of course no single essay (or book) can capture the entirety of a much-discussed text and its oft-maligned author. The best introduction to Morton as a thinker is Michael Zuckerman's astonishing essay, "Pilgrims in the Wilderness: Community, Modernity, and the Maypole at Merry Mount," *New England Quarterly* 50 (1977): 255–77. Other important works on Morton include Karen Ordahl Kupperman's superb "Thomas Morton, Historian," *New England Quarterly* 50 (1977): 660–64, and her exemplary *Indians and English: Facing off in Early America* (Ithaca, 2000), where she draws on Morton's writing; and Donald F. Connors, *Thomas Morton* (New York, 1969), which is especially strong in tracing the ways that later writers, across the nineteenth and twentieth centuries, drew on Morton's writings. Heath's and Connors's studies can be read alongside Jack Dempsey's *Thomas Morton of "Merrymount": The Life and Renaissance of an Early American Poet* (Scituate, Mass., 2000), the only recent full-length study of Morton, and Dempsey's edition of *New English Canaan* (Scituate, Mass., 2000), which draws from and extends Charles Francis Adams Jr.'s pioneering scholarship. An earlier brief exploration of Morton's life and a different gloss on *New English Canaan* can be found in Minor W. Major, "Thomas Morton and His New English Canaan" (Ph.D. diss., University of Colorado, 1957). Charles Francis Adams Jr.'s contemporary B. F. DeCosta produced two essays worthy of attention: a short biographical sketch, "Morton of Merry Mount," that appeared in the *Magazine of American History* 8 (1882): 81–94, and "Morton's *New English Canaan*," *New-England Historical and Genealogical Register* 48 (1894): 329–31, in which he reported that Morton's book was so powerful that some readers copied it for themselves, a reminder of the ongoing practice of scribal publication.

Scholars have also pored over Morton's text, analyzing it from a variety of angles. Among the best are Edith Murphy's incisive reading in "'A Rich Widow, Now to Be Tane Up or Laid Downe': Solving the Riddle of Thomas Morton's 'Rise Oedipeus,'" *William and Mary Quarterly*, 3rd ser., 53 (1996): 755–68; Thomas Cartelli, "Transplanting Disorder: The Construction of Misrule in Morton's *New English Canaan* and Bradford's *Of Plymouth Plantation*," *English Literary Renaissance* 27 (1997): 258–80; and Daniel Walden, "'The Very Hydra of the Time': Morton's *New English Canaan* and Atlantic Trade," *Early American Literature* 48 (2013): 315–36, which demonstrates Walden's insight that close reading of the text will allow Morton's book to "reclaim a position alongside, rather than opposed, to the more conventional narratives of early New England and larger American colonial projects" (332). Similarly excellent is Michelle Burnham's analysis of Morton's book as a text that "depends on a courtly reading model" and offers its readers "a kind of aristocratic colonial fantasy; it promises would-be planter-gentlemen the pastoral possibilities of unlimited pleasure and leisure rather than the burden of hard labor and the necessity of sacrifice." See her "Land, Labor, and Colonial Economics in Thomas Morton's *New English Canaan*," *Early American Literature* 41 (2006): 405–28, quotations at 424 and 425.

Given the unusual history of the book's publication—its initial suppression and then its reprinting—it is not surprising that scholars have investigated the publishing history of *New English Canaan* in depth and revealed a printing history that is crucial to understanding Morton. For this vital literature see Matt Cohen, "Morton's Maypole and the Indians: Publishing in Early New England," *Book History* 5 (2002): 1–18; Cohen, *The Networked Wilderness: Communicating in Early New England* (Minneapolis, 2010); and especially Paul R. Sternberg, "The Publication of Thomas Morton's *New English Canaan* Reconsidered," *Papers of the Bibliographical Society of America* 80 (1986): 369–74. For the larger context of Morton's book within the intellectual factory of early New England and on-the-ground ways of sharing information, see Katherine Grandjean, *American Passage: The Communications Frontier in Early New England* (Cambridge, Mass., 2015). For the best insight into the culture of Swallowfield at the time Morton lived there, see Steve Hindle, "Hierarchy and Community in the Elizabethan Parish: The Swallowfield Articles of 1596," *Historical Journal* 42 (1999): 835–51.

Works that pivot either on *New English Canaan* specifically or on the circulation of knowledge about and within New England more generally make sense only if set in the larger context of what we know about Morton's era. Fortunately, there is no shortage of excellent works about early New England. For the English (and other European) migrants and the world they created, see, among many works, Virginia DeJohn Anderson, *New England's Generation: The Great Migration and the Formation of Society and Culture in the Seventeenth Century* (Cambridge, 1991); Bernard Bailyn, *The Peopling of British North America: An Introduction* (New York, 1986); John Demos, *A Little Commonwealth: Family Life in Plymouth Colony* (New York, 1970); Nick Bunker, *Making Haste from Babylon: The* Mayflower *Pilgrims and Their World* (New York, 2010); Nathaniel Philbrick, *Mayflower:*

A Story of Courage, Community, and War (New York, 2006); and Malcolm Gaskill, *Between Two Worlds: How the English Became Americans* (New York, 2014). George D. Langdon Jr.'s excellent *Pilgrim Colony: A History of New Plymouth, 1620–1691* (New Haven, 1966), includes no mention of Thomas Morton—and by doing so serves as a reminder that it is possible to tell the history of Plymouth without focusing on the maypole or the relatively small number of followers that Morton attracted to the settlement begun by Weston and Wollaston. There are exemplary studies of John Winthrop, including Francis J. Bremer's meticulous biography, *John Winthrop: America's Forgotten Founding Father* (New York, 2003); the brilliant edition of Winthrop's journal edited by Richard S. Dunn et al. as *The Journal of John Winthrop, 1630–1649* (Cambridge, Mass., 1996); and Edmund S. Morgan's *The Puritan Dilemma: The Story of John Winthrop* (Boston, 1958). But as good as the work on Winthrop is, there is less scholarship on Bradford, though there are multiple editions of his history, or on Ferdinando Gorges, for whom the best full-length works remain James Phinney Baxter, *Sir Ferdinando Gorges and His Province of Maine*, 2 vols. (Boston, 1890) and Richard A. Preston, *Gorges of Plymouth Fort: A Life of Ferdinando Gorges, Captain of Plymouth Fort, Governor of New England, and Lord of the Province of Maine* (Toronto, 1953). There is no better exploration of the religious context of the world Morton first entered in New England than Mark Peterson's "The Plymouth Church and the Evolution of Puritan Religious Culture," *New England Quarterly* 66 (1993): 570–93.

There is, of course, no shortage of works on religion in seventeenth-century New England. The best starting place is Edmund S. Morgan's *Visible Saints: The History of a Puritan Idea* (New York, 1963), the most subtle and economic reading of dissenters' tracts that exists. It is hard to fathom Morton's critique of the Pilgrims and Puritans without understanding how English Puritans thought about planning communities with no wall between church and state as well as their views on the Church of England. Among the most useful works in this vast literature are Perry Miller, *Errand into the Wilderness* (Cambridge, Mass., 1956), especially its opening eponymous essay; Francis J. Bremer, *The Puritan Experiment: New England Society from Bradford to Edwards*, rev. ed.

(Hanover, N.H., 1995); Charles L. Cohen, *God's Caress: The Psychology of Puritan Religious Experience* (Oxford, 1988); Philip F. Gura, *A Glimpse of Sion's Glory: Puritan Radicalism in New England, 1620–1660* (Middletown, Conn., 1984); David D. Hall, *Worlds of Wonder, Days of Judgment: Popular Religious Beliefs in Early New England* (New York, 1989); Charles E. Hambrick-Stowe, *The Practice of Piety: Puritan Devotional Disciplines in Seventeenth-Century New England* (Chapel Hill, 1982); Janice Knight, *Orthodoxies in Massachusetts: Rereading American Puritanism* (Cambridge, Mass., 1992); Mark A. Peterson, *The Price of Redemption: The Spiritual Economy of Puritan New England* (Stanford, 1997); Sarah Rivett, *The Science of the Soul in Colonial New England* (Chapel Hill, 2011); and Cristobal Silva, *Miraculous Plagues: An Epidemiology of Early New England Narrative* (New York, 2011). Michael P. Winship, in a dazzling feat of intellectual history, drew on Morton to fill in some of the silences in the documents left by other observers, including Bradford; see his *Godly Republicanism: Puritans, Pilgrims, and a City on a Hill* (Cambridge, Mass., 2012). Mark Peterson's monumental *The City-State of Boston: The Rise and Fall of an Atlantic Power, 1630–1865* (Princeton, 2019) is now the foundation for understanding the city that began as a village in Morton's time.

These works reveal an underlying truth that was absent from earlier histories of New England: what went on there was not, contrary to Bradford and those who thought like him, the unfolding of a preordained plan that brought success to the newcomers but instead a contested and often brutal clash between Europeans, primarily English, and Ninnimissinuok. No one has gotten at this element of the seventeenth century as powerfully as Bernard Bailyn in his brilliant *The Barbarous Years—The Peopling of British North America: The Conflict of Civilizations, 1600–1675* (New York, 2012). The events that Morton witnessed, participated in, or heard about (notably the epidemic of 1616 to 1619 and the catastrophic war of 1637) had widespread repercussions for all involved. Colonists often saw events as one tragedy unfolding after another, as Kathleen Donegan has so smartly described in *Seasons of Misery: Catastrophe and Colonial Settlement in Early America* (Philadelphia, 2014). Slavery, once presumed to be a problem in the history of the English colonies around the

Chesapeake, in the lower South, and in the West Indies, took root in New England too, starting with the capture of Ninnimissinuok by Thomas Hunt, among others. Important new work on this phenomenon includes Margaret Newell, *Brethren by Nature: New England Indians, Colonists, and the Origins of American Slavery* (Ithaca, 2015); Michael Guasco, *Slaves and Englishmen: Human Bondage in the Early Modern Atlantic World* (Philadelphia, 2014); and Wendy Warren, *New England Bound: Slavery and Colonization in Early America* (New York, 2016).

Over the past thirty or so years, following the work of historians like Cronon and Salisbury, a number of scholars have illuminated the indigenous history of the lands once dominated by the Ninnimissinuok. The best introduction to this field is Kathleen J. Bragdon, *Native People of Southern New England* (Norman, Okla., 1996), which can be supplemented by other vital work, including Alfred A. Cave, "Why Was the Sagadahoc Colony Abandoned? An Evaluation of the Evidence," *New England Quarterly* 68 (1995): 625–40; Lucianne Lavin, *Connecticut's Indigenous Peoples: What Archaeology, History, and Oral Traditions Teach Us about Their Communities and Cultures* (New Haven, 2013); Andrew Lipman, *Saltwater Frontier: Indians and the Contest for the American Coast* (New Haven, 2015); Jonathan K. Patton, "Considering the Wet Homelands of Indigenous Massachusetts," *Journal of Social Archaeology* 14 (2014): 87–111; Patricia E. Rubertone, *Grave Undertakings: An Archaeology of Roger Williams and the Narragansett Indians* (Washington, D.C., 2001); and William S. Simmons, *Spirit of the New England Tribes: Indian History and Folklore* (Hanover, N.H., 1986). The barbarity of the Pequot War has generated its own poignant scholarship; for insightful works see Alfred Cave, *The Pequot War* (Amherst, Mass., 1996); Michael L. Fickes, "'They Could Not Endure That Yoke': The Captivity of Pequot Women and Children After the War of 1637," *New England Quarterly* 73 (2000): 58–81; Michael Freeman, "Puritans and Pequots: The Question of Genocide," *New England Quarterly* 68 (1995): 278–93; Ronald Dale Karr, "'Why Should You Be So Furious?': The Violence of the Pequot War," *Journal of American History* 85 (1998): 876–909; Andrew Lipman, "'A Meanes to Knitt Them Togeather': The Exchange of Body Parts in the Pequot War," *William and Mary Quarterly*, 3rd ser., 65

NOTE ON SOURCES

(2008): 3–28; Benjamin Madley, "Reexamining the American Genocide Debate: Meaning, Historiography, and New Methods," *American Historical Review* 120 (2015): 98–139; and Matthew S.
Muehlbauer, "'They . . . Shall No More Be Called Peaquots but Narragansetts and
Mohegans': Refugees, Rivalry, and the Consequences of the Pequot
War," *War and Society* 30 (2011): 167–76. The potential causes of the
devastating epidemic of the late 1610s received extensive treatment
in John S. Marr and John T. Cathey, "New Hypothesis for Cause
of Epidemic among Native Americans, New England, 1616–1619,"
Emerging Infectious Diseases 16 (2010): 281–86.

There is a certain seductive quality to *New English Canaan*. I am
hardly alone in making that observation. After all, John, John
Quincy, Charles Francis Sr., and Charles Francis Adams Jr. read the
book and understood its significance for the history of Massachusetts. Literary luminaries including Nathaniel Hawthorne, William
Carlos Williams, Robert Lowell, and Philip Roth saw something
about the shaping of the American character in Morton's and his
followers' disdain for Bradford, Standish, Endecott, Winthrop, and
the rest of the Pilgrims and Puritans.

But Morton's story is about more than one book. No study of
him is complete if based wholly or even primarily on the text of *New
English Canaan*. Evidence about him not published during his life-
time is crucial. Here the most important materials can be found in
the papers and journal of John Winthrop and the documents generated by the trials about the Miller estate in Swallowfield, many of
which can be found in Charles Edward Banks, "Thomas Morton
of Merry Mount," *Proceedings of the Massachusetts Historical Society*,
3rd ser., 58 (1924–25): 147–93, which is based on manuscripts from
Chancery and the Star Chamber in the English National Archives
(formerly the Public Record Office). Similarly, Gorges's efforts to
undermine the Pilgrims and the Puritans, which never circulated
in book form like *New English Canaan*, reveal why Winthrop and
his colleagues in Massachusetts Bay needed to exile Morton twice.
The best rendering of the rather complex series of machinations of
the mid-1630s can be found in Charles M. Andrews, *The Colonial
Period of American History*, 4 vols. (New Haven, 1934–39), vol. 1, *The*

Settlements, especially 400–429, which also includes extensive material about Gorges. Gorges's efforts to control Maine are smartly documented in Hannah Farber, "The Rise and Fall of the Province of Lygonia, 1643–1658," *New England Quarterly* 82 (2009): 490–513. Details about the quo warranto of 1635 need to be pieced together from different sources: Thomas Hutchinson's *History of Massachusetts* (Boston, 1764); *Hutchinson Papers,* publications of the Prince Society (Albany, 1865); G. D. Scull, "The 'Quo Warranto' of 1635," *New-England Historical and Genealogical Register* 38 (1884): 209–16; and *Proceedings of the American Antiquarian Society* (Cambridge, Mass., 1867), 53–131, which contains the surviving minutes of the Council for New England, with the material on the quo warranto on 119–30. The American Antiquarian Society (AAS) materials also appeared separately as *Records of the Council for New England* (Cambridge, Mass., 1867); the quo warranto material in this edition is at 71–82. The New England case needs to be set into the larger English legal context, which has been thoroughly explained in Paul D. Halliday, *Dismembering the Body Politic: Partisan Politics in England's Towns, 1650–1730* (Cambridge, 1998); Catherine F. Patterson, *Urban Patronage in Early Modern England: Corporate Boroughs, the Landed Elite, and the Crown, 1580–1640* (Stanford, 1999); and Patterson, "Quo Warranto and Borough Corporations in Early Stuart England: Royal Prerogative and Local Privileges in the Central Courts," *English Historical Review* 120 (2005): 879–906.

Charles Francis Adams Jr. believed that Morton's story demanded a wide audience. Picking up a family tradition that dated at least as far back as his great-grandfather John, his intellectual relationship with Morton began with a long article on the maypole in the *Atlantic,* which ran in two parts in May and June 1877. He followed with his edition of *New English Canaan* in 1883 and his verbal portrait of Morton in *Three Episodes of Massachusetts History* in 1892. Morton, he understood, knew something that was almost impossible to measure from a distance of over 250 years—that the English settlement of New England rested on the actions of those who were there, many of whom battled with each other for the future direction of this new homeland, rather than on plans hatched across the Atlantic. Now, with the four hundredth anniversary of the English arrival at New Plymouth looming on the horizon, the time seems right to invest that story with the sense of contingency it deserves. The dissenters bemoaned their loss of ideological purity and their declension from an inspiring goal. Eventually their heirs realized that they had to accept the corruptions of daily life. Morton, for his part, saw a different kind of tragedy—an inability for all involved to escape from the cataclysm enfolding the Ninnimissinuok. New England could have been a promised land, he believed, but it was not to be because of the victory of his enemies.

Notes

Adams, *NEC*	Thomas Morton, *New English Canaan*, ed. Charles Francis Adams Jr. (Boston: Prince Society, 1883).
CO	Colonial Office Papers, the National Archives, Kew, U.K.
HEH	Henry E. Huntington Library, San Marino, Calif.
MHS	Massachusetts Historical Society
NEC	Thomas Morton, *New English Canaan* (Amsterdam, 1637)
Proc MHS	*Proceedings of the Massachusetts Historical Society*
TNA	The National Archives, formerly the Public Record Office, Kew, U.K.
WMQ	*William and Mary Quarterly*

PROLOGUE

1. John Adams to Thomas Jefferson, October 12, 1812, and July 15, 1813, Adams Family Papers, MHS. The letters between them relating to Morton and early New England history, with the exception of one that Adams began but never finished, can be found in *The Adams-Jefferson Letters: The Complete Correspondence between Thomas Jefferson and Abigail and John Adams*, 2 vols., ed. Lester J. Cappon (Williamsburg and Chapel

Hill, 1959), 2:311–25; and *The Papers of Thomas Jefferson: Retirement Series*, 14 vols. to date, ed. J. Jefferson Looney (Princeton, 2004–), 5:386–90, 508–13, 583–85, 595–96, and 6:137–39, 145–46.

2. Adams to Jefferson, October 12, 1812.

3. For Washington's recommendation, see George Washington to John Adams, February 20, 1797, in Founders Online (founders.archives. gov; accessed July 23, 2018, from the original at the MHS [Adams Family Papers, reel 383]); and Washington to John Quincy Adams, June 25, 1797, in *Papers of George Washington: Retirement Series*, 3 vols. to date, ed. Dorothy Twohig et al. (Charlottesville, 1998–), 1:210–11. For John Quincy receiving news of his new assignment, see John Quincy Adams, *Diaries*, 2 vols., ed. David Waldstreicher (New York, 2017), 1:77–78. For the younger Adams's time in Prussia, see *Memoirs of John Quincy Adams*, 12 vols., ed. Charles Francis Adams (Philadelphia, 1874–77), 1:195–247. For his literary ambitions, see Paul C. Nagel, *John Quincy Adams: A Public Life, a Private Life* (New York, 1997), 118–23; and James Traub, *John Quincy Adams: Militant Spirit* (New York, 2016), 103–4.

4. Adams to Jefferson, October 12, 1812.

5. Adams to Jefferson, October 12, 1812. For Adams's understanding of the name, see Scraps of the History of Mount Wollaston with Notes, October 19 and October 27, 1802, sheet 4, MHS.

6. Adams to Jefferson, October 12, 1812. The property had come into the possession of Adams from his wife Abigail's grandfather John Quincy; see Nagel, *John Quincy Adams*, 6.

7. Jefferson to Adams, December 28, 1812. Wollaston, who had arrived in Plymouth in 1624, never reached Virginia because he turned for England instead of sailing to the Chesapeake, though the details came to light only through examination of the records of the High Court of Admiralty; see H. Hobart Holly, "Wollaston of Mount Wollaston," *American Neptune* 37 (1977): 5–25. Jefferson also informed Adams that the copy that John Quincy Adams had picked up in Berlin was the second edition of *New English Canaan*, an erroneous opinion but one supported by a catalog Jefferson possessed of the library of the Society for the Propagation of the Gospel in Foreign Parts. Jefferson's claim that the 1637 copy in Adams's possession was a second edition came from [White Kennett], *Bibliotecæ Americanæ Primordia: An Attempt towards Laying the Foundation of an American Library . . . Humbly Given to the Society for the*

Propagation of the Gospel in Foreign Parts (London, 1713), 77 (alleged 1632 edition), 82 (1637 edition).

8. Adams to Jefferson, January 26, 1813; Jefferson to Adams, May 27, 1813; Adams to Jefferson, May 29, 1813 (quotation); translation of Eclogue IV:1 from *Virgil: Eclogues, Georgics, Aeneid 1–6*, trans. W. R. Fairclough (Cambridge, Mass., 1916). The unsent letter, dated February 2, 1813, in the Adams Family Papers at MHS, bears no recipient's name but continued the thread that Adams had initiated in his prior letters.

9. Adams turned to other historians of the region to fill in yet other details of the earliest days of Mount Wollaston, which he identified as being on the property of one John Quincy who had died in 1767, not his own son but a relative of his wife Abigail, who had been "one of the council for the Province." See Adams, Scraps of the History of Mount Wollaston, sheet 1.

10. Adams, Scraps of the History, sheets 3, 11.

11. Adams, Scraps of the History, sheet 7.

12. Adams, Scraps of the History, sheet 7.

13. Adams, Scraps of the History, sheet 19.

14. Bernard Bailyn, "Butterfield's Adams: Notes for a Sketch," *WMQ*, 3rd ser., 19 (1962): 238–56, quotation at 244.

15. Diary of Charles Francis Adams, vol. 1, entry for September 6, 1824, in MHS Digital Edition: Adams Papers (accessed July 6, 2017).

16. *Memoirs of John Quincy Adams*, 8:155–56.

17. Edward Arber, ed., *A Transcript of the Registers of the Company of Stationers of London*, 5 vols. (Birmingham, 1875–77, 1894), 4:283; S.P. 16/382/17, TNA; see *Calendar of State Papers, Domestic Series, Charles I, 1637–1638* (London, 1869), 257, for a note about the seizure of Morton's book.

18. When Charles Francis Adams Jr. edited *New English Canaan* in the late nineteenth century, he noted that there was a copy of the book in the library of the Society for the Propagation of the Gospel in Foreign Parts in London on which someone had written (in pen) that it had been published in 1632, a detail picked up in Justin Winsor, *Narrative and Critical History of America*, 8 vols. (Boston, 1884–89), 3:348. That copy is now in the possession of the British Library. There are four copies in that collection, with one bearing that inked date on the title page. Winsor, the librarian of Harvard College and a renowned bibliophile, was

skeptical about what he had seen. See J[ustin] W[insor], "Massachusetts Bay, 1620–1630," and "Massachusetts Bay, 1630, et seq.," *Harvard College Library Bulletin* 1 (1879): supplement 9:195–96 and supplement 10:244–45. Adams concluded that any mention of a copy being published in England was erroneous; the only printing besides that from Amsterdam in 1637 was by the historian and editor Peter Force, who lacked a complete title page when he published Morton's text in his collection of tracts in the 1830s. See Adams, *NEC*, 99–104. The best study of the book's checkered printing history is Paul R. Sternberg, "The Publication of Thomas Morton's *New English Canaan* Reconsidered," *Papers of the Bibliographic Society of America* 80 (1986): 369–74. See also *"New English Canaan" by Thomas Morton of "Merrymount": Text and Notes*, ed. Jack Dempsey (Scituate, Mass., 2000), xxviii–xxxi; and Matt Cohen, *The Networked Wilderness: Communicating in Early New England* (Minneapolis, 2010), 50. The New Haven bookseller William Reese, who had the book for sale, noted that only two copies had come to auction over the past generation. See *America Before 1700*, Wm. Reese Co. catalog 271 (New Haven, n.d.), item 61. There are at least two surviving manuscript copies produced by individuals who saw the value in the text in an age when no printer issued a new edition; see B. F. DeCosta, "Morton's *New English Canaan*," *New-England Historical and Genealogical Register* 48 (1894): 329–31. For Adams's copy, see the note for the entry in the Diary of Charles Francis Adams for September 6, 1824; that copy is now in the collection of the Boston Athenaeum. "The old Accounts of the first Settlement of the Colonies, are very Curious," Benjamin Franklin had written to Peter Collinson when *New English Canaan* and other books arrived, "and very acceptable to the Library Company, who direct me to return their hearty Thanks for your Kindness in sparing them to the Library." Franklin to Collinson, June 26, 1755, in Leonard Labaree et al., eds., *The Papers of Benjamin Franklin*, 43 vols. to date (New Haven, 1959–), 6:84n. An earlier list of this shipment in Franklin's hand indicates the books arrived at the Library on May 24, 1755.

19. There remains some ambiguity about the year that Morton returned, which was either 1624 or 1625, but most evidence suggests he arrived in 1624.

20. For the context see Bernard Bailyn, *The Barbarous Years—The*

Peopling of British North America: The Conflict of Civilizations, 1600–1675
(New York, 2012), 321–64, esp. 345–47.

21. The extent of Winthrop's service was evident to the earliest
historians of New England; see [Edward Johnson], *A History of New-
England. From the English Planting in the Yeere 1628 untill the Yeere 1652*
(London, 1654), 48. Johnson's work is known today for the running head
that appears in this first edition: "Wonder-Working Providence of Sions
Saviour, in New England." If not otherwise specified, biographical details of major figures in this book come from *American National Biography* and the *Oxford Dictionary of National Biography*.

22. Roth, *The Dying Animal* (New York, 2001), 60.

CHAPTER I. HOMELANDS

1. For one explanation of Morton's obscure origins, see Jack Dempsey, *Thomas Morton of "Merrymount": The Life and Renaissance of an Early
American Poet* (Stoneham, Mass., 2000), 5–9. The absence of documen-
tation has led to varied estimates for his likely birth; the literary critics
Leslie A. Fiedler and Arthur Zieger claimed that he was born in London circa 1590 and could have been Catholic or Anglican; see Fiedler
and Zieger, eds., *O Brave New World: American Literature from 1600 to
1840* (New York, 1968), 678. Another biographer has estimated that he
was likely born in 1579 or 1580; see Donald F. Connors, *Thomas Morton*
(New York, 1969), 17.

2. See David Harris Sacks, *The Widening Gate: Bristol and the Atlantic
Economy, 1450–1700* (Berkeley, 1991); Peter E. Pope, *Fish into Wine: The
Newfoundland Plantation in the Seventeenth Century* (Chapel Hill, 2004).

3. The elder Hakluyt's chambers and geographic knowledge were
detailed by his younger cousin in Hakluyt, *The Principall Navigations and
Voiages of the English Nation* (London, 1589), 2ʳ. Bradford claimed that
Morton was "a kind of pettifogger of Furnival's Inn," presumably to suggest that he dealt with less important legal affairs; see Bradford, *Of Plymouth Plantation*, ed. Samuel Eliot Morison (New York, 1952), 205. John
Adams, in his unpublished history of Quincy, recognized Bradford's
effort to delegitimize Morton's legal work when the Pilgrim referred to
his nemesis as a "pettifogger"; see Adams, Scraps of the History, sheet 1.

4. The label Ninnimissinuok includes multiple groups, including

the Nipmuck, Wampanoag, Narragansett, and Massachusett, who had extensive linguistic, economic, political, familial, and social ties. Roger Williams, in his *Key to the Language of America* (first published in 1643), argued that before the arrival of Europeans the local Natives referred to themselves as *"Nínnuock, Ninnimissinnûwock, Eniskee-tompaûwog,* which signifies *Men, Folke,* or *People."* See Roger Williams, *A Key into the Language of America; or, An Help to the Language of the Natives in That Part of* AMERICA, *called* NEW-ENGLAND (London, 1643), A3ᵛ; and Kathleen J. Bragdon, *Native People of Southern New England* (Norman, Okla., 1996), xi–xiii.

5. For the larger context, see Margaret M. Bruchac, "Earthshapers and Placemakers: Algonkian Indian Stories and the Landscape," in Claire Smith and H. Martin Wobst, eds., *Indigenous Archaeologies: Decolonizing Theory and Practice* (London, 2005), 56–80.

6. All names here can be found in William Bright, *Native American Placenames of the United States* (Norman, Okla., 2004); see also J. Hammond Trumbull, *Indian Names of Places, etc. in and on the Borders of Connecticut* (Hartford, 1881); Trumbull, *The Composition of Indian Geographical Names: Illustrated from the Algonkin Languages* (Hartford, 1870; repr., New York, 2015).

7. Williams, *Key into the Language of America,* 114–18.

8. Winslow, *Good Newes from New England: A True Relation of Things Very Remarkable at the Plantation of Plimoth in New England* (London, 1624), 52–53. See also William S. Simmons, *Spirit of the New England Tribes: Indian History and Folklore* (Hanover, N.H., 1986), 39.

9. Williams, *Key into the Language of America,* 127.

10. William Baylies, "Description of Gay Head, 1786," *Memoirs of the American Academy of Arts and Sciences* 2 (1793): 150–55; Simmons, *Spirit of the New England Tribes,* 174–75; see also Mabel Frances Knight, "Wampanoag Indian Tales," *Journal of American Folklore* 38 (1925): 134–35.

11. See Jonathan K. Patton, "Considering the Wet Homelands of Indigenous Massachusetts," *Journal of Social Archaeology* 14 (2014): 87–111, esp. 90–91 (directions) and 101–3 (canoes). Widespread participation of Ninnimissinuok in whaling, which required craft more substantial than a dugout canoe, apparently developed only at the end of

the seventeenth century; see Daniel Vickers, "The First Whalemen of Nantucket," *WMQ*, 3rd ser., 40 (1983): 560–83.

12. Bragdon, *Native People of Southern New England*, 89 (agriculture), 191–92 (wetlands); Winslow, *Good Newes from New England*, 57.

13. *NEC*, 18. This statement that the Natives drew on Greek and Latin aroused the ire of J. H. Trumbull, a linguist Adams had consulted when preparing his edition of the text; see Adams, *NEC*, 123n2.

14. *NEC*, 18–19. As Roger Williams wrote, "By occasion of their frequent lying in the Fields and Woods, they much observe the Starres, and their very children can give Names to many of them": Williams, *Key into the Language of America*, 79–80, quotation at 80.

15. *NEC*, 19–22; Adams, *NEC*, 129n.

16. *NEC*, 24–26.

17. *NEC*, 26.

18. *NEC*, 54.

19. See William Cronon, *Changes in the Land: Indians, Colonists, and the Ecology of New England* (New York, 1983), 19–33; Carolyn Merchant, *Ecological Revolutions: Nature, Gender, and Science in New England*, 2nd ed. (Chapel Hill, 2010), 74–85; Brian Donahue, *The Great Meadow: Farmers and the Land in Colonial Concord* (New Haven, 2007), 35–53; Lucianne Lavin, *Connecticut's Indigenous Peoples: What Archaeology, History, and Oral Traditions Teach Us about Their Communities and Cultures* (New Haven, 2013), 192–269.

20. The European practice of describing the look of indigenous Americans originated with Columbus, who then set the pattern for other ethnographic depictions of the dress, gender roles, and daily practices of peoples across the Western Hemisphere; see Margaret Hodgen, *Early Anthropology in the Sixteenth and Seventeenth Centuries* (Philadelphia, 1964); Stuart B. Schwartz, ed., *Implicit Understanding: Observing, Reporting, and Reflecting on the Encounters between Europeans and Other Peoples in the Early Modern Era* (Cambridge, 1994); Karen Ordahl Kupperman, *Indians and English: Facing Off in Early America* (Ithaca, 2000); and Joyce Chaplin, *Subject Matter: Technology, the Body, and Science on the Anglo-American Frontier, 1500–1676* (Cambridge, Mass., 2001).

21. *NEC*, 28–30.

22. *NEC*, 30–32.

23. *NEC*, 47-48. The nineteenth-century historian Francis Parkman, one of Adams's experts, could not imagine what authority Morton had in mind, nor did he believe that indigenous Canadians (the alleged source of the story) had ever encountered an Iberian; see Adams, *NEC*, 166n1.

24. *NEC*, 42-43, quotation at 43.

25. *NEC*, 33 (Natives as role models), 38-40 (reputation).

26. *NEC*, 24.

27. *NEC*, 34-36. Williams defined the term as "priest"; see his *Key into the Language of America*, 119. The figure of the juggler or conjuror, already known to the English through the work of Thomas Harriot, notably the illustrated edition of *A Briefe and True Report of the New Found Land of Virginia* (Frankfurt-am-Main, 1590), B3 (should be B2ᵛ but misnumbered in the original), remained a fixture in European descriptions of eastern North America; see Peter C. Mancall, "Illness and Death among Americans in Bernard Picart's *Cérémonies et Coutumes Religieuses*," in Lynn Hunt, et al., eds., *Bernard Picart and the First Global Vision of Religion* (Los Angeles, 2010), 271-87.

28. *NEC*, 40-41.

29. *NEC*, 41-42; Andrew Lipman, *The Saltwater Frontier: Indians and the Contest for the American Coast* (New Haven, 2015), 54-124. One good that Morton claimed interior groups traded were "curious silver reles," but not even Charles Francis Adams Jr., with his team of experts, could figure out what this meant and so he attributed it to a printer's error; see Adams, *NEC*, 159n2.

30. *NEC*, 27-28. In *New England's Prospect* Wood had noted that "it is natural to all mortals to worship something, so do these people, but exactly to describe to whom their worship is chiefly bent is very difficult." See Wood, *New England's Prospect*, ed. Alden Vaughan (Amherst, Mass., 1977), 100-102, quotation at 100.

31. *NEC*, 49-50; Williams, *Key into the Language of America*, 116; see also Adams, *NEC*, 167n2.

32. *NEC*, 51-52.

33. *NEC*, 50.

34. Pope, *Fish into Wine*, 15-20.

35. See Alden T. Vaughan, *Transatlantic Encounters: American Indians in Britain, 1500-1776* (New York, 2006), 1-20; Peter C. Mancall, "The Raw and the Cold: Five English Sailors in Sixteenth-Century Nunavut,"

WMQ, 3rd ser., 70 (2013): 3-40; Mancall, *Hakluyt's Promise: An Elizabethan's Obsession for an English America* (New Haven, 2007), 102-27.

36. Hakluyt, *Principall Navigations Voiages and Discoveries of the English Nation* (London, 1589), 506-825; Hakluyt, *Principal Navigations Voyages Traffiques & Discoveries of the English Nation*, 3 vols. (London, 1598-1600), vol. 3.

37. Hakluyt remained interested in North America after the turn of the century, and authored a pamphlet to support the struggling Virginia Company in 1609, but he had wider interests as well, including in the southwest Pacific. He passed on his new manuscripts to the minister Samuel Purchas, who incorporated Hakluyt's unpublished papers in an even larger, five-volume collection in 1625. On Hakluyt's later years, see Mancall, *Hakluyt's Promise*, 195-235; for what Purchas got from Hakluyt, among his other sources, see John Parker, "Contents and Sources of Purchas his Pilgrimes," in L. E. Pennington, ed., *The Purchas Handbook*, 2 vols. (London, 1997), 2:464.

38. John Brereton, *A Briefe and True Relation of the Discoverie of the North Part of Virginia* (London, 1602), 12-13 (list of commodities), 7 (fertility of the land), 6 (quickly sprouting plants), 9-10 (copper), 11 (health of the English), 5 (ease of fishing); Wood, *New England's Prospect*, ed. Vaughan, 32-33, quotation at 32.

39. Brereton, *Briefe and True Relation*, 10-11 (appearance of the Natives), 9 (sign language), 6 (tobacco), 11 (conversation). For the ways that Europeans understood how Americans consumed tobacco, see Peter C. Mancall, "Tales Tobacco Told in Sixteenth-Century Europe," *Environmental History* 9 (2004): 648-78.

40. Rosier's report was published as *A True Relation of the Most Prosperous Voyage Made This Present Year, 1605, by Captain George Waymouth, in the Discovery of the Land of Virginia, Where He Discovered, Sixty Miles Up, a Most Excellent River, Together with a Most Fertile Land.* See *Rosier's Narrative of Waymouth's Voyage to the Coast of Maine, in 1605, with Remarks by George Prince* (Bath, Maine, 1860), 4-15, 18, 21-22, 30.

41. *Rosier's Narrative*, 23-24, quotations at 23.

42. *Rosier's Narrative*, 25; Harriot, *Briefe and True Report of the New Found Land of Virginia*, 29.

43. *Rosier's Narrative*, 29 (captives), 24 (quotation).

44. *Voyages of Samuel de Champlain*, 2 vols., trans. Charles Pomeroy

Otis (Boston, 1880), 2:76-77. For the larger context, see David Hackett Fischer, *Champlain's Dream: The European Founding of North America* (New York, 2008), 182-92.

45. See W. Jeffrey Bolster, "Putting the Ocean in Atlantic History: Maritime Communities and Marine Ecology in the Northwest Atlantic, 1500-1800," *American Historical Review* 113 (2008): 19-47.

46. Champlain, *Voyages*, 2:77-79. For the culture of gift giving that Champlain would have known, see Natalie Zemon Davis, *The Gift in Sixteenth-Century France* (Oxford, 2000).

47. Smith, *A Description of New England* (London, 1616), 1-2.

48. Smith, *Description of New England*, 7-10. For what Smith believed was the range of the Massachusetts' settlements, see Philip L. Barbour, ed., *The Complete Works of Captain John Smith (1580-1631)*, 3 vols. (Chapel Hill, 1986), 1:329n.

49. Smith, *Description of New England*, 10-12. Smith claimed that the Dutch had "2 or 3000 Busses, Flat bottomes, Sword pinks, Todes, and such like" (12).

50. Smith, *Description of New England*, 16-17; Mauricio Obregón, ed., *The Barcelona Letter of 1493, the Landfall Controversy, and the Indian Guides* (New York, 1991), 66.

51. Smith, *Description of New England*, 17-18, 40; Mancall, *Hakluyt's Promise*, 128-55; A. L. Beier, *Masterless Men: The Vagrancy Problem in England, 1560-1640* (London, 1985).

52. Smith, *Description of New England*, 26 ("Paradise"), 43-45 ("North parts").

CHAPTER 2. PARTNERS

1. Will of George Miller of Swallowfield, March 4, 1616 (proved March 20, 1616), PROB 11/127, 203-304, TNA. The will is dated 1615 according to the Julian calendar, which did not mark the start of the new year until March 25.

2. The document is EL 6195, 34a^v-36a^r, HEH (this manuscript is bound into EL 6162). For a superb analysis and edition of this rare text, see Steve Hindle, "Hierarchy and Community in the Elizabethan Parish: The Swallowfield Articles of 1596," *Historical Journal* 42 (1999): 835-51.

3. The will does not contain the date of his death, but it does note

that Alice proved his will in London on March 20, sixteen days after he signed it.

4. See Christopher L. Tomlins and Bruce H. Mann, eds., *The Many Legalities of Early America* (Chapel Hill, 2001).

5. Malcolm Gaskill, *Between Two Worlds: How the English Became Americans* (New York, 2014), 64; Nathaniel Philbrick, *"Mayflower": A Story of Courage, Community, and War* (New York, 2006), 24–29.

6. The most detailed accounts of Gorges and his family and their efforts to create their own provinces in New England can be found in Richard A. Preston, *Gorges of Plymouth Fort: A Life of Ferdinando Gorges, Captain of Plymouth Fort, Governor of New England, and Lord of the Province of Maine* (Toronto, 1953); James Phinney Baxter, *Sir Ferdinando Gorges and His Province of Maine*, 2 vols. (Boston, 1890); Henry S. Burrage, *The Beginnings of Colonial Maine, 1602–1658* (Portland, Maine, 1914); and Andrews, *Colonial Period*, 1:320–43, 375–99.

7. *Proc MHS*, 3rd ser., 58 (1924–25):192–93; Certificate of behavior of George Miller the younger of Swallowfield regarding two pews in Swallowfield parish church belonging to Mr Phipps, lord of Sheepridge manor, ms D/EJR/Q1, Berkshire Record Office, Reading. In this period it was common for noblewomen to marry soon after they turned nineteen and gentry, at least in Canterbury (for which there has been sustained analysis), were about twenty-one and three-quarters. See Peter Laslett, *The World We Have Lost: England Before the Industrial Ages*, 3rd ed. (New York, 1984), 82.

8. Morton v. Humphreys, C 3/368/10, TNA; *Proc MHS*, 3rd ser., 58 (1924–25): 165–67.

9. *Proc MHS*, 3rd ser., 58 (1924–25):167–69. On the range of Chancery's actions and its history, see P. Tucker, "The Early History of the Court of Chancery: A Comparative Study," *English Historical Review* 115 (2000): 791–811; and Henry Horwitz and Patrick Polden, "Continuity or Change in the Court of Chancery in the Seventeenth and Eighteenth Centuries?" *Journal of British Studies* 35 (1996): 24–57.

10. *Proc MHS*, 3rd ser., 58 (1924–25): 169–70.

11. *Proc MHS*, 3rd ser., 58 (1924–25): 170.

12. See Edward P. Cheyney, "The Court of Star Chamber," *American Historical Review* 18 (1913): 727–50; Thomas G. Barnes, "Star Chamber Mythology," *American Journal of Legal History* 5 (1961): 1–11.

13. *Proc MHS*, 3rd ser., 58 (1924–25): 171–73.

14. *Proc MHS*, 3rd ser., 58 (1924–25): 173–74.

15. *Proc MHS*, 3rd ser., 58 (1924–25): 175–79.

16. *Proc MHS*, 3rd ser., 58 (1924–25): 180–81.

17. *Proc MHS*, 3rd ser., 58 (1924–25): 181–86.

18. The text lists the payment as "50ii," using a shorthand for 50 libor, or pounds.

19. *Proc MHS*, 3rd ser., 58 (1924–25): 186–88.

20. Charles Francis Adams, *Three Episodes of Massachusetts History*, 2 vols. (Boston, 1896), 1:163–64. The exact date of Morton's departure remains unknown.

21. *Proc MHS*, 3rd ser., 58 (1924–25): 189–91.

22. Spelling of indigenous names varied from one text to another. These Natives were also called Manida and Skidwarres/Skidwares/Skettwarroes; see Alden T. Vaughan, *Transatlantic Encounters: American Indians in Britain, 1500–1776* (New York, 2006), 57–60. As Vaughan noted, the one named Tahanedo went to the house of Sir John Popham, one of Gorges's allies, and Amoret went to John Slany, who was the Newfoundland Company's treasurer; see *Transatlantic Encounters*, 61.

23. The biographical details that follow here come primarily from a long "Memoir" by James Phinney Baxter for the Prince Society, which appeared in his edition of writings by and related to Gorges. See Baxter, *Gorges and His Province of Maine*, 1:1–198, esp. 67–68 (captives), 4 (1066), 14–16 (military experience), 111 (marriage), 44–59 (plot against the queen and regaining his position at Plymouth). For additional details, see C. M. Macinnes, *Ferdinando Gorges and New England* (Bristol, 1965), 2 (knighted by Essex); and John Latimer, *Annals of Bristol in the Seventeenth Century* (Bristol, 1900), 27.

24. The details of his involvement can be found in Baxter, *Gorges and His Province of Maine*, 1:188–96; see also Latimer, *Annals of Bristol in the Seventeenth Century*, 126–27.

25. See Latimer, *Annals of Bristol in the Seventeenth Century*, 27–28.

26. Smith, *Description of New England*, 49–50.

27. Ferdinando Gorges, "A Briefe Narration of the Originall Undertakings of the Advancement of Plantations into the Parts of America," in *America Painted to the Life* (London, 1658), 3. Gorges's history was published posthumously by his grandson (with whom he shared his name).

The text was reprinted with editorial apparatus in Baxter, *Gorges and His Province of Maine*, 2:1-81.

28. *A Briefe Relation of the Discovery and Plantation of New England* (London, 1622), A3ᵛ-[A4ᵛ], quotation at [A4ʳ]. Gorges's name does not appear as the author of the pamphlet, but the dedication is signed "The President and Concell of New-England" when Gorges was its president. Three years later the text appeared again in Samuel Purchas's massive collection, *Purchas His Pilgrimes*, 5 vols. (London, 1625), 4:1827-32.

29. Gorges, "Briefe Narration," 4-5.

30. For details of what happened on that mission, which never reached New England, see the account of John Stoneman, the ship's pilot: "The Voyage of M. Henry Challons Intended for the North Plantation of Virginia, 1606," in *Purchas His Pilgrimes*, 4:1832-37.

31. *A Briefe Relation*, Bᵛ.

32.William Strachey, *The Historie of Travell into Virginia Britania* (1612), ed. Louis B. Wright and Virginia Freund, Publications of the Hakluyt Society, 2nd ser., 103 (London, 1953), 173.

33. Strachey, *Historie of Travell*, 173.

34. *A Briefe Relation*, Bᵛ-B2ʳ.

35. Biard, Relation for 1612, in Reuben Gold Thwaites, ed., *The Jesuit Relations and Allied Documents*, 73 vols. (Cleveland, 1896-1901), 2:45-47. For a discussion of what happened at Sagadahoc, with analysis of Biard's claims, see Alfred A. Cave, "Why Was the Sagadahoc Colony Abandoned? An Evaluation of the Evidence," *New England Quarterly* 68 (1995): 625-40.

36. *A Briefe Relation*, B2ʳ⁻ᵛ; Seymour V. Connor, "Sir Samuel Argall: A Biographical Sketch," *Virginia Magazine of History and Biography* 59 (1951): 162-75, esp. 168-69.

37. Gorges to Cecil, [presumably] February 7, 1608, Hatfield House, quoted in Baxter, *Gorges and His Province of Maine*, 1:84.

38. Letter of the Council of the Virginia Company to Gorges, February 17, 1608, in Corporation Archives of Plymouth, in Baxter, *Gorges and His Province of Maine*, 1:91 ("frozen"), 90.

39. *A Briefe Relation*, B2ᵛ-B3ʳ. The English could not have known it at the time, but these years were likely the coldest of the seventeenth century, with ice choking previously navigable sea lanes across the

North Atlantic; see Sam White, *A Cold Welcome: The Little Ice Age and Europe's Encounter with North America* (Cambridge, Mass., 2017), 3-4.

40. Gorges, "Briefe Narration," 12.

41. *A Briefe Relation*, B3^r.

42. Smith, *The Generall History of Virginia, the Somer Iles, and New England* (1624) in Barbour, ed., *Complete Works of Captain John Smith*, 2:403.

43. Gorges, "Briefe Narration," 13-15. Gorges identified the captain as Henry Harley, but more recent scholars have corrected the record. See Baxter, *Gorges and His Province of Maine*, 2:20n (argues for Harley). Vaughan, *Transatlantic Encounters*, 65; and Barbour, ed., *Complete Works of Captain John Smith*, 1:293 both identify him as Harlow.

44. See J. E. C. Hill, "Puritans and 'The Dark Corners of the Land,'" *Trans. Royal Historical Society* 13 (1963): 77-102.

45. Gorges, "Briefe Narration," 15; Vaughan, *Transatlantic Encounters*, 65-67.

46. Gorges, "Briefe Narration," 4, 15-16.

47. *A Briefe Relation*, B3^r. For the range of Hunt's efforts, see Wendy Warren, *New England Bound: Slavery and Colonization in Early America* (New York, 2016), 3-6.

48. *A Briefe Relation*, B3^v; see also Vaughan, *Transatlantic Encounters*, 57-58.

49. In the early decades of the nineteenth century the Pequot author William Apess, who had published the first indigenous autobiography in the United States in 1829, referred to Hunt's activities in a pamphlet he published commemorating the death of Metacom (known to the English as King Philip), who had been killed in the mid-1670s. Apess saw the history of seventeenth-century New England as a series of crimes committed by the English. Among them was Hunt's capture of thirty natives. "This inhuman act of the whites," Apess commented, "caused the Indians to be jealous forever afterward." "How inhuman it was in those wretches," he continued, "to come into a country where nature shone in beauty, spreading her wings over the vast continent," and claim that they had the best intentions in mind for the continent's indigenous peoples. "How they could go to work to enslave a free people and call it religion," he fumed, "is beyond the power of my imagination and outstrips the revelation of God's word." William Apess, "Eulogy

on King Philip, as Pronounced at the Odeon, in Federal Street, Boston" (1836), in *On Our Own Ground: The Complete Writings of William Apess, a Pequot*, ed. Barry O'Connell (Amherst, Mass., 1992), 279. In the text Apess misidentified Hunt as Henry Harly, but from the context it is evident he meant Hunt.

50. *A Briefe Relation*, C2ᵛ-C3ʳ. For Epenow's involvement, see Emmanuel Altham to Sir Edward Altham, September 1623, in Sydney V. James Jr., ed., *Three Visitors to Early Plymouth*, 2nd ed. (Bedford, Mass., 1997), 27n. On the causes of death in early Jamestown, see Carville Earle, "Environment, Disease, and Mortality in Early Virginia," in Thad W. Tate and David L. Ammerman, eds., *The Chesapeake in the Seventeenth Century: Essays on Anglo-American Society* (Chapel Hill, 1979), 96-125; and Karen Ordahl Kupperman, "Apathy and Death in Early Jamestown," *Journal of American History* 66 (1979): 24-40.

51. *A Briefe Report*, Dʳ-[D4ʳ], Eᵛ-E2ʳ, quotations at Dʳ ("disasters"), Dᵛ (Rome, etc.), [D4ʳ] (whales), D2ᵛ (Natives), Eᵛ-E2ʳ. For the ways that Europeans understood weather and temperature in this age, see Karen Ordahl Kupperman, "The Puzzle of the American Climate in the Early Colonial Period," *American Historical Review* 87 (1982): 1269-89.

52. See George Peckham, "A True Reporte of the Late Discoveries and Possession . . . of the Newfound Landes . . . by . . . Sir Humphrey Gilbert," in David B. Quinn and Alison O. Quinn, eds., *New American World*, 5 vols. (New York, 1979), 3:34-60. The text dates from 1583, the year Gilbert died at sea while returning from Newfoundland.

53. "Warrant to Prepare a Patent for the Northern Company of Virginia," from Trade Papers, State Paper Office, 5:55, reprinted in John Poor, *A Vindication of the Claims of Sir Ferdinando Gorges as the Father of English Colonization in America* (New York, 1862), 108-9.

54. The patent, dated November 3, 1620, is in CO 5/902, 1-28; see esp. 2 (Gorges's role), 3 (name of the proposed colony), and 26 (conversion). See also Charles E. Clark, *The Eastern Frontier: The Settlement of Northern New England, 1610-1763* (New York, 1970), 16-17; and Charles M. Andrews, *The Colonial Period of American History*, 4 vols. (New Haven, 1934), 1:320-26. The expansive claim was even broader than that understood by Smith, who thought that New England should run from 41 to 45 degrees north latitude; see Smith, "Letter to Francis Bacon," in Barbour, ed., *Complete Works of Captain John Smith*, 1:378.

55. "A Letr to Sr Thomas Coventrie," November 3, [1620], in Poor, *Vindication*, 109–18.

56. CO 1/1, no. 47, March 3, 1620; Latimer, *Annals of Bristol in the Seventeenth Century*, 73.

57. *Acts of the Privy Council of England* 38 (1932): 51.

58. "Letr to Thomas Coventrie," 110.

59. Retrospective clinical diagnosis is often imprecise, in part because of the ways that observers recorded symptoms. For this epidemic, see John S. Marr and John T. Cathey, "New Hypothesis for Cause of Epidemic among Native Americans, New England, 1616–1619," *Emerging Infectious Diseases* 16 (2010): 281–86. For mortuary practices that might have facilitated transmission, see James W. Bradley, "European Contact and the Continuity of Mortuary Ceremonialism on Cape Cod: An Update from the Corn Hill Site, Truro, MA," *Archaeology of Eastern North America* 26 (1998): 189–99.

60. Historians estimate that the bubonic plague that arced across Europe from 1347 to 1349 likely killed about one-third of the population, though the death rate could have climbed to two-thirds in regions where food shortages, perhaps produced by an inability to bring in crops or tend livestock, followed pestilence. See Alfred W. Crosby, *Ecological Imperialism: The Biological Expansion of Europe, 900–1900* (Cambridge, 1986), 52–53. Such death rates reshaped the culture and society of the survivors, often in unexpected ways, as the experience of plague in fourteenth-century Europe demonstrated; see David W. Herlihy, *The Black Death and the Transformation of the West* (Cambridge, Mass., 1997).

61. On the relationship between malnutrition and mortality in early America, see David S. Jones, "Virgin Soils Reconsidered," *WMQ*, 3rd ser., 60 (2003): 703–42.

62. Smith, *New Englands Trials*, 2nd ed. (London, 1622), [B4^r]. The modern place-names are in Barbour, ed., *Complete Works of Captain John Smith*, 1:428n. Though Smith seems to have learned of the epidemic by 1619, he did not mention it in the first edition of *New Englands Trials*, which appeared in 1620.

63. "Cushman's Discourse," in John Masefield, ed., *Chronicles of the Pilgrim Fathers* (London, 1910), 229–30.

64. Emmanuel Altham to Sir Edward Altham, September, 1623, 29.

65. *NEC*, 23.

66. For Gorges's interest in the region, see Robert E. Moody, ed., *The Letters of Thomas Gorges, Deputy Governor of the Province of Maine, 1640–1643* (Portland, Maine, 1978). The younger Gorges mentioned Morton only once in his correspondence; see Thomas Gorges to Sir Ferdinando Gorges, [September? 1641] (55).

67. *A Briefe Relation*, sig, B^r.

68. See Edward Waterhouse, *Declaration of the State of the Colony and Affaires in Virginia. With a Relation of the Barbarous Massacre* (London, 1622); Bailyn, *Barbarous Years*, 100–106; James Horn, *A Land as God Made It: Jamestown and the Birth of America* (New York, 2005), 255–78.

69. On one notable storm and its consequences, see Louis B. Wright, *A Voyage to Virginia in 1609*, 2nd ed. (Charlottesville, 2013); Lorri Glover and Daniel B. Smith, *The Shipwreck that Saved Jamestown: The Sea Venture and the Birth of America* (New York, 2008).

70. Gorges, "Briefe Narration," 11.

CHAPTER 3. EXILES

1. Bradford noted that Wollaston had appeared in 1624 or 1625. Charles Francis Adams Jr. stated that there was no evidence he had appeared in the region before 1625. Subsequent research indicates that Wollaston had arrived there by 1624, suggesting that Morton was there by then as well. See Holly, "Wollaston of Mount Wollaston," 21–25, and Gaskill, *Between Two Worlds*, 86. For Adams, see his edition of *New English Canaan*, 1–4.

2. See Cohen, *The Networked Wilderness;* and Katherine Grandjean, *American Passage: The Communications Frontier in Early New England* (Cambridge, Mass., 2015).

3. William Bradford, *A Relation or Journall of the Beginning and Proceedings of the English Plantation Setled at Plimoth in New England* (London, 1622), [1]; George D. Langdon Jr. *Pilgrim Colony: A History of New Plymouth, 1620–1691* (New Haven, 1966), 12–14.

4. Bradford, *Relation or Journall*, 3; Bradford, *Of Plymouth Plantation*, 42n, 86.

5. See Michael P. Winship, *Godly Republicanism: Puritans, Pilgrims, and a City on a Hill* (Cambridge, Mass., 2012), esp. 60–64 (with the quotation at 63); and Edmund S. Morgan, *Visible Saints: The History of a Puritan Idea* (1963; repr., Ithaca, 1965), 17–32.

6. On the migration, see Virginia DeJohn Anderson, *New England's Generation: The Great Migration and the Formation of Society and Culture in the Seventeenth Century* (Cambridge, 1991); Bernard Bailyn, *The Peopling of British North America: An Introduction* (New York, 1986), 24-25; Bailyn, *Barbarous Years*, 365-78; and Nicholas Canny, "English Migration into and across the Atlantic during the Seventeenth and Eighteenth Centuries," in Canny, ed., *Europeans on the Move: Studies on European Migration, 1500-1800* (Oxford, 1994), 64. For the number of the Leiden church, see Philbrick, *Mayflower*, 21; for the number in Plymouth by 1628, see Michael Zuckerman, "Pilgrims in the Wilderness: Community, Modernity, and the Maypole at Merry Mount," *New England Quarterly* 50 (1977): 255; for the English and Scots dissenters in Leiden, see Keith L. Sprunger, "Other Pilgrims in Leiden: Hugh Goodyear and the English Reformed Church," *Church History* 41 (1972): 46-60.

7. Bradford, *Of Plymouth Plantation*, 58.

8. Bradford, *Of Plymouth Plantation*, 61-62.

9. Bradford, *Of Plymouth Plantation*, 62.

10. Bradford, *Of Plymouth Plantation*, 87.

11. Those verses from the Geneva Bible, the version the Pilgrims likely used: "Then Moses went from the plain of Moab up into Mount Nebo unto the top of Pisgah that is over against Jericho: and the Lord showed him all the land of Gilead, unto Dan, / And all Naphtali and the land of Ephraim and Manasseh, and all the land of Judah, until the utmost sea: / And the South, and the plain of the valley of Jericho, the city of palm trees, unto Zoar. / And the Lord said unto him, This is the land which I sware unto Abraham, to Isaac and Jacob, saying, I will give it unto thy seed: I have caused thee to see it with thine eyes, but thou shalt not go over thither. / So Moses the servant of the Lord died there in the land of Moab, according to the word of the Lord."

12. Bradford, *Of Plymouth Plantation*, 62.

13. Bradford, *Of Plymouth Plantation*, 62-63. The full verse in the Geneva Bible reads: "Praise the Lord, because he is good: for his mercy endureth forever. / Let them which have been redeemed of the Lord, show how he hath delivered them from the hand of the oppressor. / And gathered them out of the lands, from the East and from the West, from the North and from the South. / When they wandered in the desert and

wilderness out of the way, and found no city to dwell in, / Both hungry and thirsty, their soul fainted in them. / Then they cried unto the Lord in their trouble, and he delivered them from their distress, / And led them forth by the right way, that they might go to a city of habitation. / Let them therefore confess before the Lord his loving kindness, and his wonderful works before the sons of men."

14. On the conditions that the migrants found, see Cronon, *Changes in the Land*, 19–33.

15. Bradford, *Of Plymouth Plantation*, 111; John Pory to the Earl of Southampton, January 13, 1622/1623 and later, and Emmanuel Altham to Sir Edward Altham, September 1623, in James, *Three Visitors to Early Plymouth*, 11, 24. For those early tensions, see Phineas Pratt, *A Declaration of the Affairs of the English People That First Inhabited New England*, ed. Richard Frothingham Jr. (Boston, 1858). Pratt offered a detailed retrospective history of the early years of Plymouth in a manuscript he wrote in 1662, which Increase Mather drew from in 1677.

16. Mark A. Peterson, "The Plymouth Church and the Evolution of Puritan Religious Culture," *New England Quarterly* 66 (1993): 570–93.

17. Langdon, *Pilgrim Colony*, 2, 8–9, 16–17. The modern city of Plymouth, built on the foundations from the *Mayflower* migrants and their followers, is at 41.52 degrees north latitude, according to the United States Geological Survey.

18. Winship, *Godly Republicanism*, 119–23; Langdon, *Pilgrim Colony*, 17–20.

19. Bradford, *Of Plymouth Plantation*, 133; Winship, *Godly Republicanism*, 121.

20. Bradford, *Of Plymouth Plantation*, 116.

21. CO 1/1, March 3, 1620.

22. *Records of the Council for New England* (Cambridge, Mass., 1867), 59–60, 63.

23. *Records of the Council for New England*, 67, 73.

24. *Records of the Council for New England*, 73–75.

25. *Records of the Council for New England*, 76–78.

26. CO 1/2, no. 14, December 30, 1622.

27. *Records of the Council for New England*, 79 (migrants and fees), 85 (apprentices), 89 (Lord Gorges's ship), 96.

28. Bradford, *Of Plymouth Plantation*, 135; Gorges, "Briefe Narration," 51–54; see also "Records of the Council for New England," *Proceedings of the American Antiquarian Society* (1857): 59.

29. Bradford, *Of Plymouth Plantation*, 137–38; see also Andrews, *Colonial Period*, 1:338–43; and Burrage, *Beginnings of Colonial Maine*, 156–57.

30. Bradford, *Of Plymouth Plantation*, 142–44. On the decline of wetlands and the long-term impact, see Cronon, *Changes in the Land*, 122–26. On the health of New England livestock, see Virginia DeJohn Anderson, *Creatures of Empire: How Domestic Animals Transformed Early America* (New York, 2006), 141–52.

31. Bradford, *Of Plymouth Plantation*, 147–49. The scriptural references are to Psalms 10:10 and Jeremiah 41:6.

32. Bradford, *Of Plymouth Plantation*, 149.

33. Bradford, *Of Plymouth Plantation*, 150–51.

34. Bradford did not provide the date of the trial, but noted that Lyford wrote a letter on August 22, 1624, "a month or two" after its conclusion; see Bradford, *Of Plymouth Plantation*, 158–59, quotation at 158.

35. Bradford, *Of Plymouth Plantation*, 151–53.

36. Bradford, *Of Plymouth Plantation*, 157–58.

37. After the court's sentence Lyford, having been discovered to be a serial adulterer by his wife, moved to Virginia, where he took up a ministerial post at Martin's Hundred. Oldham, for his part, after trying to return to the Plymouth area, also went to Virginia before heading back north, where a dispute led to his death at the hands of Algonquians, perhaps Pequots since Bradford claimed this was one of the causes of the war of 1637. See Bradford, *Of Plymouth Plantation*, 158–69, 169n, quotation at 159; "Minutes of the Council and General Court, 1622–1629," *Virginia Magazine of History and Biography* 31 (1923): 214; Eric Klingelhofer and William Henry, "Excavations at Martin's Hundred Church, James City County, Virginia: Techniques for Testing a 17th Century Church Site," *Historical Archaeology* 19 (1985): 98; Ivor Noël Hume, *Martin's Hundred* (Charlottesville, 1991), 64–65. The best summary of the relations between the Pilgrims and Oldham and Lyford can be found in Winship, *Godly Republicanism*, 122–33.

38. Bradford, *Of Plymouth Plantation*, 37n., 170–72.

39. Bradford, *Of Plymouth Plantation*, 177–78, quotation at 178. As

Bradford wrote in his first history, the colonists went to visit the Massachusetts "partly to make Peace with them, and partly to procure their trucke." Bradford, *Relation or Journall*, 57.

40. Bradford, *Of Plymouth Plantation*, 194.

41. Bradford, *Of Plymouth Plantation*, 194-96.

42. Bradford, *Of Plymouth Plantation*, 197-202; "Plymouth Company Accounts" for 1628, signed by Sherley, in *Massachusetts Historical Society Collections* 1 (1825): 199-201.

43. On the merchants' collection of wampum, see Paul Otto, "'This Is That Which . . . They Call Wampum': Europeans Coming to Terms with Native Shell Beads," *Early American Studies* 15 (2017): 1-36. See also Marc Shell, *Wampum and the Origins of American Money* (Urbana, Ill., 2013). On the far-reaching impact of colonizers recognizing the utility of wampum, see Neal Salisbury, *Manitou and Providence: Indians, Europeans, and the Making of New England, 1500-1643* (New York, 1982), 148-52; and Christopher L. Miller and George R. Hamell, "A New Perspective on Indian-White Contact: Cultural Symbols and Colonial Trade," *Journal of American History* 73 (1986): 311-28.

44. Bradford, *Of Plymouth Plantation*, 202-4, quotations at 203.

45. Bradford, *Of Plymouth Plantation*, 205.

46. Bradford, *Of Plymouth Plantation*, 204-6, quotation at 205. The song verses are in *NEC*, 133-35. For the height of the pole and the renaming, see Adams, *Three Episodes*, 1:175-77; and Adams, *NEC*, 277.

47. Emma Griffin, *England's Revelry: A History of Popular Sports and Pastimes, 1660-1830* (Oxford, 2005), 26.

48. Frederick J. Furnivall, ed., *Phillip Stubbes's Anatomy of the Abuses of England in Shakspere's Youth, ad. 1583* (London, 1877-79), 146-48.

49. Furnivall, *Anatomy of Abuses*, 149-50; L. A. Govett, *The King's Book of Sports* (London, 1890), 52-54.

50. Bradford, *Of Plymouth Plantation*, 206-7, quotation at 207. On the accuracy of guns of this era, see Chaplin, *Subject Matter*, 80-81.

51. *Governor William Bradford's Letter Book* (Bedford, Mass., 2001), 41.

52. King James I, responding to reports of the sale of firearms to Natives in New England, banned what he called "disorderly trading" there in 1622, but the earliest law regulating Native use of guns in Plym-

outh took effect in 1644 when the colony fined any colonist who repaired "any guns or armes for the Indians," suggesting that at least some already possessed such weapons. In 1651 New Plymouth banned colonists from allowing any Native servants to possess a gun, but it was not until 1676, in a period of widespread war in New England, that providing arms to Natives became a capital crime. "A Proclamation Prohibiting Interloping and Disorderly Trading to New England in America," November 6, 1622, in *Stuart Royal Proclamations*, vol. 1, *Royal Proclamations of King James I, 1603–1625*, Oxford Scholarly Editions Online (accessed May 18, 2016); William Brigham, ed., *The Compact and Charter and Laws of the Colony of New Plymouth* (Boston, 1836), 76 (1644), 94 (1651), 178 (1676). Despite any existing laws, Natives acquired firearms soon after Europeans arrived; see Angela R. Riley, "Indians and Guns," *Georgetown Law Journal* 100 (2012): 1675–1745, esp. 1685–93.

53. Bradford, *Of Plymouth Plantation*, 207–8.

54. *Bradford's Letter Book*, 41.

55. Bradford, *Of Plymouth Plantation*, 208.

56. Bradford, *Of Plymouth Plantation*, 209; "A Proclamation Prohibiting Interloping and Disorderly Trading."

57. Bradford, *Of Plymouth Plantation*, 209–10.

58. [Samuel Maverick], *A Briefe Discription of New England and the Several Townes Therein* (Boston, 1885), 10 (this edition is based on Maverick's manuscript of 1660); Bradford, *Of Plymouth Plantation*, 206.

59. Bradford, *Of Plymouth Plantation*, 206; Nathaniel Morton, *New-England's Memoriall* (Cambridge, 1669), 70; *Bradford's Letter Book*, 41–42.

60. *Bradford's Letter Book*, 43–44.

61. Bradford, *Of Plymouth Plantation*, 210.

62. Bradford, *Of Plymouth Plantation*, 215–16, 216n; Langdon, *Pilgrim Colony*, 32–33.

63. Add Mss. 35124, 23, British Library, London; *The Winthrop Papers*, 6 vols. (Boston, 1863–92), 2:44. For Winthrop's experience at the court, see Francis J. Bremer, *John Winthrop: America's Forgotten Founding Father* (New York, 2003), 144–46.

64. In 1644 there is a reference to the daughter of a Thomas Wigge gaining possession of lands recently confiscated from a Catholic landholder, but there is no mention about how the elder Wigge (or his wife) had died; see Add Mss. 61681, British Library.

65. John Winthrop, *The Journal of John Winthrop, 1630–1649*, ed. Richard S. Dunn et al. (Cambridge, Mass., 1996), 39.

66. Nathaniel B. Shurtleff, ed., *Records of the Governor and Company of the Massachusetts Bay in New England*, 5 vols. (Boston, 1853–1854), 1: 74–75.

67. Thomas Dudley to the Lady Bridget, Countess of Lincoln, March 12 and 28, 1630/1, in Everett Emerson, ed., *Letters from New England: The Massachusetts Bay Colony, 1629–1638* (Amherst, Mass., 1976), 74.

68. Winthrop, *Journal*, 39n.

69. Bradford, *Of Plymouth Plantation*, 216–17.

70. Winthrop, *Journal*, 39n.

71. The literature on Williams and Hutchinson is voluminous; see, among many other sources, Shurtleff, *Records* 1:160–61; Francis J. Bremer, *The Puritan Experiment: New England Society from Bradford to Edwards*, rev. ed. (Hanover, N.H., 1995), 62–70; Bailyn, *Barbarous Years*, 449–56; Roger Williams, *On Religious Liberty*, ed. James C. Davis (Cambridge, Mass., 2008), 7–15; Williams, "The Bloudy Tenent of Persecution" (originally published London, 1644), in Edmund S. Morgan, ed., *Puritan Political Ideas, 1558–1794* (1965; repr., Indianapolis, 2003), 203–18; Deborah Lucas Schneider, "Anne Hutchinson and Covenant Theology," *Harvard Theological Review* 103 (2010): 485–500; David D. Hall, ed., *The Antinomian Controversy, 1636–1638*, 2nd ed. (Durham, N.C., 1990); Ann F. Withington and Jack Schwartz, "The Political Trial of Anne Hutchinson," *New England Quarterly* 51 (1978): 226–40; Morgan, *Visible Saints*, 109–12; Perry Miller, *The New England Mind: The Seventeenth Century* (Cambridge, Mass., 1954), 388–92.

72. Winthrop, *Journal*, 53.

CHAPTER 4. CUTTHROATS IN CANAAN

1. *Proc. MHS* 20 (1882–83): 64–65.

2. Winthrop, *Journal*, 124, 535–38.

3. See Clark, *Eastern Frontier*, 18–19; Andrews, *Colonial Period*, 1:400–402.

4. For Gorges's actions in England during these years, see Preston, *Gorges of Plymouth Fort*; and Andrews, *Colonial Period*, 1:403–10.

5. William Bradford, *History of Plymouth Plantation, 1620–1647*, 2 vols. (Boston, 1912), 2:136–39.

6. Bradford, *History of Plymouth Plantation*, 2:139–42, quotations at 139 and 140; see also Morton, *New-England's Memoriall*, 85–86.

7. Thomas Wiggin to Master Downing, August 31, 1632, CO 1/6, no. 65.

8. Tho. Wiggin to Sir John Cooke, November 19, 1632, CO 1/6, no. 68.

9. Bradford, *History of Plymouth Plantation*, 2:136–45, quotations at 145; see also Morton, *New-England's Memoriall*, 86–89.

10. Winthrop, *Journal*, 536.

11. Here are those verses from the King James Version, which Morton was likely to have used. Verse 4: "And Jonah began to enter into the city a day's journey, and he cried, and said, Yet forty days, and Nineveh shall be overthrown." Verses 9–10: "Who can tell if God will turn and repent, and turn away from his fierce anger, that we perish not? / And God saw their works, that they turned from their evil way; and God repented of the evil, that he had said that he would do unto them; and he did it not."

12. "And Samson went and caught three hundred foxes, and took firebrands, and turned tail to tail, and put a firebrand in the midst between two tails. / And when he had set the brands on fire, he let them go into the standing corn of the Philistines, and burnt up both the shocks, and also the standing corn, with the vineyards and olives."

13. Winthrop, *Journal*, 537–38.

14. Winthrop, *Journal*, 536–37, 536n.

15. Winthrop, *Journal*, 538. Morton referred to Winthrop in this last passage as Minerva, a reference to the governor's skills; see Winthrop, *Journal*, 538n.

16. The text of the Massachusetts Bay Charter mentioned that it bore the seal attached by ribbons (see Shurtleff, *Records*, 1:28), and though now detached, the seal and ribbons remain with the charter in the Massachusetts Archives.

17. The document, dated 1674, is CO 1/6 November 4, 1631 to November 1, 1638 (accessed via Proquest July 31, 2018), hereafter cited as Minutes of the Council for New England; the material from 1631 to 1638 was printed in *Records of the Council for New England* (Cambridge, Mass., 1867), 97–131.

18. Minutes of the Council for New England, 59^{r-v} (patents), 61^{r-v} (town).

19. Minutes of the Council for New England, [66^r]–67^r (1632 orders), 65^v (Dutch ships), 65^r (Massachusetts Bay Company).

20. *Acts of the Privy Council of England: Colonial Series*, 6 vols. (London, 1908–12), 1:184–85.

21. The two entries are for November 23 and 24, 1635, in KB 21/12, 11–11^v, TNA.

22. Minutes of the Council for New England, 76^v, 77^r.

23. See M. T. Clanchy, *From Memory to Written Record: England, 1066–1307*, 3rd ed. (Oxford: Wiley-Blackwell, 2013), 31, 44–45, 309–28.

24. See Paul D. Halliday, *Dismembering the Body Politic: Partisan Politics in England's Towns, 1650–1730* (Cambridge, 1998), 26–27, 162–64, quotation at 163; Catherine F. Patterson, *Urban Patronage in Early Modern England: Corporate Boroughs, the Landed Elite, and the Crown, 1580–1640* (Stanford, 1999), 89, 151, 168, 173–74, 279–80n8, 299n8; Patterson, "Quo Warranto and Borough Corporations in Early Stuart England: Royal Prerogative and Local Privileges in the Central Courts," *English Historical Review* 120 (2005): 879–906.

25. Egerton Ms 2395, British Library; [Thomas Hutchinson], *A Collection of Original Papers Relative to the History of the Colony of Massachusetts Bay* (Boston, 1769), 101–3; G. D. Scull, "The 'Quo Warranto' of 1635," *New-England Historical and Genealogical Register* 38 (1884): 209–16, quotation at 216; Order of the Privy Council, May 3, 1637, CO 1/9, no. 49; minutes of the Court of King's Bench, 1637, CO 1/9, no. 50; the king's manifesto for the government in New England, July 23, 1637, CO 1/9, no. 60; Minutes of the Council for New England, 70^r–71^v.

26. *Records of the Council for New England*, 80–81.

27. Morton to the King, [June 21, 1636], Court of Requests, Charles XXXVIII, part 3, reprinted in *Proc. MHS*, 3rd ser., 59 (1925–26): 92–95, quotation at 93.

28. *Plymouth Church Records, 1620–1859* (New York, 1920), 1:89–91. Nathaniel Morton recognized that the issue in London dealt with Massachusetts Bay, not New Plymouth, but he knew as well that the threat to colonial religious practice would spread to the region, which explains why he wrote about this in his history of the early church in Plymouth.

29. Winthrop, *Journal*, 262; also Winthrop journal, HM 39724, HEH, 25–26.

30. The back-and-forth can be found in William Hubbard, *A General History of New England from the Discovery to MDCLXXX* (1680; 2nd ed. [Boston, 1898]), 263–72. The petition is reprinted in Ebenezer Hazard, ed., *Historical Collections*, 2 vols. (Philadelphia, 1792–94), 1:435–36.

31. *The Autobiography and Correspondence of Sir Simonds D'Ewes*, 2 vols., ed. James O. Halliwell (London, 1845), 2:117–18; Baxter, *Gorges and His Province of Maine*, 171–73. For D'Ewes as a chronicler, see *The Journal of Sir Simonds D'Ewes*, ed. Wallace Notestein (New Haven, 1923), vii–xvii.

32. See Conrad Russell, *The Fall of the British Monarchies, 1637–1642* (Oxford, 1991), 27–146; and Kevin Sharpe, *The Personal Rule of Charles I* (New Haven, 1992), 769–824.

33. Baxter, *Gorges and His Province of Maine*, 173–74; Andrews, *Colonial Period*, 1:421–22; Winthrop, *Journal*, 224; Burrage, *Beginnings of Colonial Maine*, 233–34.

34. Minutes of the Council for New England, 76^v, 77^r, 78^r.

35. There were perhaps twenty editions and translations of Columbus's reports by 1500; see J. H. Elliott, *The Old World and the New, 1492–1650* (Cambridge, 1970), 9.

36. Ramusio, *Navigationi et viaggi*, 3 vols. (Venice, 1554–59). The American materials can be found in the third volume, which appeared in print before the second: Ramusio, *Terzo volume delle navigationi et viaggi nel quale si contengo le navigatione al Mondo Nuovo* (Venice, 1556).

37. Richard Eden, *The Decades of the Newe Worlde or West India* (London, 1555).

38. See, e.g., Richard Willes, ed., *The History of Travayle in the West and East Indies* (London, 1577).

39. On Hakluyt's methods and collections, see Mancall, *Hakluyt's Promise*.

40. See Peter C. Mancall, *Fatal Journey: The Final Expedition of Henry Hudson—A Tale of Mutiny and Murder in the Arctic* (New York, 2009).

41. For the publishing history, see the excellent modern edition by Vaughan, *New England's Prospect*, 1–3. As the movement that would be-

come the American Revolution began to gather steam, one unidentified scholar appended a long prefatory note to a 1764 edition of Wood's work that linked a text describing the environment and indigenous peoples of southern New England in the early 1630s to then current debates about the role of the colonies in the British imperial system. The Prince Society reprinted this edition in 1868.

42. *NEC*, A2^{r-v}.

43. Bradford, *Relation or Journall.*

44. *NEC*, 5–6, 8.

45. See, e.g., Bernard Picart and Jean-Frédéric Bernard, *The Ceremonies and Religious Customs of the Various Nations of the Known World.* 6 vols. (London, 1733–1739), 3:1–12.

46. See Thomas Moffat, *Insectorum sive Minimorum Animalium* (London, 1634), which would later appear in an English-language translation as the final section of Edward Topsell, *The Historie of Four-Footed Beastes* (London, 1658).

47. *NEC*, 11–15, quotations at 14 and 15.

48. *NEC*, 16–17.

49. *NEC*, 44.

50. *NEC*, 44–45.

51. *NEC*, 45–47.

52. *NEC*, 43.

53. *NEC*, 51.

54. *NEC*, 54.

55. *NEC*, 55.

56. See Humphrey Gilbert, *A Discourse of a Discoverie for a New Passage to Cataia* (London, 1576); and Richard Hakluyt, *Divers Voyages Touching the Discovery of America and the Ilands Adjacent* (London, 1582), q^{r-v}. For transportation as a policy, see A. Roger Ekirch, *Bound for America: The Transportation of British Convicts to the Colonies, 1718–1775* (Oxford, 1990).

57. *NEC*, 56–58, quotations at 57 ("Platoes Comonwealth") and 176 (ale drinking).

58. *NEC*, 59–60.

59. *NEC*, 60–61. As the literary critic Michelle Burnham has observed, Morton's language was so effusive that "sentence after sentence

struggles to make language rich enough to describe the wealth of the country." See her "Land, Labor, and Colonial Economics in Thomas Morton's *New English Canaan*," *Early American Literature* 41 (2006): 405–28, quotation at 414.

60. *NEC*, 62–66, quotation at 64.

61. *NEC*, 67–69.

62. *NEC*, 69–70. Adams, relying on the authority of the nineteenth-century American ornithologist John James Audubon, believed that the English writer exaggerated a bit in this measurement; see Adams, *NEC*, 192n3.

63. *NEC*, 71–73, quotations at 73; Minutes of the Council for New England, 77^r. For the wider phenomenon of Europeans' obsession with American birds, including hummingbirds, see Alessandra Russo et al., eds., *Images Take Flight: Feather Art in Mexico and Europe, 1400–1700* ([Munich], 2015).

64. *NEC*, 78–83.

65. *NEC*, 74–75.

66. *NEC*, 77–78. Morton noted that the "stones" of the muskrat could also be used to make excellent perfume, a trait that other Europeans attributed to the castor sacs of a beaver. See *NEC*, 81. On the properties of beaver tails and castoreum, see Edward Topsell, *Naturall Historie of Foure-Footed Beastes* (London, 1607), 44–50.

67. Adams pointed out that the rock was actually porphyry, not marble; see Adams, *NEC*, 215n2.

68. *NEC*, 83–86. In 1609 Hakluyt, in an effort to build interest for the Virginia venture, had translated a tract that spoke of potential riches to be found in North America, adding in his preface that indigenous allies of the first colonists had told them of nearby mines. See [Richard Hakluyt, trans.], Gentleman of Elvas, *Virginia Richly Valued, by the Description of the Maine Land of Florida, Her Next Neighbor* (London, 1609), A3^r. On the widespread belief among the English that they would locate mines in the Western Hemisphere, see Karin Amundsen, "Metallurgy, Mining, and English Colonization in the Americas, 1550–1624" (Ph.D. diss., University of Southern California, 2017).

69. *NEC*, 86–87.

70. *NEC*, 86–91.

71. *NEC*, 92, 94–95.

72. *NEC*, 93. Adams and his team identified the modern place-names; see Adams, *NEC*, 229-30.

73. *NEC*, 94-96.

74. *NEC*, 93.

75. *NEC*, 96-98. Morton was not alone in his claims about learning the language of New England's indigenous peoples. In addition to Roger Williams, whose *Key into the Language of America* appeared in 1643, William Wood included a vocabulary in *New England's Prospect*, and John Pory wrote in January 1623 that he had "collected a small dictionary," noticing that the vocabulary of Natives around Chesapeake Bay resembled that of the people of southern New England. See Vaughan's edition of Wood's *New England's Prospect*, 117-24; and Pory to the Earl of Southampton, January 13, 1622/1623 and later, in James, ed., *Three Visitors to Early Plymouth*, 13.

76. *NEC*, 99-100.

77. See Burnham, "Land, Labor, and Colonial Economics," esp. 410-18.

78. In addition to this part of his book being even more self-serving than the rest, it was also, as Adams pointed out in his edition, the part with the most "errors." Adams dismissed Morton's brief opening chapter, which focused on an initial pact between the locals and the Pilgrims, as "a confused, rambling account of the familiar Indian incidents which took place during the first year after the landing at Plymouth," found another section "wholly confused and misleading," and noted that yet another part revealed Morton's "rambling, incoherent" style and "confused the events of one year with those of another." Adams's notes are more extensive throughout this section than in the rest of the book, a device that the nineteenth-century editor used to distance himself from any endorsement of Morton's version of the history of this period. See Adams, *NEC*, 243n1, 247n1, 259n1.

79. *NEC*, 104-5.

80. *NEC*, 106-8, quotation at 107.

81. *NEC*, 111-12. The name stuck for years. Adams claimed that Morton had gotten the translation wrong, but that was irrelevant in the 1630s since virtually none of Morton's readers, with the exception of those who knew Roger Williams's work, could have offered a correc-

tion. And because Williams's book did not appear in print until six years after Morton's, it is likely that no one could have known better. See Adams, *NEC*, 252–54, quotation at 254. Adams pointed out that the linguist J. Hammond Trumbull had claimed that Morton mistranslated the term, which should have been "*wotawquenauge*, which means 'coatmen,' or men wearing clothes, the *waútacone-nûaog* of Williams": Adams, *NEC*, 254n1.

82. *NEC*, 114.

83. *NEC*, 118–20.

84. *NEC*, 121. On this point Morton's calculation was a bit off; unlike in Virginia, the sex ratio of English migrants to New England tended to be balanced, which facilitated family formation and reproduction; see Anderson, *New England's Generation*, 20–23; and John Demos, *A Little Commonwealth: Family Life in Plymouth Colony* (New York, 1970), 192.

85. *NEC*, 124–25, quotation at 125.

86. *NEC*, 126–28, quotation at 128. Morton here likened the man's errand to actions that had challenged Cervantes's Quixote.

87. *NEC*, 132–38; quotations at 135 and 138; Morgan, *Visible Saints*, 75–76.

88. *NEC*, 139–45, quotations at 139.

89. *NEC*, 156–57.

90. *NEC*, 158–59.

91. Numbers 22:20–34.

92. *NEC*, 163–64.

93. *NEC*, 164.

94. *NEC*, 178–79.

95. *NEC*, 180–82.

96. *NEC*, 182 ("Counsell table"), 188 (Separatists and repentance).

97. *NEC*, 23.

CHAPTER 5. ACOMENTICUS

1. Winthrop, *Journal*, 492.

2. Winthrop, *Journal*, 187.

3. Winthrop, *Journal*, 189–91.

4. Winthrop, *Journal*, 191–92. Williams had lived in Plymouth

and Massachusetts, but he became unwelcome in both. Nonetheless, he maintained the respect of colonists for his abilities with the Natives, including the Wampanoags, who tended to him in the winter of 1635–36 when he was banished from Massachusetts. By early 1636 he had begun a new settlement along the shores of Narragansett Bay that would become the colony of Rhode Island. Bradford, who had earlier been happy to see Williams leave Plymouth (as he wrote in 1633), valued his intervention in a tense moment after a colonist murdered a Narragansett in 1638; see Bradford, *Of Plymouth Plantation*, 257, 300.

5. Winthrop, *Journal*, 207.

6. Winthrop, *Journal*, 207–8. Justification, as the historian Edmund Morgan has explained, was "the imputation of Christ's righteousness to man" and sanctification "the gradual improvement of a man's behavior in obedience to God." Morgan, *Visible Saints*, 67.

7. Winthrop, *Journal*, 208–9.

8. Winthrop, *Journal*, 209–10; for the context, see Morgan, *Visible Saints*, 64–138.

9. Winthrop, *Journal*, 211.

10. Winslow to Winthrop, April 17, 1637, in *Winthrop Papers*, 3:391–92.

11. Winthrop, *Journal*, 212–14; Winthrop to Bradford, [May 20], 1637, in *Winthrop Papers*, 3:417–19, also in Bradford, *Of Plymouth Plantation*, 394–96.

12. Winthrop, *Journal*, 214–17; see also *Winthrop Papers*, 3:422–26.

13. Williams to the Governor of Massachusetts, May 13, 1637, and Williams to Sir Henry Vane and Winthrop, [May 15, 1637], in *Winthrop Papers*, 3:410–14, quotation at 414.

14. Winthrop, *Journal*, 218.

15. Winslow to Winthrop, May 22, 1637, in *Winthrop Papers*, 3:419–20, quotation at 420.

16. On the lack of information about Vincent, see the brief prefatory note in P. Philip Vincent [P. Vincentius], "A True Relation of the Late Battell Fought in New England, between the English, and the Salvages: With the Present State of Things There (1637)," ed. Paul Royster, *Electronic Texts in American Studies*, paper 35 (accessed April 28, 2016).

17. Vincent, "True Relation," 9–12.

18. Vincent, "True Relation," 15–19, quotation at 15.

19. Vincent, "True Relation," 8–9.

20. [Johnson], *History of New-England*, S2ᵛ–S3ʳ.

21. John Underhill, *Newes from America; or, A New and Experimentall Discoverie of New England; Containing, a True Relation of Their War-like Proceedings These Two Yeares Last Past, with a Figure of the Indian Fort, or Palizado* (London, 1638), 2–3, 6–16, 32–35. (All page numbers refer to the electronic edition by Paul Royster, *Electronic Texts in American Studies*, paper 37 [accessed April 30, 2016].)

22. Underhill, *Newes from America*, 35–36.

23. Underhill, *Newes from America*, 1–2.

24. Daniel Patrick to the Governor and Council of War in Massachusetts, June 19, 1637, in *The Winthrop Papers*, 5 vols. ([Boston], 1929–1947), 3:430–31; Winthrop, *Journal*, 222.

25. Williams to Winthrop, c. June 21, 1637, in *Winthrop Papers*, 3:433–34, quotations at 434.

26. See Israel Staughton to the Governor and Council of Massachusetts, [August 14, 1637]; Richard Davenport to Winthrop, [c. August 23, 1627]; Roger Williams to Winthrop, [September 9, 1637]; Williams to Winthrop, [c. October 26, 1637], in *Winthrop Papers*, 3:481–83, 490–91, 494–96, 500–501. Davenport claimed that other Natives would "bee glad to make women of all the Pecots now," but in the margin wrote the word "slaves." See *Winthrop Papers*, 3:491, 491n.

27. Michael L. Fickes, "'They Could Not Endure That Yoke': The Captivity of Pequot Women and Children After the War of 1637," *New England Quarterly* 73 (2000): 59–60.

28. Winthrop, *Journal*, 224, 187. The patent to Gorges, dated April 3, 1639, is in CO 5/902, 61–92.

29. Karen Ordahl Kupperman, *Providence Island, 1630–1641: The Other Puritan Colony* (Cambridge, 1993), 172, 178, 335, quotation at 178.

30. For the context, see Warren, *New England Bound*, 25–36.

31. Winthrop, *Journal*, 260–61.

32. Bradford, *Of Plymouth Plantation*, 296.

33. Mason, *A Brief History of the Pequot War*, ed. Thomas Prince (Boston, 1736), 4, 8–10.

34. Winthrop, *Journal*, 177.

35. Winthrop, *Journal*, 332.
36. Winthrop, *Journal*, 332-33.
37. Winthrop, *Journal*, 333.
38. Winthrop mentions Morton's arrest in a series of memoranda that were not part of his journal; see *Journal*, appendix C, 759. See also *Winthrop Papers*, 4:464.
39. Winthrop, *Journal*, 535.
40. Winthrop, *Journal*, 535-38.
41. Shurtleff, *Records*, 2:90.
42. Winthrop, *Journal*, 538-39; Winslow to Winthrop, [1643], in *Winthrop Papers*, 3:175; Winslow to Winthrop, [January 1644], in *Winthrop Papers*, 4:428.
43. Underhill, *Newes from America*, 18; see also Winthrop, *Journal*, 187, 432.
44. Charles Edward Banks, *History of York Maine*, 2 vols. (1931; repr., York, Maine, 1990), 1:435-39.
45. Thomas Gorges to Sir Ferdinando Gorges, [September? 1641], in Robert E. Moody, ed., *The Letters of Thomas Gorges* (Portland, Maine, 1978), 55.
46. Patent of Gorges to Cleeve, January 27, 1636, in James Finney Baxter, *George Cleeve of Casco Bay, 1630-1667, with Collateral Documents* (Portland, Maine: Gorges Society, 1885), 216-21.
47. Gorges to Henry Vane, John Winthrop, et al., August 23, 1637, and Richard Vines to John Winthrop, January 9, 1643, in Baxter, *Cleeve of Casco Bay*, 224-26, quotations at 226, 233-36. On Morton representing Cleeve and Tucker, see Matthew Cradock to John Winthrop, March 15, 1636[/37], in *Winthrop Papers*, 3:378-79.
48. Grant of Casco Neck and Hog Island . . . to George Cleeve, May 23, 1643, in Baxter, *Cleeve of Casco Bay*, 246-50.
49. Hannah Farber, "The Rise and Fall of the Province of Lygonia, 1643-1658," *New England Quarterly* 82 (2009): 490-513.
50. Charter of Agamenticus, 1641, in Banks, *History of York*, 1:435-39.
51. Petition of Morton to the Court at Boston, [May 1645?], vol. 38b: Judicial, 1640-1658, 220, Massachusetts Archives, Boston. Adams, in his edition of *New English Canaan*, plausibly argued for the date of

May 1645 since the petition was endorsed by Thomas Dudley in his time as governor; he served in that capacity from May 14, 1645 to May 6, 1646. See Adams, *NEC*, 90.

52. Petition of Morton, 220–220a.

53. Will of Morton, *Proc MHS*, 3rd ser., 58 (1924–25): 163–64.

54. Other than Winthrop's comment, Morton disappears from the historical record after May 23, 1643, when he served as a witness to the sale of Casco Neck and Hog Island to George Cleeve; the deed is reprinted in Baxter, *Cleeve of Casco Bay*, 246–50.

55. Banks, *History of York*, 1:160.

56. Winthrop, *Journal*, 492n, 535–39. In the seventeenth century about 60 percent of men in New Plymouth lived to at least age seventy, and over one-fourth (28.4 percent) lived until age eighty. By contrast, only 8.3 percent of the population in England reached age sixty in 1631, and the number increased to only 9.7 percent by 1661. See Demos, *Little Commonwealth*, 193; Laslett, *The World We Have Lost*, 111.

57. Along these lines, Bradford's description of another epidemic in 1634 similarly attributed the catastrophe to the unflinching hand of the almighty; see Bradford, *Of Plymouth Plantation*, 270–71.

58. Baxter, *Gorges and His Province of Maine*, 1:151–57 (fur trade and initial distributions), 181–83 (division of land), 185–87 (Agamenticus), 196 (bequest and sale to Massachusetts).

CHAPTER 6. LEGACIES

1. Morton, *New-England's Memoriall*, A3ᵛ, 68–72. This Morton had long experience in Plymouth, having arrived in July 1623 when he was perhaps eleven years old; in addition to the *Memoriall* he wrote the history of the first church in Plymouth, and for that task too he drew on his uncle's manuscripts; see *Plymouth Church Records, 1620–1859* (New York, 1920), 1:xv–xvi.

2. Bradford, *Of Plymouth Plantation*, xxviii–xxx; Thomas Prince, *A Chronological History of New-England in the Form of Annals*, 2 vols. (Boston, 1736), 1:85 ff. (use of Bradford), 167 (Morton at Ma-re Mount), 176–77 (the removal of Morton in 1628); William Hubbard, *A General History of New England* (Cambridge, 1815), 101–5 (Morton at Ma-re Mount). As David Hall has noted, some "texts that remained unpublished, like William Bradford's history of Plymouth, could be consulted in an ar-

chive." See Hall, "Readers and Writers in Early New England," in Hugh Amory and David D. Hall, eds., *A History of the Book in America*, 5 vols., vol. 1, *The Colonial Book in the Atlantic World* (New York, 2007), 142.

3. John Hancock, *A Memorial of GOD's Goodness* (Boston, 1739), 18.

4. Thomas Hutchinson, *The History of the Colony of Massachusetts-Bay, from the First Settlement Thereof in 1628. Until Its Incorporation with the Colony of Plimoth* . . . *in 1691* (Boston, 1764), 7-8 (Morton at Ma-re Mount), 48-53 (Gorges's efforts to claim at least some of New England). After his death Hutchinson's history was published again, another way that Bradford's interpretation of Morton survived; see Hutchinson, *The History of Massachusetts, from the First Settlement Thereof in 1628, until the Year 1750*, 2 vols. (Salem, 1795), 1:15 (Morton), 50-54 (Gorges and the quo warranto). On Hutchinson's book, see Lawrence S. Mayo, "Thomas Hutchinson and His *History of Massachusetts Bay*," *Proceedings of the American Antiquarian Society* (1931): 321-39. On Hutchinson's life and difficult relations with other colonists, see Bernard Bailyn, *The Ordeal of Thomas Hutchinson* (Cambridge, Mass., 1974).

5. [Johnson], *History of New-England*, [Q4^v]-R^r.

6. Winthrop, *Journal*, 105; [Maverick], *A Briefe Discription of New England*, 15-18. See also Maverick to the Earl of Clarendon, n.d., in [*The Clarendon Papers*], *Collections of the New-York Historical Society* 2 (1869): 40-41; Minutes of the Council for New England, 60^v (Maverick among the council members). Maverick's book, like Bradford's, survived only in manuscript form until the nineteenth century.

7. See the notes about this copy's provenance (the local call number is Am 1637 Mor 260.o), Library Company of Philadelphia; and Franklin to Collinson, June 26, 1755.

8. John Winthrop, *A Journal of the Transactions and Occurrences in the Settlement of Massachusetts and the Other New-England Colonies* . . . *and Now First Published from a Correct Copy of the Original Manuscript* (Hartford, 1790), unpaginated editor's preface (history of the manuscript and its use), 21 (Morton's first banishment from Massachusetts), 208 (the quo warranto), 352-55 (the 1644 encounter with the presentation of Morton's letter). Despite its claim to being correct, this edition has Morton being killed off in 1640, which Winthrop might have preferred, but it was another enemy of the colony, John Mason, who succumbed, which Winthrop had previously recorded in his journal for 1636. For an ex-

ample of a manuscript copy of a portion of Winthrop's journal, see HM 39724, HEH, a copy created by an unknown scribe sometime around 1743, an act of creation testifying to the ongoing value that some saw in Winthrop's account of the colony's founding.

9. See Adams, Scraps of the History, sheets 3 and 11.

10. *Monthly Anthology and Boston Review*, June 1810, 420–25, quotations at 420; *Monthly Anthology and Boston Review*, July 1810, 49–55, quotations at 54–55. The *Anthology* was produced by a group of Boston publishers eager to draw attention to their efforts, and among the contributors was Adams, whose copy was presumably the one used for the excerpts. The group lasted only from 1804 to 1811, but it helped spawn two major literary institutions: the *North American Review*, which began in 1815, and the Boston Athenaeum, which was founded in 1811. Though it is impossible to know for certain if Adams was the editor, his family had ties to the magazine and Adams had provided one of his father's letters (written in 1755) to the *Anthology*, a fact that Charles Francis Adams acknowledged later; see the notes attached to John Adams to Nathan Webb, October 12, [1755?], and the entry for August 13, 1833, in the Diary of Charles Francis Adams, both in MHS Digital Edition: Adams Papers (accessed August 10, 2017).

11. See Connors, *Thomas Morton*, 124–25.

12. Irving also drew on Bradford's version of the Pequot War, which he saw depicting "the cold blooded detail of indiscriminate butchery." See Irving, "Traits of Indian Character," in *Washington Irving: History, Tales and Sketches* (New York: Library of America, 1983), 1005–6 (using Morton), 1010 (on the Pequot War).

13. A. C., "Thomas Morton of Mount Wollaston," *New-England Galaxy and United States Literary Advertiser,* June 15, 1821, 4 (accessed via Proquest, September 30, 2018).

14. An American [Lydia Maria Child], *Hobomok: A Tale of Early Times* (Boston, 1824), 11.

15. [Catherine Maria Sedgwick], *Hope Leslie; or, Early Times in the Massachusetts*, 2 vols. (New York, 1827), 2:43–44, quotation at 44.

16. The manuscript is acquisition number 1928.M-19.928, Clements Library, University of Michigan, Ann Arbor. For Drake, see the obituary notices in the *American Booksellers' Guide* 2, no. 7 (1875): 222; and the *New York Genealogical and Biographical Record* 6, no. 4 (1875): 197.

For the existence of Bartlet's copy, see DeCosta, "Morton's *New English Canaan*," 329. Bartlet turned to writing history in the 1850s and became a member of the Massachusetts Historical Society in 1858; he died while still working on a history of the Episcopal Church in America. See Edmund F. Slafter, "Memoir of the Rev. William Stoodly Bartlet," *Proc. MHS* (1886): 430-34. The practice of writing out parts of Morton's book continued into the twentieth century: Mrs. Nehemiah Perry, the historian of the Dorothy Ripley Chapter of the Daughters of the American Revolution, copied out portions of *New English Canaan* from the copy in the Pequot Library in Southport, Connecticut, and deposited them with the DAR; see *Daughters of the American Revolution Magazine* 51 (1917): 185.

17. The first appearance of the story, attributed to "the author of the Gentle Boy" but not to Hawthorne by name, was in *The Token and Atlantic Souvenir: A Christmas and New Year's Present* (Boston: Charles Bowen, 1836), 283-97.

18. G. Harrison Orians, "Hawthorne and 'The Maypole of Merry-Mount,'" *Modern Language Notes* 3 (1938): 159-67; and, especially, J. Gary Williams, "History in Hawthorne's 'The Maypole of Merry Mount,'" *Essex Institute Historical Collections* 108 (1972): 173-89.

19. Hawthorne, "The May-Pole of Merry Mount," in *Twice-Told Tales* (Boston, 1837), 77-94, quotations at 77 ("jollity and gloom," allegory), 87 ("future complexion," "banner-staff"), 88 ("darksome figures," "Puritan of Puritans"), 93 ("severest Puritan"), 92 ("zealot").

20. Hawthorne, "Main-Street," in Hawthorne, *The Snow-Image, and Other Tales* (London, 1851), 34-61, quotation at 45; see also Hawthorne, *Tales and Sketches* (New York, 1982), 1034; Brenda Wineapple, *Hawthorne: A Life* (New York, 2003), 199, 245.

21. John L. Motley, *Merry-Mount: A Romance of the Massachusetts Colony*, 2 vols. (Boston, 1849); the physical description of Morton is on 1:10. For the history, see Motley, *The Rise of the Dutch Republic: A History*, 3 vols. (London, 1856). A decade before Motley turned to Morton, he had written a different two-volume work relating to New England's history entitled *Morton's Hope*, but though he dealt extensively with Native history, his note at the end indicates that he used sources other than *New English Canaan*, thereby suggesting that his title was perhaps inspired by Thomas Morton but the protagonist named Morton has no

obvious connection to the historical figure. See Motley, *Morton's Hope; or, The Memoirs of a Provincial*, 2 vols. (New York, 1839); the historical note is on 2:298.

22. Longfellow, "The Landlord's Tale: The Rhyme of Sir Christopher," in *Tales of a Wayside Inn* (Boston, 1880), 305. Longfellow had published an earlier edition of *Tales* in 1863, but it did not include this poem.

23. "The May-Pole of Merry Mount" appeared in these editions: *Twice-Told Tales*, 2 vols. (Boston, 1842), 1:65–83; *Twice-Told Tales*, 2 vols. (Boston, 1851), 1:67–82; *Twice-Told Tales*, 2 vols. (Boston, 1865), 1:52–67.

24. It remains a feature of the American literary canon now available in the Library of America edition of Hawthorne's writings; see Hawthorne, *Tales and Sketches* (New York, 1982).

25. See Hawthorne, *Twice-Told Tales*, ed. Wallace Stegner (New York, 1966), x–xi; the story appears on 273–84.

26. Samuel G. Drake, *The History and Antiquities of Boston* (Boston, 1856), iii (twenty-five years of work), 36–39, quotation at 37–38.

27. Drake, *History and Antiquities of Boston*, 48–50, 49n.

28. Drake, *History and Antiquities of Boston*, 113–15, 126–27, 114n (man in bilboes), quotations at 115n, 126n.

29. *The Diary of John Quincy Adams*, ed. Allan Nevins (New York, 1951), 484; the false date on the title page is in Force, ed., *Tracts and Other Papers, Relating Principally to the Origin, Settlement, and Progress of the Colonies in North America*, 4 vols. (Washington, D.C., 1838).

30. The society's act of incorporation, constitution, and subscribers can be found in Champlain, *Voyages*, 1:[306]–16.

31. Boston, 1865.

32. Adams Jr., "The May-Pole of Merrymount," *Atlantic*, May and June 1877, 557–67 and 686–97.

33. For information about the publication of these books, see Adams, *Three Episodes*, opposite the title page.

34. Adams, *NEC*, [v]. Charles Francis Adams Jr. was one of the *less* voluble members of his clan; the microfilm version of the papers of three generations starting with John stretch more than five miles, most of it dominated by John, John Quincy, and Charles Francis Sr.; when the letterpress edition concludes, there will be eighty to one hundred volumes. See Bailyn, "Butterfield's Adams," 239.

35. *Cambridge Tribune*, September 17, 1921, 7 (accessed via the Cambridge Public Library website, April 21, 2015).

36. For Putnam, see Curtis M. Hinsley, "From Shell-Heaps to Stelae: Early Anthropology at the Peabody Museum," in "Objects and Others: Essays on Museums and Material Culture," ed. George W. Stocking Jr., special issue, *History of Anthropology* 3 (1988): 49–74.

37. Slafter, "Memoir of Samuel de Champlain," in Champlain, *Voyages*, 1:1–204.

38. Adams, *NEC*, vi.

39. *Bulletin of the Bureau of American Ethnology* 25 (Washington, D.C., 1903).

40. John Eliot, *The Indian Primer; or, The Way of Training Up Our Indian Youth in the Good Knowledge of God*, ed. John Small (Edinburgh, 1877), i.

41. See the conveyance of land from Thomas Dilla to Nathaniell Cuper, September 1701, in Ives Goddard and Kathleen J. Bragdon, eds., *Native Writings in Massachusett*, 2 vols. (Philadelphia, 1988), 1:58–61 (the original ms is HM 3993[1], HEH); and the Mashpee petition of June 11, 1752, in Goddard and Bragdon, *Native Writings*, 1:370–73.

42. See Jean M. O'Brien, *Firsting and Lasting: Writing Indians out of Existence in New England* (Minneapolis, 2010).

43. See Ruth Wallis Herndon and Ella Wilcox Sekatau, "The Right to a Name: The Narragansett People and Rhode Island Officials in the Revolutionary Era," *Ethnohistory* 44 (1997): 433–62.

44. The most famous example was the Mashpee writer William Apess, whose writings are in *On Our Own Ground*. But Apess was not alone; see Lisa Brooks, *The Common Pot: The Recovery of Native Space in the Northeast* (Minneapolis, 2008).

45. For the survival of these histories and what can be found in them, see Bragdon, *Native People of Southern New England*; Bruchac, "Earthshapers and Placemakers"; and Simmons, *Spirit of the New England Tribes*.

46. Goddard and Bragdon, *Native Writings*, xv; Wôpanâak Language Restoration Project (wlrp.org), accessed March 13, 2017.

47. Leslie Fiedler and Arther Zeiger, eds., *O Brave New World: American Literature from 1600 to 1840* (New York, 1968), 380; Andrews,

Colonial Period, 1:332–33; Karen Ordahl Kupperman, "Thomas Morton, Historian," *New England Quarterly* 50 (1977): 660–64, quotation at 662; Salisbury, *Manitou and Providence*, 159.

48. Chas S. Clifton, *Her Hidden Children: The Rise of Wicca and Paganism in America* (Lanham, Md., 2006), 39–41, quotations at 41.

49. "Revels at Merrymount Today," http://ancientlights.org/revels (accessed July 20, 2018).

50. "A Proclamation . . . [by] Deval L. Patrick," March 1, 2011, Archives Division of the Secretary of the Commonwealth's Office, obtained from the Office of the Governor of Massachusetts, July 30, 2018.

51. Helen Augur, "A Pagan Ghost at the Puritans' Feast," *New York Times Magazine*, June 29, 1930, 6, 21, quotation at 21 (accessed via Times-Machine, September 30, 2018).

52. *Boston Globe*, July 2, 1930, 14; July 3, 1930, 5; July 8, 1930, 1, 17; July 9, 1930, 1; July 10, 1930, 32; July 11, 1930, 7 (accessed via newspapers.com, September 30, 2018).

53. Williams added that this madness continued: "Mather defends the witchcraft persecutions." Williams, "The May-Pole at Merry Mount," in *In the American Grain* (1933; repr., New York, 2009), 75–80, quotations at 79 and 80.

54. Benét, "The Devil and Daniel Webster," *Saturday Evening Post*, October 24, 1936, subsequently published as a stand-alone novella (New York, 1937).

55. Lowell, *Endecott and the Red Cross*, in *The Old Glory* (New York, 1965), 3–59, quotation at 6.

56. Philip Roth, *The Dying Animal* (New York, 2001), quotations at 59 (Shakespeare) and 60 (sex).

57. Roth, *The Dying Animal*, 61–62.

58. See Mason I. Lowance Jr., *The Language of Canaan: Metaphor and Symbol in New England from the Puritans to the Transcendentalists* (Cambridge, Mass., 1980), 13–15.

59. Shurtleff, *Records*, 1:19.

Acknowledgments

Thomas Morton sailed across the Atlantic Ocean four times, providing posterity with a story that has been told time and again. He told his own story, and so did his enemies. Whatever the merits of my version, there would be no story to be told without the disputes that set these people against each other and without the many traces, however imperfect, that Morton left in historical records on both sides of the Atlantic.

I could not have completed this version of Morton's life without abundant support—the kind of support I suspect Morton could have used on many occasions, like when he was stranded on the Isles of Shoals or shackled in bilboes. Fortunately, the interventions I needed were attainable, especially from the University of Southern California, which provided ample support for me to write this book. In particular, I thank Amber Miller and Steve Kay as well as the Undergraduate Research Assistant Program from the USC Provost's Office for funding a steady stream of exemplary research assistants, including Lance Good, Alex Hofmann, Serena Jarwala, Emily Levine, Will Orr, Avery Wendell, and especially Madeline Adams, Megan Hansford, Marissa Roy, and Madeline White. I wrote and revised much of this book at the Huntington Library with the unflagging support of Steve Hindle and his predecessor, Roy Ritchie. In addition, I received crucial support, especially in gathering the visual materials and tracking down copies of *New English Canaan*, from scholars and archivists at the Clements Library at the University of Michigan (with thanks to Andrew Rutledge), the Library of Congress (with assistance from Julie Miller), the John Carter Brown Library, the Library Company of Philadelphia, the Boston Athenaeum, the Maine Historical Society, the Huntington, and the Massachusetts Historical Society (especially Sabina Beauchard). I owe the inspiration for the opening of this book to the incomparable Sara Georgini, who told me about John Adams's unpublished history of Mount Wollaston and was my guide through the treasures of the Adams Papers at the MHS.

Whatever coherence this book has owes much to a community of historians who spent time reading over various parts. I thank my hosts at Yale (especially Steve Pincus), Princeton (notably Sarah Rivett and Wendy Warren), and Georgetown (particularly Alison Games) for seminars that enabled me to clarify certain parts of the argument. I thank Becky Wrenn for the two maps she drew for this book, showing that the setting for much of the action in this book was well peopled before the English arrived and that Gorges's claims posed a substantial threat to the religious dissenters who arrived before his claim became reduced in the late 1630s. Along the way I profited from the expertise of many who shared their thoughts and time, including Karin Amundsen, Zara Anishlansin, Bud Bailyn, Juliana Barr, Mary Bilder, Daniela Bleichmar, Amy Braden, Bill Deverell, Ellen Dooley, Alejandra Dubcovsky, Bob Frankel, Anne Goldgar, Jim Green, Paul Halliday, David Hancock, Cynthia Herrup, Steve Hindle, Drew Lipman, Mary Beth Norton, Barbara Oberg, Lindsay O'Neill, Nathan Perl-Rosenthal, Josh Piker, Keith Pluymers, Neil Safier, Carole Shammas, Karin Wulf, and Tim Gustafson, who told me about the appearance of Morton in Roth's *Dying Animal.* During a sabbatical when I wrestled with an undisciplined manuscript I had ideal companions in Dan Richter and Mark Valeri, the former sharing his unparalleled expertise in seventeenth-century Anglo-American and indigenous politics and the latter his dazzling erudition about early American religious practice. I received close readings of various stages of the manuscript from John Demos, Lara Heimert, Eric Hinderaker, and Lou Masur, and finely honed, enormously detailed reports from Mark Peterson and Chris Grasso, without whom this book would have been far poorer. I also thank my copy editor, Robin DuBlanc, the press's senior manuscript editor Margaret Otzel and editorial assistant Eva Skewes, and Cynthia Ingham, who provided careful proof reading and prepared the index. Deirdre Mullane, my longtime agent, also offered a crucial critique, as did my editor Adina Berk, who brought the manuscript to Yale when I feared it might be as lost as those Pilgrims thought they were in 1620.

I dedicate this book to Lisa, Sophie, and Nicholas, for their assistance with stylistic and legal clarity . . . and for helping me find a path.

Index

The letter *f* following a page number denotes a figure.